MOTHERS

SONS

06/02

MOTHERS

&

SONS

*Feminism, Masculinity, and
the Struggle to Raise Our Sons*

EDITED BY
Andrea O'Reilly

ROUTLEDGE
NEW YORK AND LONDON

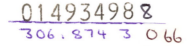
Published in 2001 by
Routledge
29 West 35th Street
New York, NY 10001

Published in Great Britain by
Routledge
11 New Fetter Lane
London EC4P 4EE

Library of Congress Cataloging-in-Publication Data

Mothers & Sons / edited by Andrea O'Reilly.
  p. cm.
  Includes bibliographical references and index.
  ISBN 0–415–92489–8 — ISBN 0-415-92490-1 (pbk.)
  1. Mothers and sons. 2. Feminism 3. Sex role. I. Title: Mothers and sons.
  II. O'Reilly, Andrea, 1961–

HQ755.85 .M73 2001
306.874'3—dc21   00–059242

CONTENTS

ACKNOWLEDGMENTS   *vii*

INTRODUCTION *Andrea O'Reilly*   *1*

I MOTHERING AND MOTHERHOOD   *23*

1
WHO ARE WE THIS TIME? AN EXCERPT FROM *AMERICAN MOM*
Mary Kay Blakely   *25*

2
MOTHERING SONS WITH SPECIAL NEEDS: ONE PEACEMAKER'S CHALLENGE
Jacqueline Haessly   *42*

3
MASCULINITY, MATRIARCHY, AND MYTH: A BLACK FEMINIST PERSPECTIVE
Claudette Lee and Ethel Hill Williams   *56*

4
MOTHERS, SONS, AND THE ART OF PEACEBUILDING
Linda Rennie Forcey   *71*

5
IN BLACK AND WHITE: ANGLO-AMERICAN AND
AFRICAN-AMERICAN PERSPECTIVES ON MOTHERS AND SONS
Andrea O'Reilly   *91*

would, as always, like to thank my children, Jesse, Erin, and Casey O'Reilly-Conlin. Since they were quite young, they have graciously accepted that books and a computer are a normal part of mothering. More recently, as they have become young adults, their belief in, and respect for my feminist scholarship, and their seemingly endless encouragement and sage advice, have sustained me and made me a better writer, thinker, and teacher.

I would like to dedicate this book to my first-born child, my sixteen-year-old son, Jesse O'Reilly-Conlin. When I first learned that I was pregnant I hoped for a daughter, believing that with a girl-child I could better live and serve feminism. Thank you Jesse for proving me wrong. I am a wiser, more hopeful, and courageous feminist because of you. In being the good man that you are, you also have shown me and others that sons as well as daughters may create the "feminist new world" that we want for both men and women.

INTRODUCTION

Andrea O'Reilly

"Few subjects so provoke anxiety among feminists," Robin Morgan writes, "as the four-letter word *sons*" (38). "We've thought and talked about, written and read about, mothers and daughters," Morgan continues, "but with a few notable exceptions we've averted our eyes from The Other Touchy Subject. Yet that subject goes to the heart of practicing what we claim to believe, that 'the personal is political.' It goes to the crux of power and of patriarchy—even though it also grazes the living nerves of love" (38).

In September 1997 the Centre for Feminist Research at York University hosted an international conference entitled "Mothers and Daughters: Moving into the Next Millennium" attended by more than one hundred and fifty speakers from around the world. Throughout the weekend, as participants probed the myriad and complex issues that mothers and daughters face at the start of a new millennium, we also, over coffee and at dinner, began to talk about our sons. The women, those who were mothers of sons and others who were concerned about boys today, began to ask, at first with some hesitation and then with increasing urgency, whether we, in our academic and personal interest in the mother-daughter relation, had in some fundamental way wronged our sons, let them down or simply forgotten them. Had we, in our negligence or disinterest, academic and otherwise, given our sons up to patriarchy, done to them what we have spent our lives fighting against for ourselves and for our daughters? Has feminism, as Babette Smith argues in *Mothers and Sons*, "failed the mothers of sons" (ix)? Whether feminism has failed sons or not, it has, as Nancy Backes suggests in her recent article, forgotten them. "Although [the mother-son] relationship, is one of life's most permanent and powerful relations," writes Backes, "mothers and sons have not been much studied."[1] The mother-son relationship, it would seem, is indeed, as Linda Forcey notes in her book *Mothers of Sons*, a "taboo topic" (2).

In response to this silence surrounding the mother-son relation, the Centre for Feminist Research at York University and the newly formed Association for Research on Mothering planned for the fall of 1998 a follow-up conference on "Mothers and Sons: Challenges and Possibilities."[2] Attended by more than seventy speakers from a dozen countries, the conference sought to identify and investigate the salient issues of this emerging field of feminist inquiry. On the eve of the first day of the conference, moments before the opening reception, an earthquake hit Toronto, causing the buildings at the York conference site to shake. And though the earthquake was a minor one and did not result in any damage, it nonetheless, became *the* topic of conversation that evening, particularly among local participants, as earthquakes are rare occurrences in southwestern Ontario. On the final morning of the conference, an unexplained power failure at York put the lights out in the conference building, leaving many participants stranded in darkened washrooms and hallways. By the end of the conference weekend, participants were convinced that these most unusual, perhaps even supernatural, occurrences were portents, testifying to the significance of this conference on mothers and sons. We joked that while a feminist conference on mothers and sons had indeed caused the earth to move, the complexities of the issues raised at this very same conference left most of us stumbling in the dark intellectually. This volume, developed from the conference, seeks to move forward, as the earth did on the eve of the conference, the feminist dialogue on mothers and sons and to shed new light on this important relationship that has increasingly engaged the minds and hearts of mothers and feminist academics alike.

Organizing the chapters of the book proved to be a difficult task because of the complex interrelation of the topics and issues raised. In the end, after many revisions I decided upon a triad thematic arrangement to reflect and expand upon what emerged as the three central, albeit overlapping, themes of the conference. The first section, "Mothering and Motherhood," looks at women's mothering and considers the various ways that the institution of motherhood oppresses women, circumvents mother-son attachment, and causes boys to be raised sexist and masculine, as it is defined in patriarchal culture. Mothers must, the contributors argue, redefine mothering in ways that accord them authority and authenticity that, in turn, will enable them to challenge the patriarchal dictates of both motherhood—for themselves—and masculinization for their sons. The next section, "Men and Masculinities," examines the various ways feminist mothers seek to dismantle, destabilize, and deconstruct normative patterns of male socialization and traditional definitions of masculinity. The contributors argue that the masculinity our culture requires boys to assume is harmful to them and society at large. "Mothers and Sons: Connections and Disconnections," the section that concludes the book, challenges the assumption, both lay and academic, that sons must separate from their mothers to achieve psychological wellness and maturity. The contributors contend that in fact it is mother and son *disconnection* that harms men psychologically. This section imagines and investigates ways to foster mother-son connection; as well, it identifies and interrogates those cultural forces that cause disconnection.

Mothering and Motherhood

In *Of Woman Born: Motherhood as Experience and Institution*, Adrienne Rich distinguishes between two meanings of motherhood: "the potential relationship of any woman to her powers of reproduction and to children; and the institution which aims at ensuring that that potential—and all women—shall remain under male control" (13). Across cultures and throughout history most women mother in the institution of motherhood; that is, women's mothering is defined and controlled by the larger patriarchal society in which they live. It has long been recognized in the "Mothers and Daughters" scholarship that mothers who raise daughters in accordance with patriarchal motherhood enact and perpetuate patriarchal strictures of gender socialization.[3] Mothers must therefore, according to this literature, reject patriarchal motherhood if they hope to raise empowered daughters. Daughters need, according to Rich, "mothers who want their own freedom and ours. . . . The quality of a mother's life—however embattled and unprotected—is her primary bequest to her daughter, because a woman who can believe in herself, who is a fighter, and who continues to struggle to create livable space around her, is demonstrating to her daughter that these possibilities exist" (247).

Writing of lesbian mothering in *Politics of the Heart*, Baba Cooper describes this mothering as radical mothering: "involving children in disloyalty to the culture the mother is expected to transmit at the expense of woman-bonding and female empowerment" (238). Women must, as Rich has argued on many occasions, be outlaws from the institution of motherhood and engage in gynocentric mothering that nurtures the power of their female selves and that of their daughters. Whether it be termed courageous mothering as Rich describes it, or radical mothering as defined by Cooper, this practice of mothering calls for the empowerment of daughters *and* mothers and recognizes that the former is only possible with the latter. As Judith Arcana writes, "If we want girls to grow into free women, brave and strong, we must be those women ourselves" (33). Women must, in other words, mother against motherhood.

The emergent feminist scholarship on the mother-son relationship also emphasizes the importance of interrogating and dismantling the patriarchal institution of motherhood. In the mother-daughter literature it is recognized that in order for mothers to instill agency, authority, and authenticity in their growing daughters, the mothers must model these same attributes in their own daily lives. In contrast, the teaching of anti-sexism and the undermining of masculine socialization are the explicit goals of feminist mothering of sons. Feminist mothering of sons, in other words, seeks to destabilize the normative practice of masculinization. Some writers on the mother-son relation go on to argue that the institution of motherhood fosters both sexism and patriarchal masculinity and thus mothers must reject traditional motherhood in order to bring about the gender transformation they wish for themselves and their sons. Judith Arcana, for example, in *Every Mother's Son* (1983), the first book-length study of the mother-son relationship, argues that traditional motherhood positions mothers as secondary to, and in service to, children and men. "Though children of both sexes," Arcana writes, "put their mothers in the position of servants . . . mothers of sons, whether we feel it in the moment or not, are inadvertently reinforcing the sexist premise that women exist to serve men. . . . Men learn from infancy to expect and solicit selflessness and cherishing care at the hands of women" (101, 102). While "daughters learn from our mothers to *be mothers*," to give in that disastrously self-destructive way that has been honored by men as true motherhood; sons learn *to expect such treatment from women*" (102). Given that women's secondary status is enforced in both the gender arena (service to men), and in the maternal realm (service to children), mothers must, if they hope to raise nonsexist men who reject traditional masculinity, challenge both patriarchal imperatives: women are to serve both men and children.

Contemporary feminist writing on the mother-and-son relation, examines, as did Arcana's early work, the interconnectedness of traditional manhood and traditional motherhood and argues, similar to Arcana, that in order to change the way men experience and define masculinity, women must change the way they define and experience motherhood. This theme is explored in the first section of this volume. Writing from a variety of maternal standpoints and drawing upon both experience and theory, the contributors seek to imagine and implement "mothering against motherhood." Each author in her own way positions herself as an outlaw from the institution of motherhood, and resists in both word and deed what Toni Morrison defines in another context as "the master narrative" of motherhood. Motherhood, as we know, is a cultural construction that varies with time, place, and family circumstance; there is no one essential or universal experience of motherhood. However, the diverse meanings and experiences of mothering become marginalized and erased through the construction of an official definition of motherhood that, in turn, becomes codified as the official and only meaning of motherhood; alternative meanings of motherhood are marginalized and rendered illegitimate. The real and normal script of motherhood, according to the hegemonic narrative, is performed by white, heterosexual, middle-class, able-bodied women who are married and raising their children in a nuclear family, preferably as stay-at-home mothers. The authors, whether by choice or circumstance, refuse this patriarchal maternal role and mother their sons outside and against the institution of motherhood. This mode of mothering, the contributors argue, enables them to thwart the destructive process of traditional masculine socialization and thus raise healthier and happier boys.

Mary Kay Blakely, in the opening chapter of this section, describes both herself *and* her two sons as "'outlaws from the institution of motherhood,' as Adrienne Rich described those who drift—or flee from traditional rules and expectations." Blakely's chapter, a narrative of her outlaw journey through motherhood, details with both humor and honesty the various maternal identities—"a working mother, a divorced mother, a poor mother, an almost-remarried mother, a comatose mother, a long-distance mother, and, finally, a deliberately single mother"—she acquired, whether by choice or circumstance, as an expatriate of motherhood. "The real life of mothers," Blakely writes, "[bears] little resemblance to the plot outlined in most of the books and articles [we] read." And while the reality of motherhood may be, in Blakely's words, "painful or compromising," it is nonetheless, "prefer[able] to the national game of Let's Pretend—the fantasy in which we are all supposed to pass for perfect mothers, living in the traditional version of a perfect family." Audre Lorde once wrote, "The strongest lesson I can teach my son is the same lesson I teach my daughter: how to be who he wishes to be for himself. And the best way I can do this is to be who I am and hope that he will learn from this not how to be me, which is not possible, but how to be himself" (77). Feminist writers on the mother-daughter relationship argue that mothers must act and speak from truth and authenticity if they hope to achieve empowerment for themselves and their girl children. A mother of sons also must, Blakely argues, mother from a place of truth and authenticity and model for her son resistance so that he may, in Audre Lorde's words, "move to that voice within himself, rather than to those raucous, persuasive or threatening voices from outside, pressuring him to be what the world wants him to be" (77). Therefore, "[while] getting bounced from the game [of Let's Pretend] into actual life," Blakely writes, "is invariably traumatic," it is better for us and our sons.

The second chapter by Jacqueline Haessly also narrates the author's exile from the institution of patriarchal motherhood and argues, as did Blakely's piece, that as an outlaw she was a better mother for herself and her sons. Blakely came to be an outlaw through both choice and circumstance as a "working" and later as a divorced and single mother and as a feminist mother. Haessly's "drift," to use Rich's term, from traditional motherhood was occasioned by her commitment to "feminist parenting for justice and peace" and her (and her husband's) decision to adopt four special needs children, three of whom were boys. Traditional motherhood is not informed by a peacemaking or feminist child-rearing philosophy, nor does the normative discourse of the good mother in the perfect family take into account the lived realities of raising children with special needs. It is assumed that the children, as with the mother and father, are in good mental and physical health, are able-bodied, are of the same race/ethnicity as their (presumably white) opposite-sex parents, and are biologically related to them. In this chapter Haessly details the aims and challenges of "peaceful" parenting and those of raising special needs children. "While all families may experience challenges in their efforts to promote peace in the family," writes Haessly, "there are special challenges for families with special needs sons." She explains that "Peacemaking in the family is about creating peaceful environments where everyone can feel safe." Children who have been abused or abandoned, in particular, need such a space; as well they need nurturing touch. However, with sons, this, as Haessly explains, "pose[s] greater challenges because the culture itself and peer pressure have boys turning away from demonstrative contact with both fathers and mothers." As with Blakely, Haessly was able to be a good and effective mother for her children—and in particular her adopted special needs sons—and nurture them well and safely into adulthood only as an outlaw from the institution of motherhood.

The third chapter in this section, "Masculinity, Matriarchy, and Myth: A Black Feminist Perspective" by Claudette Lee and Ethel Williams, moves us from narrative to theory in considering how women mother sons against and outside the institution of motherhood. Lee and Williams argue that the harsh cultural realities of being black in America—racism, poverty, and the inordinately high rate of black male incarceration—have necessitated, in their words, "that black women take a different approach to both feminism and the parental relationship with their sons." African-American mothering of sons is specifically racially determined in its concern for sons' safety and in its emphasis on survival. "The major challenge, however, to a black mother raising sons today," as Lee and Williams explain, "remains the same as that of yesterday," or what Sara Ruddick defines "as the central constitutive, invariant aim of maternal practice" (19). African-American mothering, they go on to explain, "differs in its need to impose a sense of awareness of a racially oppressive society, and how to survive physically, mentally, and emotionally in an environment often hostile to the existence of blacks, especially black males." Black mothering is also concerned with wanting children, in Williams and Lee's words, "to be comfortable with their blackness, to be secure, to be proud, and to be able to love." African-American mothers of sons, from necessity, mother in ways different from what is prescribed in the normative ideology/institution of motherhood. Moreover, it is this specific African-American practice/philosophy of mothering, Lee and Williams emphasize, that enables black mothers to keep their sons safe in a hostile world and raise them to be men proud of their African-American ancestry and identity.

The next chapter in this section, "Mothers, Sons, and the Art of Peacebuilding" by Linda Forcey, revisits and expands upon the theme of mothering and peacemaking first raised by Haessly in her chapter on special needs sons. Mothers of sons, according to Forcey, understand their work as mothers of sons to be that of "peacekeepers and peacemakers" and they interpret peace as meaning "the absence of conflict" or "peace at any price." This definition of both peace and women's role as "peacemakers" impedes, Forcey argues, the formation and implementation of "genuine peacebuilding at the familial and larger public levels." Mothering becomes constructed as peacemaking, as Forcey explains, because our culture assumes that women are, by virtue of either biology, socialization, or both, best suited to the task of nurturance and peacemaking and that the duty of children-rearing is, and should be, the sole responsibility of mothers. Genuine peacebuilding in both the home and the world at large, Forcey emphasizes, requires that mothers reject the responsibility assignment and redefine child rearing as a truly shared activity. Her chapter concludes by investigating the various ways we may redefine motherhood and considers, in turn, how true peacebuilding facilitates, and is facilitated by, this redefinition of motherhood.

My chapter, which concludes the section, examines three schools of feminist thought with respect to mothers and sons to determine how women's maternal role/identity and the mother-son relation are represented in each. The chapter opens referencing the ancient myths of Jocasta/Oedipus and Clytemnestra/Orestes. These patriarchal narratives both in their ancient forms and in their modern renditions enact maternal erasure and enforce mother-son separation. The chapter goes on to argue that maternal erasure and disconnection are central as well to early Anglo-American feminist thought on mothers and sons, which tended to downplay and devalue women's role and identity as mothers. The chapter considers how recent Anglo-American feminist writings on mothers and sons call into question the patriarchal and early feminist perspective on maternal displacement to emphasize mother-son connection. Finally, the chapter reviews recent African-American feminist thought on mothers and sons to explore both its emphasis on maternal presence and involvement and its specific, racially determined mode of rearing sons. The new feminist perspectives—Anglo-American and African-American—the chapter concludes, by highlighting maternal agency, authority, and responsibility and in foregrounding mother-son connection, have imagined and made possible a truly feminist narrative of mothers and sons.

Men and Masculinities

Robert Bly in his best-selling book, *Iron John*, argues that the modern man "is not happy . . . he is life preserving but not life giving . . . his life is full of anguish and grief" (2–4). Morever, modern men are, according to Bly, "soft." They have discovered their "feminine side" but have left unexplored their true essential masculinity: "Many men say to me that they literally don't know what the word man means" (234). Healing occurs, Bly argues, only when men get in touch with their essential masculinity and free what he calls "the wild man inside." The son must "move from the mother's realm to the father's realm" (ix). "When women, even women with the best intentions" writes Bly "bring up a boy alone, he may in some way have no male face, or he may have no face at all" (17). The journey to manhood therefore requires "a clean break from the mother" (19) because the American male grows up with too much mothering and not enough fathering. He suffers from what Bly calls "father hunger."

Feminist theory has long critiqued Bly's misogynist and mother-blaming narrative of manhood and has argued that the "wild man" masculinity championed by Bly is harmful to men themselves and society at large.[4] And while many feminists would agree with Bly that we as a culture now face, in the jargon of media pundits, a "crisis in masculinity," they see neither hypermasculinity nor heightened male bonding as the solution. The emergent literature on masculinity written by men argues that while sons learn that they are beneficiaries of power and privilege, they pay a high price for this status. Michael Kaufman, for example, describes masculinity as "an idealized version of what it means to be male . . . a collective hallucination . . . a state of mind and a story of how to behave" (25, 32, 29). Having been socialized to repress and deny emotions associated with the feminine—empathy, vulnerability, compassion, gentleness—and taught to tough it out on their own through our culture's valorization of independent, individualistic (and fully individuated) masculinity, men grow into manhood deeply wounded and isolated. Masculinity then becomes a facade or a place of refuge, where men seek to convince themselves and others that they are as brave and strong as the idealized version of masculinity purports them to be. Writers on masculinity, men and women alike, agree that masculinity, as with femininity, is a cultural construct that exits in a constant state of flux, its meaning continually shifting in response to changing economic, political, and social times. While most men today, as Carol Tavris has observed, "reject the John Wayne model of masculinity, they seem less sure than women about what should replace it" (49). Likewise, men and, to a lesser degree, women seem uncertain about *how* they would go about creating these desired new masculinities. Generally, writers on masculinity reject Bly's father-son attachment thesis and see a change in traditional gender socialization practices as a way to engender new masculinities. However, what is curiously absent or downplayed in the new masculinity literature is the relationship a son has with his mother, and she with him. The notable exception is William Pollack's 1998 book *Real Boys: Rescuing Our Sons from the Myths of Boyhood,* examined in the final section of the introduction.

"Traditionally, Western culture," as Sharon Abbey notes in her chapter in this book, "celebrated the powerful connections that develop between mothers and sons. However, we have recently lost sight of much of this wisdom recently and, as a result, have closed off channels for its appropriate expression." This, I would suggest, explains, at least in part, the absence and/or marginalization of the mother-son relationship in the new masculinity literature. Evidence of this marginalization may be found even in feminist, woman-authored works on masculinity such as Susan Faludi's recent best-selling book *Stiffed: The Betrayal of the American Man.* Significantly, the words "mother" and "motherhood" in the book's exceptionally detailed index have only a handful of entries while the word "father" yields close to a hundred listings. The book argues that men of the baby boom generation have been betrayed or stiffed by their own fathers and the fathers of male culture—bosses, teachers, corporations—because the idealized manhood they have been guaranteed and promised as their birthright is no longer theirs for the taking. These sons, according to Faludi, as Lillian Robinson notes in her review, "far from mastering society, nature and the cosmos, . . . have been acted upon by social forces that make them feel not only that they're not powerful, but that they're not men" (3). "The handiest scapegoat for masculine impotence," as Robinson continues, "is the rise of feminism. . . . [and for the disinherited white males], people of colour [were targeted] for taking what belonged by right to them" (3).

The economic transition from industry to service, from production to consumption, redefined the way men and the culture at large view manhood. Where once manhood was demonstrated by utility, today manhood is largely displayed, in Faludi's words, in an "ornamental" manner, similar to the way our culture has traditionally defined the feminine. "The fifties housewife," explains Faludi, "stripped of her connection to a wider world and invited to fill the void with shopping and the ornamental display of her ultra-femininity, could be said to have morphed into the nineties man, stripped of his connections to a wider world and invited to fill the void with consumption and a gym-bred display of his ultra-masculinity" (40). In contrast, manhood demonstrated by utility was, again in Faludi's words, "defined by character, by the inner qualities of stoicism, integrity, reliability, the ability to shoulder the burdens, the willingness to put others first, the desire to protect and provide and sacrifice" (38). Significantly, Faludi defines this as "a maternal conception of manhood" (38). These are the same qualities recoded as masculine," writes Faludi, "that society has long recognized in women as the essence of *motherhood*. Men were useful insofar as they mastered skills associated with the private realm of the feminine" (38). Maternal manhood affirms and depends upon what may be termed male mothering; older men are both expected and required to provide nurturance and guidance to younger men under their charge, whether they be sons, employees, apprentices, friends, junior colleagues, or peers. The loss of male mothering and the transition from a maternal concept of manhood to an ornamental masculinity are, according to Faludi, the cause of the current crisis in masculinity.

I raise Faludi's argument not to debate it, but rather to demonstrate how current masculinity scholarship, even by writers like Faludi who advocate the return of manhood to its traditional maternal characteristics, marginalizes actual mothers and their relationship to their sons. While Faludi may affirm male mothering and maternal manhood, actual mothers play little or no role in either her critique of ornamental masculinity or her vision of a new utilitarian manhood. In contrast, the feminist maternal perspective on masculinities, as evidenced by the chapters in this section, foregrounds a mother's relationship with her son and positions it as pivotal to the changes we seek both for our sons and for the larger patriarchal society. In their introduction to a special feature of *Feminism and Psychology* on "Mothering Sons: A Crucial Feminist Challenge," editors Robyn Rowland and Alison M. Thomas assert that "women, [both for ourselves] and for our sons . . . will no longer put up with the old version of masculinity" and will ask instead: "How, as mothers of sons, are we to respond to this challenge?" (93). This concern and question inform each chapter of this section.

Alison M. Thomas in the first chapter, appropriately entitled "Swimming against the Tide: Feminists' Accounts of Mothering Sons," examines the aims and challenges of feminist mothering of sons. Drawing upon the findings of a qualitative research study, Thomas identifies three salient themes in contemporary feminist thought on mothering and masculinity. The first topic, "[mothers'] efforts to encourage an alternative and more positive style of masculinity," details the many ways mothers, in the words of Elsie Jay, writing in the special issue *Feminism and Psychology*, "[seek to create] a new man—sensitive, expressive, nonviolent, respectful, and loving of women." Societal and at times familial—fathers, grandparents—resistance

concludes, "while men can do the tasks and work of mothering, it is the larger 'social relations and social organization' of mothering and fathering that preclude men from being socially accepted as, or wanting to be called, 'mothers.'" Doucet's research alerts us to the complexity and difficulty of feminist mothering of sons and, in particular, its aim of destabilizing traditional masculine socialization in a culture so thoroughly gender-stratified in school, work, and families.

Mother and Son Connections and Disconnections

The hegemonic narrative of mother and son attachment—as scripted in parenting books, psychoanalytic theory, and popular wisdom—assumes that sons must separate from their mothers in order acquire a "normal" masculine identity. A close and caring relationship between a mother and her son is pathologized as aberrant, while a relationship structured upon separation is naturalized as the real and normal way to experience mother-son attachment. Olga Silverstein and Beth Rashbaum write in *The Courage to Raise Good Men*: "[Our culture believes] that a male child must be removed from his mother's influence in order to escape the contamination of a close relationship with her. The love of a mother—both the son's for her, and hers for him—is believed to feminize the boy, to make him soft, weak, dependent, homebound . . . only through renunciation of the loving mother, and identification with the aggressor father does the boy . . . become a man" (11). In other words, in Western culture we see mother-son separation as both inevitable and desirable.

Recently, feminist theorists on the mother-son relation and some masculinity writers have begun to challenge this received narrative of mothers and sons by calling into question the central and organizing premise of patriarchally mandated mother-son separation, namely that this process is both natural, hence inevitable, and "good" for our sons. These writers argue that while we may perceive mother and son separation to be a natural process, it is, in reality, a culturally scripted and orchestrated act. The assumption that boys will withdraw and distance themselves from their mothers as they grow into manhood belies the fact that it is mothers—aware that mother-son connection and closeness are disparaged in our culture and thus ever-vigilant that they not be "overclose" with their sons—who both initiate and direct this separation. "By expecting our sons to cut off from us," Silverstein and Rashbaum write, "we make sure that they do" (159). Whether the son is fully cognizant of this sudden or subtle detachment, he nonetheless, according to these writers, experiences it as a profound and inexplicable loss that leaves him feeling vulnerable and alone precisely at the moment when he is required to become brave and strong. Janet Sayers explains in *Boy Crazy*: "The result, paradoxically, of mothers and sons being separated from each other, and being early distanced from knowing each other's thoughts—in the name of such distance being necessary for making boys become manly, tough, and self-contained—is that boys often experience the adolescent feelings as quite the reverse. They often experience these changes as making them feel unmanly, weak, and uncontained. This, in turn . . . often causes them to become even more distanced, detached and divided, both from others and from themselves" (28). The force of such a separation, as William Pollack observes in his recent *Real Boys: Rescuing Our Sons from the Myths of Boyhood*, "is so hurtful to boys that it can only be called a trauma—an emotional blow of damaging proportions . . . [a] relational rupture [that] profoundly affects the psychology of most boys—and of most men—forever" (12, 27).[5] To save our sons who are destined to become these detached and wounded men and to change the patriarchal world in which they and we live, we as a culture must, as Silverstein and Rashbaum conclude, recognize that "the real pain in men's lives stems from their estrangement from women" and "face up to the longing [of sons for mothers], its power, its persistence throughout a men's life, its potential for destruction when unacknowledged" (225).

The chapter that opens this section, "Raising Relational Boys" by Cate Dooley and Nikki Fedele, draws upon relational theory to develop "a model of parenting-in-connection." In their work with three thousand mothers of sons as well as adult sons and couples, Dooley and Fedele find that "boys with a secure maternal connection develop stronger interpersonal skills and enjoy healthier relationships as adults." However, the world in which our sons live, first as boys and later as men, demands both disconnection and domination. Boy culture, as it is called by Dooley and Fedele among others, straightjackets boys into specific and rigid gender identities that discourage, if not disallow, sentiments of care and relations of connection. In opposition to boy culture, and to counter its dictates of disconnection, mothers and fathers must practice what they term "parenting in connection." "The goal," as Dooley and Fedele explain, "is to enhance connection and to circumvent distance and separation" and to move toward reconnection when disconnection does occur, as it invariably will. Mothers must model and teach to their sons specific behaviors and strategies that will enable them to stay in connection. The chapter concludes by looking at four stages in the mother-son relationship—the early years, middle years, teenage years, and college/adult years—in order to identify the cultural dictates of disconnection found in each stage and detail the various ways mothers may "counter these cultural influences and keep sons on the path of relational development."

As Fedele and Dooley's chapter considers the assorted cultural imperatives of detachment and the myriad ways they may be confronted, the following chapter "Attachment and Loss" by Janet Sayers, describes the psychological and cultural costs of failing to address mother-son disconnection. Examined by Sayers in this chapter are, in her words, "the ill effects on men's mental health" caused by "[sons] prematurely losing attachment to their mothers, when . . . they are pressured to forge a male identity separate from, and superior to, that of their mothers and women generally." Drawing upon men's memories and dreams and with reference to two clinical illustrations, Sayers explores the many and diverse manifestations of this male malaise, including stammering, recurring nightmares, self-division, schizophrenia, suicide, and manic self-glorification. Calling upon the voices of men remembering their boyhood years, Sayers delineates in poignant detail how boys were forced to detach from their mothers and deny, displace, and disguise the pain caused by this disconnection. One boy, who had been instructed from infancy to keep his feelings in check, describes how, at his mother's funeral when he was eleven, he could not cry but felt instead "a tautness around his chest." This tautness, in both a literal and figurative sense, signifies the repressed pain of disconnected boys that so often manifests itself in the maladies examined by Sayers.

Amia Lieblich's chapter, "Mother-Son Relationships in the Shadow of War," moves the discussion of mother-son connection/disconnection from the psychological realm to the political-public domain. The aim of her chapter, as she explains, is "to explicate how the mother-son relationship in modern Israel is deeply linked to the sociopolitical circumstances in which private life is embedded, and in particular to the ongoing state of war and hostility in the Middle East." Of interest to Lieblich are the ways in which the private domain of the mother-son relationship interacts with, and is constructed by, the cultural-political sphere. She traces the interface of the private and public realm along three distinct, though intersecting, thematic lines: "the mother-son relationship in the context of obligatory military service . . . ; motherhood of soldiers as a political position; and the voice of mothers as mourners." Obligatory military service, though occurring in the public realm, gives rise to mother-son disconnection in the private sphere. As the time approaches for the son's service, he will turn to his father and distance himself from his mother, as she will with him, because they live in a country where all men engage in combat training and often war, while women do not, and thus there emerges for mothers and sons a seemly impassible divide of gendered differences. In contrast, mothers who have lost sons to war and who bespeak, in a public voice, their grief and resistance to militarism seek reconnection with their deceased sons. "My first duty towards Yoni, the child who keeps living inside me" says one bereaved mother, "is to say the truth all the time, never to be silenced again." Mothers must, Lieblich concludes, "enter the public arena in Israel for their sons' sake, for their own sake, and for the sake of the future."

The chapter that closes this section and the book as a whole is written by a son, Douglas Sadao Aoki, with Japanese calligraphy by June Yuriko Aoki, his mother. Aoki's piece, "This Is Leave-Taking: Mothers, Signatures, and Countermemory," is a theoretical and narrative inquiry into how the author's subjectivity as a son and a man is constructed and negotiated in and through the language and history of his motherline. Detailing his mother's reminiscences of her mother and, in turn, that mother's memory of her mother—significations of what Aoki terms the generative definition of motherhood—Aoki recounts the countermemory that his mother has constructed for him. The maternal countermemory is inscribed, both literally and figuratively, in the materiality, or what linguist Saussure calls the signifier, of his mother's calligraphy. This writing, as Aoki explains, "is the materiality of my mother's hand, in all of its equivocality of flesh and ink" and it exists apart from and against the logocentricism of Western, patriarchal thought, which privileges the signified (meaning of the word) over the signifier (the actual or material word itself). The calligraphy thus signifies a countermemory and bequeaths to the son a specific maternal genealogy of mother-son connection.

Conclusion

This volume on mothers and sons is evidently an academic work written by women and a man whose thinking is very much shaped by the university environment in which they research and teach. However, I want to conclude this introduction by suggesting that the issues raised in this collection are "anything but academic." I am the mother of a sixteen-year-old son.

Like many other mothers, I am aware that our close and caring relationship has developed despite and in defiance of the patriarchal dictates of mother and son disconnection. I recognize as well that my son's healthy sense of self remains at risk in a culture where hypermasculinization is all-pervasive. I wonder and worry that both he and our relationship may not be strong enough, secure enough, to weather the patriarchal storm. And like many other mothers, I wonder and worry about all our sons.

I began the introduction to this book in the fall of 1999 when residents of Toronto woke one morning to read a front-page newspaper story of the brutal beating to death of fifteen-year-old Matti Baranovski in a park one Sunday evening. Matti, swarmed by a gang of boys, was knocked to the ground and kicked in the head until he was rendered unconscious. The sadness and anger were palpable in the city that autumn; alone and in groups, as we grieved Matti's death, we struggled to comprehend how boys, some as young as fourteen, could have committed such an unspeakable act. The same fall I attended a Remembrance Day assembly at my daughters' elementary school; as I listened to the poems and songs, sorting out paragraphs for this introduction in my mind, I looked around me at the prepubescent boys and realized that though Canada is not officially "at war," it raises its sons, as do many other countries, to be warriors. And today I conclude this introduction just having heard on the radio the news that a six-year-old boy shot to death a six-year-old girl who was his classmate in a school in Michigan. These events and others have caused the media and some academics to declare, in the parlance of natural catastrophes, a state of national emergency for men in contemporary culture. While I would hesitate to define it as "crisis in masculinity" as they do, I do agree that "our boys are in trouble." I understand that both the causes and solutions are complex and varied. Any analysis that does not take into account poverty, racism, classism, ableism, heterosexism, capitalism, consumerism, materialism, the increasing economic disparity between rich and poor, the scarcity of good and well-paying jobs, militarism, media violence, the loss of neighborhood in the inner city, crime, lack of access to health care (in the United States and increasingly in Canada), the deterioration of public education, the glorification of violence and competition in sport, and so on, can provide only partial answers. Nonetheless, and to return to the topic of this book, it is my belief that the hope we need and the changes we seek may be found in the mother-son relationship, as mothers and sons alike strive to redefine manhood, motherhood, and the relationship they have with one another. The mother and son relationship, as Silverstein and

Rashbaum conclude, "offers us one of our greatest hopes for transforming ourselves and the world in which we live—if we will but have the courage to make the necessary changes" (241).

NOTES

1. As evidence of this, Backes cites the United States Library of Congress, which lists only seven titles between 1968 and the mid 1990s with "mothers and sons in literature" as a descriptor. Please see her article "Beyond the 'World of Guilt and Sorrow': Separation, Attachment, and Creativity in Literary Mothers and Sons" in *The Journal of the Association for Research on Mothering* 2:1(Spring/Summer 2000), pp. 28–45.

2. Founded in the fall of 1998, The Association for Research on Mothering (ARM) is the first international feminist organization devoted specifically to the topic of mothering and motherhood. ARM is an association for scholars, writers, activists, professionals, agencies, policy makers, educators, parents, and artists. Its mandate is to provide a forum for the discussion and dissemination of feminist—academic and community grassroots—research, theory, and praxis on mothering-motherhood. It is committed in both membership and research to the inclusion of *all* mothers: First Nations mothers, immigrant and refugee mothers, working-class mothers, lesbian mothers, mothers with disabilities, mothers of color, and mothers from other marginalized groups. ARM also publishes biannually *The Journal of the Association for Research on Mothering*. The journal is an integral part of community building both for researchers—academics and grassroots—and for mothers interested in the topic of motherhood. Each issue of the journal highlights a particular motherhood theme or topic and showcases the newest and best in maternal scholarship as well as featuring numerous book reviews. Furthermore, through poetry, photography, and artwork, the journal gives voice to women's lived experiences of mothering in all their complexity and diversity. Please visit ARM's website for more information about the Association and its journal: http://www.yorku.ca/crm.

3. This is examined at length in my two recent articles on Anglo-American feminist theory and the mother-daughter relation: "Across the Divide: Contemporary Anglo-American Feminist Theory on the Mother-Daughter Relationship," in *Redefining Motherhood: Changing Identities and Patterns*, ed. Sharon Abbey and Andrea O'Reilly (Toronto: Second Story Press, 1998), 69–91; and "Mothers, Daughters and Feminism Today: Empowerment, Agency, Narrative," *Canadian Woman Studies* 18:2 & 3 (Summer/Fall 1998): 16–21. See also the introduction to *Mothers and Daughters: Connection, Empowerment, and Transformation*, ed. Andrea O'Reilly and Sharon Abbey (New York: Rowman and Littlefield, 2000).

4. For an excellent feminist critique of Bly and the Mythopoetic Men's Movement

see *Women Respond to the Men's Movement,* ed. Kay Leigh Hagan (San Francisco: Harper Collins, 1992). And for an excellent overview of mother-blaming, more generally, see Paula Caplan's *The New Don't Blame Mother* (Routledge 2000).

5. See also Paul Kivel's recent parenting book, *Boys Will Be Men: Raising Our Sons for Courage, Caring and Community* (Gobriola Island, BC: New Society Publishers, 1999). "Boys and young men," writes Kivel, "need female parents fully in their lives. . . . We do not need men to step in and 'correct' a pattern of 'over-mothering' by separating sons from women and initiating them into men's mysteries" as Robert Bly and kind would theorize. "Mothers," Kivel continues, "are not the problem; men are not the solution. There is no evidence that women-raised sons are inadequate or incompetent or lacking in any way at all, even though there are lots of assertions and attempts to demonstrate so" (42–3).

WORKS CITED

Arcana, Judith. *Every Mother's Son.* New York: Anchor Press/Doubleday, 1983.

Backes, Nancy. "Beyond the 'World of Guilt and Sorrow': Separation, Attachment and Creativity in Literary Mothers and Sons." *The Journal of the Association for Research on Mothering* 2:1 (Spring/Summer 2000): 28–45.

Bly, Robert. *Iron John.* New York: Vintage, 1990.

Cooper, Baba. "The Radical Potential in Lesbian Mothering of Daughters." In *Politics of the Heart: A Lesbian Parenting Anthology.* Edited by Sandra Pollack and Jeanne Vaughn. Ithaca, NY: Firebrand Books, 1987. 233–240.

Faludi, Susan. *Stiffed: The Betrayal of the American Man.* New York: W. Morrow and Co., 1999.

Forcey, Linda. *Mothers of Sons: Toward an Understanding of Responsibility.* New York: Praeger, 1987.

Hagan, Kay Leigh, ed. *Women Respond to the Men's Movement.* San Francisco: Harper Collins, 1992.

Kaufman, Michael. *Theorizing Masculinities.* Thousand Oaks, CA: Sage, 1994.

Kivel, Paul. *Boys Will Be Men: Raising Our Sons for Courage, Caring and Community.* Gobriola Island, BC: New Society Publishers, 1999.

Lorde, Audre. "Man Child: A Black Lesbian Feminist's Response." In *Sister Outsider: Essays and Speeches.* New York: Quality Paperback Book Club, 1993. 72–80.

Morgan, Robin. "Every Mother's Son." In *Lesbians Raising Sons.* Edited by Jess Wells. Los Angeles: Alyson Books, 1997. 38–59.

O'Reilly, Andrea. "Across the Divide: Contemporary Anglo-American Feminist Theory on the Mother-Daughter Relationship." In *Redefining Motherhood: Changing Identities and Patterns.* Edited by Sharon Abbey and Andrea O'Reilly. Toronto: Second Story Press, 1998. 69–91.

———. "Mothers, Daughters and Feminism Today: Empowerment, Agency, Narrative." *Canadian Women's Studies* 18: 2 & 3 (Summer/Fall 1998): 16–21.

O'Reilly, Andrea, and Sharon Abbey, eds. *Mothers and Daughters: Connection, Empowerment, and Transformation.* New York: Rowman and Littlefield, 2000.

Pollack, William. *Real Boys: Rescuing Our Sons from the Myths of Boyhood.* New York: Random House, 1998.

Rich, Adrienne. *Of Woman Born: Motherhood as Experience and Institution.* New York: W.W. Norton, 1986.

Robinson, Lillian M. (Faludi review) "Fatherless Figures." *The Women's Review of Books* 17:4 (Jan 2000): 1, 3–4.

Rowland, Robyn, and Alison M. Thomas. "Mothering Sons: A Crucial Feminist Challenge." *Feminism and Psychology* 6 (1996): 93–154.

Ruddick, Sara. *Maternal Thinking: Toward a Politics of Peace.* New York: Ballantine Books, 1989.

Sayers, Janet. *Boy Crazy: Remembering Adolescence.* London: Routledge, 1998.

Silverstein, Olga, and Beth Rashbaum. *The Courage to Raise Good Men.* New York: Viking, 1994.

Smith, Babette. *Mothers and Sons: The Truth about Mother-Son Relationships.* Sydney: Allen & Unwin, 1995.

Tavris, Carol. *The Mismeasure of Woman.* New York: Simon and Schuster, 1992.

I

MOTHERING AND MOTHERHOOD

1

WHO ARE WE THIS TIME?

AN EXCERPT FROM
AMERICAN MOM

Mary Kay Blakely

With swelling regret and a kind of damp pride, I traveled twenty-five hundred miles to Arizona State University the summer of 1992 with my son Ryan, a high-school wrestler and English-class con man, and left him to fend for himself in the desert. I was excruciatingly aware that by the same time the next year my younger son, Darren, then in the process of shedding his reputation as "the good child" and revealing his wilder self, would begin a similarly expanded independence. The mental countdowns that began on New Year's Day for the past two years—"nine months to go before he leaves home"— were like reverse pregnancies. The deep breathing exercises I learned twenty years ago in preparation for having a baby came in handy again, during the prolonged psychological contractions of letting my sons go.

Then, as now, wild speculations and vague worries about what to expect invaded my sleep with a barrage of questions: Who *is* this person coming along next? What kind of mother am I supposed to be *now?* The questions never stopped coming and the answers, from year to year, were never the same. In the ongoing dialectic of motherhood, opposite realities could be simultaneously true: two decades ago, my sons were the most lovable and stimulating creatures on the planet; they were also the most draining and fractious human beings I'd ever known. Now I didn't want my grown sons, my daily buddies, to leave home; I also couldn't wait for their ravenous appetites and deafening music to go. The cultural myth that mothers universally dread the "empty nest" is only half-correct. "The truth is," said my friend M-Lou, a reliably blunt reporter of what was just ahead on the motherhood learning curve, "they leave home just before you would kill them."

By the time my babies were ready to leave, they had acquired the muscled bulk of young giants and tended to travel in team-sized packs. My heavily trafficked nest was straining at the seams. A twenty-year labor, for even the hardiest of mothers, is one long, sweaty haul. While I welcomed retirement from active duty, I nevertheless found it difficult to turn off old habits of mind. The closer we came to the delivery date, the more frequent my examinations—I kept scrutinizing their behavior, their manners, especially their "attitude." One week I would be astounded by signs of growing confidence and ingenuity; the next, I would be alarmed by gaping holes in their socialization. ("Only three months to go—is that enough time to clean this kid up so he'll pass for civilized?") Were they ready for independence? Was I?

In those pregnant months before they left, I had to keep resisting the urge to have another go at them, to commence a crash summer course in morals and manners. Every time I heard an alarming story on the news about male violence or saw them watching a raunchy video on MTV, I wondered how the values I had tried to pass along would weather the next transition. I knew I faced little chance of inspiring them with any sermons about life now. My sons had both reached the cool, isolating summits of late adolescence, when children are convinced they know everything. Would they eventually learn that nobody, ever, can possess all of the truth—that as long as they are human there will always be more thinking and striving to do? "Dominance makes a ruling group stupid," the late columnist Sidney Harris once wrote about the privilege that's bestowed at birth upon certain white, heterosexual men. Would my sons resist stupidity?

As I packed the car trunk last summer with Darren's clothes, computer, barbells, and books—the sum of his material parts—I realized I was approaching that impossible state my friend Joan, a mother of five, dreamed about twenty years ago when we were both frazzled working mothers in a county auditor's office in Indiana. After squeezing in too many errands during her lunch hour and fielding phone calls from squabbling kids all afternoon, she sighed deeply and uttered a fervent wish for the day she would "become unnecessary." To be unnecessary, of course, one has to accept not being in control.

Fortunately for me, my motherhood has been out of control for most of my sons' lives. First by choice, then by circumstance, we have lived like "outlaws from the institution of motherhood," as the poet Adrienne Rich described those who drift—or flee—from traditional rules and expectations. I became an official member of this irregular band a few years after my sons were born, when their father lost his job and we became what my politically correct friend Marti calls "economically challenged." My tenure as a full-time mother was necessarily brief. Since then, I have been a working mother, a divorced mother, a poor mother, an almost-remarried mother, a comatose mother, a long-distance mother, and, finally, a deliberately single mother. The editor in chief of a national women's magazine added "unnatural mother" to my long list several years ago, after I published an essay in *The New York Times* about the mind-bending months I spent coming to terms with Ryan's request, at age thirteen, to live with his dad for a year.

"I can't understand any woman who would voluntarily give up custody of her children," the editor told her staff, calling my behavior "appalling." And she didn't even know the half of it.

By the time Ryan had proposed this domicile arrangement, our family had been through so many transformations and permutations that neither his father nor I could legitimately claim "custody" of the boys, although it took us several harrowing years of hostile negotiations to comprehend this reality. In the early custody battles, our ultimata to each other reflected the same mentality as the National Rifle Association slogan appearing on Indiana bumpers that year: "You can have my gun when you pry my cold, dead fingers from the trigger."

Our first custody agreement, translated from legal jargon, was essentially this: "Divorce me, and I'll make you regret it the rest of your life—and if you think you've seen the worst of me, just wait." Still smoldering with resentment, Howard and I were almost never talking that first year about "the best interests of the children," although we used those words. When two wounded people coming out of prolonged marital strife talk custody, the negotiations are really about money and power, and why-don't-you-*love*-me? No one should actually try to live under a treaty drafted by the newly divorced. The initial attempts are rarely more than purging exercises. Our embattled period raged on for nearly five years—the national average, Professor Judith Wallerstein reports sadly, having studied the breakdown of small civilizations such as ours. It took time, and thousands of words, before Howard and I ceased the acrimony and finally realized we were both in love with the same two boys.

However much the courts and lawyers have mangled the language—and therefore the attitudes—governing custody, we eventually understood that raising sons, like bearing arms, was less a right than a responsibility. In a civilization such as ours, a mother legitimately could be said to "have a baby," but she could never claim to own a teenager. As our sons entered their second decade, I had to keep reminding myself of the note that Salinger's Zen poet wrote in his diary about the necessary detachment a parent must strive to achieve: "A child is a guest in the house, to be loved and respected—never possessed. . . . How wonderful, how sane, how beautifully difficult and therefore true."

If I had admitted suffering terribly as a consequence of giving up custody, the women's magazine editor might have tolerated or even forgiven my departure from her norm. Martyrdom and self-sacrifice are still going concerns in the institution of motherhood. My public admission that I actually enjoyed my year of long-distance motherhood was apparently the most nettling part of my unnatural behavior. She was shocked by my admission that I would probably do it again with my younger son—which I did. Quite accidentally, I'd discovered that periodic separations helped all of us, including me, keep in vital touch with who we were and what we needed. This was a deeply threatening notion to the keepers at the gates of traditional motherhood.

All of my job titles, from Working Mom to Unnatural Mom, were deliberate career moves—with the notable exception of Coma Mom, when my illness and near-death in 1984 introduced us to a new reality none of us had anticipated. Our family values may have looked odd or painful to those who still believed there could be only one kind of family, but once we'd split from the nuclear mold—cooled off and expanded—squeezing ourselves back in would have required painful contractions for us. My sons, taking their greater independence largely for granted, were both surprised to learn, during the overwrought speeches at the Republican convention the summer Howard and I took Ryan to Arizona State, that obedience and parental consent were the operative values in "the true American family." In ours, where the hierarchy kept shifting from year to year, an abundance of mercy and nerve were the saving graces.

"If you guys aren't a real family," Ryan said, getting depressed as he listened to Rush Limbaugh on the car radio, "I guess that makes me illegitimate."

"Don't worry—we were real enough when you were born," I assured him. "We just got more and more unreal over time."

Like most middle-class women who married in the early '70s, I started out with the expectation of being the kind of traditional mother that editors in chief could admire. Since then—through natural, unnatural, and outright supernatural events—those expectations changed. Although I never planned to have such a checkered career as a mother, and certainly managed some stages more gracefully than others, each stage was critical to the next: the charmingly chaotic, physically affectionate years of our young nuclear family; the emotionally explosive and slightly radioactive period of our postnuclear family; the surprisingly fluid and eventually peaceful transition into two long-distance single-parent families. A critic in the *Times* asked recently, noting the radical changes so many families have made in the last twenty years: "Is this dysfunction or are we all just highly evolved?"

"Change takes time," the cultural adage warns those of us who long for speedier, less antagonistic evolutions. Among the outlaw mothers I know who are trying to raise children, work demanding jobs, and teach husbands and bosses that women are not happiest when out running errands, the eagerness for change is an almost physically felt pain. True, it took me many years to learn, and unlearn, what it meant to be a mother in contemporary America. But once I had those truths, I burned with the desire to live them. When I couldn't, and was paternally reminded that "change takes time," I would think: No, not true. I have changed. If you haven't, given exactly the same facts over exactly the same period, it's because *resistance* takes time.

Time is never more relative than when stretched across the full span of childhood. When my sons were toddlers, sticky and close, omnipresent and ever-needy, my days were measured out in two-hour spoonfuls between meals and naps and baths and stories. As our lives moved forward in these minute increments, I did not think it possible they would one day be leaving home "before you know it," as innumerable friends told me. After serving them some twenty thousand meals, lowering the toilet seat thousands of times, issuing countless reminders that cars need oil to run, how could a mother so centrally engaged in their growth not know it?

Can a woman really forget cooking two and a half tons of macaroni and cheese? Can she forget playing solitaire until dawn on snowy nights, waiting for the sound of tires crunching into the driveway? Can a mother really not notice that her former baby's life has changed completely when he receives, among his high-school graduation gifts, a pair of purple silk boxer shorts and a scented card written in a dainty, still Palmerized script?

No, I think a mother always knows these small incidents are adding up to Something Big. We just understand, like the fans who come faithfully to the Indy 500 every year, that it's going to be a long day.

Lurching and stalling through the early years, time moved slowly as the rookie drivers tested their limits, learned to take the curves, conferred with their pit crews. I got used to the whining noises and oily fumes, paying only half-attention through each repetitive cycle until a warning flag or frightening accident snapped my mind back on the track. Then, in the riveting final laps, time suddenly accelerated. Fixed solely on the finish line, convinced they know all they needed to know, my sons hit the pedal to the metal and ignored any further signals from the pit. They barely stopped home long enough to refuel with a favorite pot roast.

While they forged ahead with a speed that bordered on recklessness, I found myself falling back in time, seized with a ferocious desire to remember everything about this long day at the track. As twenty years of effort compressed in those final laps, I felt the stirring excitement and lumpy throat I often get in movie theaters. Living with two jocks has undoubtedly had a profound influence on my imagination, because the musical score that kept playing in my head as I watched them fling themselves into the world was not Mozart's Clarinet Concerto or Pachelbel's Canon, but the theme song from *Rocky*. I know I should be far beyond the moist, sentimental lumpiness of motherhood by now. But as it turns out, I'm not.

In those months before Ryan and Darren left home, a familiar gesture or facial expression would trigger a sudden onslaught of memories. I would see the faces and hear the voices of all the children in the family album, all the little guys who used to people my life but who have now disappeared. This happens whether a mother willingly gives up custody or not. Whenever I caught a certain provocative smile, a long-suffering frown, I would be suddenly infused with a peculiar clairvoyance. I would travel back and forth in time, remembering the first time that look appeared, knowing how often it would return to delight or haunt me. I was swamped by one of these mind floods in a shoe store last August, as Darren tried on a pair of loafers in a size that could have comfortably fit both of my feet in one shoe. I remembered the first time I saw those astonishing appendages eighteen years earlier, then attached to the smallest, most fragile human legs imaginable. Once more, I was standing woozily next to his crib in the preemie intensive care nursery, leaning against his incubator for support as I watched his labored breathing. This impatient son, who had crashed into being two months before his due date—very nearly killing us both—

lay unconscious amidst his tangle of wires and tubes while I tried to sup-press fears about underdeveloped lungs and heart muscles.

He was tininess itself, his delicate pink form stretched nakedly under sunlamps to cure his jaundice, his skinny limbs covered with dark, prenatal fuzz—cilia hair for the amniotic sea he still was supposed to be in. I watched him take a wet gulp of air and then, suddenly, stop breathing entirely. My own throat seized as the line on his heart monitor flattened. The nurse jumped up when she heard the alarm and rushed to his incuba-tor, flicking his tiny heel a few times until the rhythmic beeps of his heart returned again.

"Apnea," she said, sighing with relief. "They get so tired they forget to breathe." She then went back to her paperwork at the nursing station, lit-tle Darren Oliver went back to sleep, and I worried about brain damage for the next five years.

Darren's traumatic birth was my first brutal encounter with the reality that motherhood was not—and would never be—entirely under my control. With two sons born eighteen months apart, I operated mainly on auto-matic pilot through the ceaseless activity of their early childhood. I remember opening the refrigerator late one night and finding a roll of aluminum foil next to a pair of small red tennies. Certain that I was respon-sible for the refrigerated shoes, I quickly closed the door and went upstairs, making sure I had put the babies in their cribs instead of the linen closet. That was the same period Howard would come home from work to find his cherished domestic order dissolved in a rubble of Lincoln Logs and Legos. He would raise his eyebrows to ask, "What have you been *doing* all day?" I would shrug my shoulders to reply, "Hey—they're both still alive. I've done my job."

After I discovered the real life of mothers bore little resemblance to the plot outlined in most of the books and articles I'd read, I started relying on the expert advice of other mothers—especially those with sons a few years older than mine. This great body of knowledge is essentially an oral his-tory, because anyone who is actually doing daily motherhood has no time to write an advice book about it. Women's magazines generally feature experts like Marie Osmond or Cher, who can get through motherhood without wrinkles. I learned the most useful survival tips mainly from my friends during coffee klatsches—as outsiders dimly regarded our informal motherhood training seminars.

Most of these tips were too insignificant for the pediatricly educated to bother with, but they saved countless lives on the front. I remember trying to talk with Joan one afternoon while Ryan fussed in his playpen, flinging his rattles, teething rings, even his beloved pacifier overboard, then wailing loudly until I retrieved each item. Undoubtedly recognizing the homicidal glint in my eye as I got up for the fiftieth time, Joan asked if I had a roll of cellophane tape. I thought maybe she was going to tape his mouth shut—a thought that had begun forming darkly in my own mind—but instead she gently wrapped it, sticky side out, around his fingers on both hands. He became totally absorbed for the next half-hour, testing the tactile surface on his shirt, his nose, his hair, his toes. A toy that cost almost nothing, couldn't be thrown overboard, made no rattling noises, it was the perfect pacifier. I kept rolls of cellophane everywhere for the next three years—next to the phone, in the glove compartment, in my purse.

"Where did you learn this stuff?" I asked Joan, who possessed a wealth of small but effective techniques for preventing child-abuse.

"I don't know," she said, "I guess after five kids, I now think like one: 'What would be fun?'"

I also relied on my friends whenever I needed a sanity check. I'd completely lost my bearings one year, trying to follow potty-training instructions from a psychiatric expert who guaranteed success with his methods in three efficient days. I was stuck on step one, which stated without an atom of irony: "Before you begin, remove all stubbornness from the child." I knew this suggestion could have been written only by someone whose suit coat was still spotless at the end of the day, not someone who had any hands-on experience with an actual two-year-old. I should have questioned this authority, but there's something about being an inept toilet tutor that has a dampening effect on self-esteem. I plodded impossibly on as the three-day plan stretched into the fifth interminable week.

"What's wrong with you?" Joan asked, when I walked numbly into the faculty lounge fresh from losing another round with my baby boy. I described my trouble "removing all stubbornness." I confessed that at the rate we were going, Darren would be ten years old before he was out of diapers. "I feel so shitty—and apparently, so does he."

Joan laughed, deeply familiar by now with "the guilties." Mothers breathe guilt on the job every day, like germs in the air. She recommended I pitch the book, forget about arbitrary deadlines, and accept stubbornness as a fact of childhood ("Powerlessness corrupts," she often said). She then clued me in on a game using toilet paper rolls that Darren found so amusing, he practically lived in the bathroom for three days. Joan's theory of motherhood—the harder the developmental task, the more comedy it requires—became my own.

Every time I told Joan what a terrific mother she was, she would just smile and say, "You should know." Those words invariably prompted the story of a bad mother day. She told me about waking up once in the middle of the night, foggy-brained, unable to remember putting her two-year-old to bed. None of the usual details about the bath, the sleeper pajamas, the good-night kiss would come into focus. She got up to check on the baby and found her crib empty. Racing frantically through the house turning on lights, she finally found Patty in the kitchen, sound asleep in her high chair, her head slumped down on the tray. "At least I'd strapped her in," Joan said. "She had her seat belt on."

Nobody's perfect, we knew, but mothers are somehow expected to exceed all human limits. This is an especially preposterous ideal since mothers are likely to have more bad days on the job than most other professionals, considering the hours: round-the-clock, seven days a week, fifty-two weeks a year. You go to work when you're sick, maybe even clinically depressed, because motherhood is perhaps the only unpaid position where failure to show up can result in arrest.

Given the punishing rules—and the contemptuous labels for any mom who breaks them—mothers are naturally reluctant to admit even having bad days, let alone all the miserable details leading up to them. We all do, of course, a secret that only makes us feel more guilty. However, once my friends and I started telling the truth about how far we deviated from perfection, we couldn't stop. Joan and I regularly got together with a raucous group for Friday afternoon happy hours at the Old Gashouse downtown, where we laughed and howled like outlaws around a campsite, regaling each other with narrow escapes.

One mother admitted leaving the grocery store without her kids: "I just *forgot* them. The manager found them in the frozen foods aisle, eating Eskimo Pies." Another spooned Calamine lotion into her toddler late one night, thinking it was Pepto Bismol: "Can you *believe* it? If he hadn't gagged, I might have poisoned him." My frank and witty friends, my incredible Guilt Busters, rescued me whenever the slime hit—which happened a lot, since "mother" is the first word that occurs to politicians and columnists and popes when they raise the question: "Why isn't life turning out the way we want it?"

Most of our bad mother stories didn't look so awful in retrospect. Some, however, looked much worse. Every one of my friends has a bad day somewhere in her history she wishes she could forget but can't afford to. A very bad mother day changes you forever. Those were the hardest stories to tell, shocking tales of gin in the afternoon or broken dishes at dawn, of riveting moments when we suddenly knew, *something's wrong here . . . this isn't who I want to be.* Leaning in close and lowering our voices, passing Kleenex around our huddle, we never laughed off the guilt described in those heart-breaking confessions. Only a survivor can afford to own such difficult truths, so we always knew how each story had to end. But none of us breathed until the final resolution was spoken: "I could still see the red imprint on his little bum when I changed his diaper that night. I stared at my hands, as if they were alien parts of myself . . . as if they had betrayed me. From that day on, I never hit him again."

However painful or compromising the reality of motherhood, we preferred it to the national game of Let's Pretend—the fantasy in which we are all supposed to pass for perfect mothers, living in the traditional version of a perfect family. This public pretense not only feeds private shame, it keeps women fearfully ignorant and immobile. The players of Let's Pretend must read the daily newspapers and remain convinced their own kids have nothing to do with the statistical population who are gay, have sex, need abortions, get AIDS. The winners make it all the way around the board back to square one, Deny It, without blowing their cover. The losers have to quit the game, of course, if they draw a Chance card revealing that one of their kids is pregnant. Or dead.

Getting bounced from the game into actual life invariably is traumatic, because it is so much more impossible to deny a real dead kid than the statistical ones in the papers. A woman doesn't have to commit a bad mother day to lose her innocence. A bad mother day can also happen to her. Phyllis Schlafly had one during that same frenzied convention over family values in Houston—not a fatally bad day, but a hard one for her nonetheless. Just after she'd finished her victorious campaign for a party platform that was anti-gay, anti-choice, pro-gun, and pro-death penalty, a gay publication dropped a retaliatory bomb and "outed" her son.

It was a gross misuse of both mother and son, a political war crime by activists who let an urgent end justify the foulest means. The outing put the mainstream media in a fuzzy ethical dilemma, since facts illicitly obtained—a purloined file from the Pentagon, say, or a stolen list of porn shop customers of *Long Dong Silver*—must first legitimately be put on record before they can be publicly dissected. Cornered by reporters who kept asking if she'd heard "the news" about her son, Schlafly finally said yes, of course she'd heard—that was the point, wasn't it?

Once on record, the Sunday morning TV pundits could jaw over the illegal outing, speculating on whether it bounced Mrs. Schlafly from the leading position in Let's Pretend. Some critics righteously judged that she had "asked for it"—the same people who would argue that doing inhuman acts damages the perpetrators as much as their victims. Others rationalized that the facts were bound to leak out anyway—too many people knew, too many of whom she'd deeply offended. Why not release the information when it could have the greatest political impact? Because using a son—or daughter or brother or wife—to get to the real target is the cheapest kind of opportunism. The hypocrisy exposed by the outing was not Mrs. Schlafly's.

Interestingly, Schlafly—who is never at a loss for words before a microphone—remained almost mute on the subject. When pressed, she would say only this: She wasn't going to feed her son's private life to bloodthirsty piranhas in the media. For the first time in my long history with her, I felt like applauding. Maybe she never needed my compassion before, or maybe that's what twenty years of motherhood does to you. Someone you don't even like has a truly bad mother day—whether it happens because of her or to her—and you feel compassion for the rattled state you know she's in. In motherhood, where seemingly opposite realities can be simultaneously true, being the Christian mother of a homosexual son—let's say a very devout mother and a much-loved son—could induce a cognitive headache that might last for years.

I am more familiar with Phyllis Schlafly's loopy vision of reality than I wish, since I had to live in it for so long. She and I both started raising sons in the early '70s, though on opposite sides of the Mississippi and just about everything else. It was largely thanks to Schlafly, a popular speaker and successful campaigner from Illinois, that mothers in Indiana had so few day-care centers, sex-education programs, school desegregation plans, and women's shelters. She thought that "battered women" were a feminist plot to shame men and that shelters could only lead to the breakdown of families, which made sense to Indiana legislators. At the many hearings we both attended, I was frequently stirred by her speeches, though never to applause. When Schlafly talked, men listened. State representatives nodded and took notes, finding her vision of the Totaled Woman exactly in line with their own. She may have favored a staunch hands-off policy for government, but as a neighbor, she was in-your-face.

It's possible Schlafly may now remain mute on quite a few issues for a while, if her unwelcome news survives the initial barrage of denial. A lot of mothers with homosexual sons, Christian or not, pass through many agonizing stages before accepting reality—maybe seeking therapeutic cures, extracting promises of celibacy, or arranging dinners with one "right girl" after another. After reading about the homosexual sailor aboard the *Belleau Wood* who was beaten to death by his crew mates, so brutally, according to the *The New York Times*, "that his mother could only identify him by the tattoos on his arms," you could understand a mother's attempt to change her son. If change takes time and you've got only one life, wouldn't changing your son be easier than changing the entire Navy?

Eventually, however, one bad mother day can produce more growth than a thousand good ones. That's why they're so memorable. Once we learn *something's wrong here . . . this isn't who I want to be,* the hard work of figuring out who we *do* want to be begins in earnest. One unwelcome but deeply personal revelation about sexuality can shake up a whole lot of other long-cherished facts about biology, motherhood, religion, jobs, housing, health care, discrimination, and on and on. With certain cultural and biological facts, it doesn't matter which side of the Mississippi you live on. With six growing children, Mrs. Schlafly invited a lot of Chance cards into her life. By the summer of 1992, homosexuality didn't even make the list of major things a mother had to worry about.

A "Snapshot" feature in *USA Today* a few years earlier briefly listed the five greatest concerns parents and teachers had about children in the '50s: talking out of turn, chewing gum in class, doing homework, stepping out of line, cleaning their rooms. Then it listed the five top concerns of parents today: drug addiction, teenage pregnancy, suicide and homicide, gang violence, anorexia and bulimia. Add AIDS, poverty, homelessness. Change takes time? Between my own childhood and the advent of my motherhood— one slim generation—the culture had gone completely mad.

While my sturdy support network was a sanity saver during my sons' early childhood, it was indispensable during the mind-racking years of adolescence, when the stakes rose precipitously and upped the guilt ante beyond any individual woman's resources. In an ideal society, mothers and fathers would produce potty-trained, civilized, responsible new citizens, while government and corporate leaders would provide a safe, healthy, economically just community. It was not our luck to live in an ideal world. Given the violence and greed and myopic leadership of the past two decades, a young man coming of age in America today faces treacherous curves and dangerous potholes on the way to every destination.

By the time my sons entered the second half of high school, every one of the grim realities in *USA Today* had shown up in the lives of their classmates and friends. It was impossible to assure myself that I didn't have to worry about my sons getting involved with guns or drugs. They and I both knew kids in our neighborhood, kids who regularly sat around our own kitchen table, who were. The scary reports about racial tensions and domestic violence in America were not abstractions to us. We have always lived right down the block, right next door to them, in our "good neighborhoods" as well as the bad.

Raising sons forever changed the way I read the newspapers. Desperate for an answer to "How could this *be*?" I would read and reread stories about the six teenage "wilders" from the Bronx who brutally assaulted a jogger in Central Park and left her in a coma; the half-dozen members of the California Spur Posse who proudly tallied their sexual conquests—including that of a twelve-year-old girl; the four high-school athletes in Glen Ridge, New Jersey, who gang raped a mentally retarded young woman with baseball bats and broom handles while nine others looked on. These stories *seared* me.

My imagination would heat up and I would see six poor mothers in the Bronx, nine middle-class mothers in California, thirteen well-to-do mothers in New Jersey, feeling certain I knew exactly how their hearts must be breaking. I could imagine what might be going on inside the tortured mind of Joel Steinberg's mother, after the bloody images of Hedda Nussbaum and five-year-old Lisa Steinberg convinced a jury of her son's guilt. His mother, to the bitter end of the trial, refused to believe her son capable of such violent battery and murder. She built a defensive case against Hedda—what a lousy mother she was, a drug abuser, so out of control she must have been "asking for it." Something, anything, to explain this alien son in the news, not the boy she once knew, not the son she so carefully raised. The choices I saw for her, listening to long months of shocking testimony, were to deny reality or start weeping and never stop.

"You raise your children knowing them intimately," novelist Rosellen Brown said, "but then you reach a point where that's no longer true." It takes twenty or so years before a mother can know with any certainty how effective her theories have been—and even then there are surprises. The daily newspapers raised the most frightening questions of all for a mother of sons: Could my once-sweet babes ever become violent men? Are my sons really who I think they are?

Struck dumb with horror by the Glen Ridge trial—the four athletes, the baseball bats, how the defense insisted sexual violence wasn't a crime if the retarded woman "asked for it," how neighbors and relatives could rationalize "boys will be boys" to include this assault within normal boy behavior—my friend Elisabeth became suddenly panicked about what her own son regarded as normal. Home from college the week the story hit, he was riding the subway with her one morning when she asked—trying to sound casual as she pointed to a headline across the aisle—what he thought of the case. Whose argument did he identify with? He looked at her, dumbfounded, then caught her drift.

"Mom!" he fairly shouted. "Are you really asking if I know whether it's wrong to rape a retarded girl with a baseball bat???"

She was. She could hardly believe it herself. How could she, of all people, doubt his regularly demonstrated integrity? Because she knew, as most mothers who take the news personally do, that the integrity of every young man is under constant assault. Before reaching maturity, our sons will have been exposed to more than two hundred thousand episodes of televised violence. Professor Neil Malamuth and Edward Donnerstein determined in a college sample of "regular guys, normal men," that 66 percent had a "conquest mentality toward women." Even if I'd had the money to afford private schools and expensive neighborhoods—which I didn't—there was nowhere in America where rape, battery, violence weren't daily occurrences. Since we live in a culture where so many smart, successful, educated people from New York to California, so many high public officials all over America, could mistake a conquest mentality for normal, couldn't our sons?

I wish it were true that a mother was the most powerful influence on her children, but her singular power is for a limited time only, in early childhood, when most of us are half out of control ourselves. However diligent she may be, however dedicated, no mother can escape the larger influences of culture, biology, and fate. Culture shapes the human mind with television, books, films, friends, teachers, coaches; biology governs the body with genetic codes, some imprinted with preset timers for schizophrenia or juvenile diabetes; fate can change a young life completely,

instantly, with a motorcycle accident, a bullet, a broken neck. Even within
the remaining quarter's worth of family influence, a mother shares her
fraction of power with fathers and siblings and—especially in hard economic times—live-in relatives and friends. Until mothers become the
sayers and the makers of the culture, until we can actually live in a culture
where mothers and children genuinely matter, ours is an essentially powerless responsibility. Mothers carry out most of the work orders, but most
of the rules governing our lives are shaped by outside influences.

While the stricken mothers in the Bronx or Glen Ridge may be responsible for less than a fraction of a fraction of the blame for the violent
eruptions of their sons, women habitually receive the major share of the
blame. Long before the family-values folks damned us, we had years of
practice chastising ourselves. A friend whose daughter was diagnosed with
a learning disability spent a year wondering: Was it my fault? Was it the two
glasses of wine I had at a party, decades earlier, before the warning labels
about pregnancy appeared on liquor bottles? Another friend whose three-
year-old son developed muscular dystrophy spent the next decade
searching her soul: Was it my fault? Did his disease begin when I stepped
on the fluoroscope in the shoe store, a child myself, to admire my toes in
my Mary Janes? Had the X-rays I playfully turned on, again and again, forever damaged my son's genes? The same questions bombarded my own
mother, when my eldest brother manifested his first symptoms of manic
depression: Was it my fault? Did his mental illness begin when he was
three, when I tried to sleep through his cries from the nursery one night?
The same questions invaded my life after medical science finally pardoned
my mother by uncovering genetic factors, abundantly evident on several
branches of my family tree. As my sons approached the trigger age, it was
my turn to worry: Was it my fault? Were they more vulnerable because of
the dangerous chromosomes I brought to their gene pool? There is almost
an arrogance in the outsized guilt these questions raised—as if a mother
could bend biology, culture, and fate to her will, if only she were smart,
attentive, dedicated enough.

I was only dimly aware when I was "having a baby" two decades ago that I
was entering a partnership for life. If longevity statistics apply, my sons and
I will spend more years in our future adult relationship than all the years I
spent with them as babies, toddlers, young boys, and teens—all the loved,
"gone children" who exist only in memory now. It's ultimately absurd for a

mother in one stage of development to throw judgmental grenades at women who have moved on to another. All of us, if we succeed in the job, will eventually become out-of-control mothers, noncustodial mothers, very likely long-distance mothers. Only a fool would offer herself today as the singular role model for the Good Mother. Most of us know not to tempt the fates: the moment I felt sure I had everything under control was invariably the moment right before the principal called, reporting that one of my sons had just driven somebody's motorcycle through the high school gymnasium.

Once I'd given birth to my sons, there were no guarantees about where they would wind up, with whom, in what condition of health or sanity. "Each child represents such risk, such blind daring on its parents' parts—such possibility for anguish and pain," novelist Sue Miller wrote in *Family Pictures*. The burst of love that began with childbirth expanded over the next two decades, along with the growing realization that I could not possess my sons for long, keep them safe, guarantee them a happy life. Joy/pain, joy/pain/. . . the heartbeat of motherhood.

The shocks and goosebumps and passion of raising sons often caused in me that aching, delirious sensation Einstein once described as "the deep shudder of the soul in enchantment." For Einstein, this ache was relieved with tears when he heard the sweet swell of violins echoing through velveted symphony halls. For me, those tears often flowed in less elegant settings—often in emergency rooms, when the doctor finally emerged from behind the white curtain where one of my sons lay unconscious and announced, "He's going to be all right." I could be wearing a ratty sweatshirt splattered with blood when that quivering shudder came, but I understood what love—maybe even redemption—felt like in that moment.

Motherhood, for me, was a constantly humbling experience. However global I strived to become in my thinking over the last twenty years, my sons kept me rooted to an utterly pedestrian view, intimately involved with the most inspiring and fractious passages in human development. However unconsciously by now, motherhood informs every thought I have. It influences everything I do. More than any other part of my life, being a mother taught me what it means to be human.

If I've taught Ryan and Darren something about women and justice, my jock sons have taught me something about being a sport. In our ongoing discussions of gender politics, I've looked at the issues as urgently as ever, but through the lens of love and hope rather than anger and despair. By encouraging their greater compassion and maturity, I have grown and changed myself. Raising boys has made me a more generous woman than I really am. There are undoubtedly other routes to learning the wishes and dreams of the presumably opposite sex, but I know of none more direct, or highly motivating, than being the mother of sons.

2

MOTHERING SONS WITH SPECIAL NEEDS

ONE PEACEMAKER'S
CHALLENGE

Jacqueline Haessly

Sons with special needs present unique challenges for mothers who seek both to nurture their sons and provide opportunity for them to care for and nurture others. Special needs include medical, physical, cognitive, mental, and/or emotional conditions requiring additional and often outside care to assist with activities of daily living, and—for adopted children—special needs can also mean children who differ racially, culturally, or ethnically from the adoptive family. Each special need places added demands upon all family members, demands which can generate stress and lead to unresolved feelings of inadequacy, resentment, and guilt if not acknowledged and addressed. When the culture itself encourages mothers to be primary care-givers while encouraging sons to be recipients rather than givers of care, the task of mothering special needs sons can seem quite daunting. Add to this mix a commitment to feminist parenting for justice and peace in a society oriented toward competitiveness, militarism, and patriarchy, and one has the makings for chaos within the family. Such was the challenge faced within our family when my husband Dan and I, having birthed one son, decided to adopt four special needs children, three of them sons.

This chapter draws upon literature on parenting, special needs adoption, disability, dysfunctional families, feminist values and theory, the theory and practice of peace education, and personal experience to describe the challenges and opportunities faced by mothers of special needs sons. Through the integration of personal story with parenting and peace education theory and practice, this chapter identifies threads from the tapestries of one mother's life, the lives of our four sons, and our own family history, and examines how these threads both influence and were influenced by the practice of peacemaking values, skills, and behaviors within our family.

Threads from Our Lives

No one of us parents alone. Our parenting practices are shaped by life experiences as someone's child, as someone's friend, as someone's neighbor. We learn to parent by observing and experiencing how others parent, and by learning—from conversations, observation, books, and courses—how to parent better, or at least differently, from the way we ourselves were parented. Each parent could ask: How was I parented? What models of parenting do I know from my own childhood, in my home, and in the home of my friends and classmates? What parenting models contributed to my husband/partner's parenting patterns? How do they differ from my own? How are they the same? What challenges do these different styles present to us as a couple? How did my professional training prepare me for parenting? How was I prepared, at home and through my education and professional work, to meet the challenges of parenting sons with special needs? How do I reconcile previous parenting, education, religious, and work messages with newly discovered knowledge regarding education for peace, justice, and nonviolent conflict resolution. This chapter looks at these questions from one family's experience, my own. The multiple strands that make up the colors, textures, and patterns from my own life impacted me and eventually shaped my own parenting.

My parents brought to their marriage parenting practices gleaned from their own family histories. The oldest daughter of eleven children, my mother had cared for her sisters and brothers from an early age. She was also a surrogate wife for her father, who had lost two wives from childbearing. As an adolescent, my mother was removed from her home when she reported incidents of incest, and had no further contact with most of her family for the next fifty years. Her entire sense of self was wrapped up in her feelings of betrayal and abandonment by her father, coupled with a sense that her role in life was to take care of people—her children, her husband, and, years later, elderly parents and other relatives. My mother was a scared, hurt, angry woman who lashed out at her children both physically and verbally. She also internalized her father's pattern of rejecting his young, and began disowning, off and on over the next forty years, two of her own four children when they reached young adult years. I was one of those children.

My father was the youngest of eleven children who expected to be taken care of, a task my mother—in her need to be wanted and needed—was eager to fulfill. My father held a steady job as a bus driver but drank heavily when he was not working, and would then verbally and physically abuse his wife and children.

Decades before organizations such as Adult Children of Alcoholic and Dysfunctional Families[1] existed, and psychological and parenting literature began documenting the prevalence of abused children becoming abusive parents, I sensed that this could be so. Frightened that I might "become like my mother or father," I began reading self-help books and talking to family counsellors during my high-school years. I was trying to understand my mother and my father, and trying to learn new ways to be an adult in the somewhat topsy-turvy world of our family life in the mid-1950s. After graduating from high school and then nursing school, I worked in a psychiatric hospital for the next ten years, perhaps trying to gain greater insight into the life of my own mother and her family. While there, I learned well how to manage and subdue out-of-control women (who were our only patients) by medicating them and physically restraining their acting-out behavior. This training, too, influenced and challenged my commitment to peaceful, nonviolent parenting.

Ten years later, in the mid-1960s, I returned to college and became involved with the civil rights and antiwar protest movements. I volunteered with a peace education group, teaching peaceful resolution of conflict, alternatives to violence, and cooperative play to students and teachers in our community. This was a welcome change from the hospital setting where I had worked for ten years. At a seminar on nonviolence, I met the man who later became my husband. When we married a year later, we shared a deep commitment to personal nonviolence in our family and community life. This commitment later posed serious challenges to our parenting and family life.

As Dan and I spoke of marriage and children, and the challenges these would present in our life, we realized that we each brought very different histories to this marriage. Dan claimed that he never saw his parents fight.

I, on the other hand, had experience with parents who shouted, screamed, hit each other and us children with belts and sticks, and threw things against walls. Over time, Dan and I came to realize that neither of us ever saw a conflict resolved peacefully, through conversation and mutual agreement. By the time we married in 1972, we had each learned some theory about peaceful, nonviolent resolution of conflicts and developed some skills in resolving them. While we were each committed to resolving the ordinary conflicts that arise in a marriage in a nonviolent manner, neither of us had any real-life experience in doing so, especially amidst the pressures of daily family living.

Then Came the Children!

Our first son was born to us a year after our marriage. Dan and I attempted as best we could to model peaceful living. We shared in parenting, nurturing, and homemaking tasks. Our son played with blocks, trucks, and dolls. We restricted play with guns and other war toys. We did not own a television set. We used gender-inclusive language to talk about people's work, and he delighted me when he returned from a preschool program one wintery day talking about the "snow clown" he had made at school. As he grew old enough to play simple games, such as Chutes and Ladders and UNICEF'S LINGO, we changed the rules and played these games cooperatively rather than competitively. He did not know any other way. He was a happy, outgoing child who knew he was loved. He loved us and he was not embarrassed to show it.

Due to serious medical complications that occurred during the pregnancy, I was advised to avoid another pregnancy. Dan and I were both older when we married and because we knew the risks, we had agreed before marriage to adopt children with special needs if I did not get pregnant, or if there were complications with the pregnancy. During the next few years we foster-parented several sons and then, when our birth son was three, we began the process of adoption. Between 1976 and 1979 we adopted four special needs children, sons ages six, ten, and eleven years old and a five-year-old daughter. Our three-year-old was excited as each new child joined our family. That meant he had more folks to play with!

The special needs of these four children read like a textbook for special education teachers or school social workers: two are racially mixed; one has a genetic deformity; one suffered brain damage from family-of-origin birth trauma and was diagnosed with a cognitive disability and autism; two were diagnosed with a learning disability; and one manifests signs of attachment disorder and fetal alcohol effect. We did not know the severity of the problems and the complexity demanded for their care at the time of their placement, both because we were idealistic and naive and because, in the mid- to late 1970s, social workers still did not reveal important information about adopted children's personal, family, and medical histories.

Along with their various disabilities, each child brought his or her own personal histories, which included trauma suffered from emotional, physical, and sexual abuse and even abandonment. In addition to their personal histories, each child had been exposed, in different ways, to the competitiveness, materialism, consumerism, and militarism so prevalent in our culture.

Our six-year-old son came to our home holding a small paper bag with one change of clothing, two comic books, and a small truck—all his worldly possessions. Abandoned by his mother on his fourth birthday, abused with belts, and marked with cigarette burns on his body, he begged for acceptance and small comforts. His previous foster family went to McDonalds for a meal almost daily and to Dunkin' Donuts after church services every Sunday, practices that did not fit well with our commitment to simple living and social justice. Finding a way to balance his needs for some continuity in his life and pleasuring him in simple ways meant examining our own lifestyle choices and adapting some of them to meet his needs.

Our eleven-year-old son, who joined our family six months later, was a TV addict who suffered withdrawal symptoms when placed in a home without one. He demanded almost constant attention from us to entertain him. Weaning him from TV addiction and encouraging him to find ways to join his two younger brothers in their imaginative play or entertain himself with reading, simple art and craft projects, and other activities took hours of patience and energy. This task was made more challenging because he had a learning disability and, at age eleven, was still reading at the first grade level. We could not just plunk him down with a book and hope he would read it. His two younger brothers helped where they could, but they, too, had their own needs and interests.

Our third son, who arrived in our home a year later, just after his tenth birthday, thrived in a competitive atmosphere and made almost every household task and family outing a competitive event. Who would be first? Fastest? Best? Get more? In every way possible, he would try, and our patience was tried! Efforts to teach him to play team sports using a win-win model[2] which we had successfully taught to our three other sons proved almost impossible. By the time he moved in, we had also adapted simple family games such as Scrabble and Strategy with cooperative rules so that the contributions of younger or less skilled readers were all valued.[3] Our ten-year-old quickly challenged these rules, and the other children just as quickly picked up on the "excitement" of playing to win.

Two years later our daughter arrived with her own special needs. She had suffered brain damage as a result of family-of-origin birth trauma. While she brought much joy to our family, her needs for services from occupational, physical, speech, and language therapists and school social workers seemed unending and often took time away from meeting the needs of the other children. While each of the boys welcomed her and assisted in some way with her daily care, we discovered that she turned most for love and comfort to our ten-year-old son, the one who seemed to us to be the most competitive.

As the boys grew more comfortable in our home, they each went through five stages.[4] First, there was the honeymoon stage, where everything was loving and wonderful; next came the acting-out stage, to test if we still loved and accepted them; this was followed by the rejection stage, rejecting us before we could reject them; next came the settling-in stage, where they each began to realize that they could count on us to be here for them "no matter what"; last came the "we are family" stage, where they began to take ownership of their family relationships. These stages were not easy nor were they linear. For every move forward, there were countermoves that added tension to the family and challenged all of us. Furthermore, these stages were complicated by normal developmental stages of childhood and adolescence. For example, at a time when the ten- and eleven-year-olds would normally be choosing activities with friends and away from the family as they moved toward growing independence, these children needed time to be with the family in order to bond with us, frequently causing emotional tugs between their bonding and independence needs. As the children grew into adolescence, past histories surfaced in new ways, causing rebellions, sexual acting out, and abuse of drugs and alcohol. It seemed at times as if we were in a constant state of turmoil, made all the more challenging by each child's personal traumatic history. It was in this context that my husband and I and our children attempted to create "family," and to do so with a commitment to family peacemaking.

Parenting and Peacemaking: The Dilemma

Peacemaking in the family is about creating peaceful environments where everyone can feel safe. Family Life Educators for Peace, Nona Cannon (1987, 1992), Judith Myers-Walls (1994) and Jacqueline Haessly (1980, 1989, 1997), along with peace educators Priscilla Prutzman (1974), Stephanie Judson (1984), and James and Kathleen McGinnis (1981, 1990), identify three key themes essential for effective, peaceful parenting. They each teach that peaceful parenting depends upon creating environments where a) affirmation of self and others, respect for individual differences, and cooperation in play and work are modeled; b) conflict is resolved peacefully; and c) our global citizenship is honored and celebrated. Such an environment encourages affirmation of self and others; open and honest communication about needs, wants, dreams, hopes, and feelings; respect for all the ways that people differ within a family and beyond; respectful, nurturing touch; and cooperation in work and play. Such an environment also promotes the peaceful, nonviolent resolution of conflict. Lastly, such an environment respects the needs of others who share life with us in our global village.

As parents, Dan and I shared a commitment to family involvement in peace and justice education and action. We also talked about peace in our home. We taught peace education programs at churches, schools, conferences, and universities. Together with our children, we served meals to the hungry, gathered clothing for the needy, and wrote letters to legislators seeking justice for all. Our children participated with us in peace marches and conferences in our community and on travels to distant states. Summer vacations always included a trip to a peace conference or class. In multiple ways we involved them in the process of education and acting for peace with justice. They enjoyed the travel and the fun with friends at peace conferences and camps, but were not always happy with our constant chatter about peace and justice issues in the home, especially when they saw us model other than peaceful parenting.

While all families may experience challenges in their efforts to promote peace in the family, there are special challenges for families with special needs sons. Children who have experienced abandonment find it hard to affirm themselves, and in a society where criticism of others is common, they also find it hard to affirm others. In weekly family sharing sessions, which included fun activities such as family game times, we also included a "Just Me" notebook activity which encouraged affirmation of self and each other.

The test of our success with teaching the skill of affirmation occurred one Sunday at our church, where I was conducting a peace education program on affirmation for the adults. The teacher for the high school class was absent, and I invited these young people, who included one of our sons, to join us. Their group remained apart, assisted by the father of one of the students. As I led the entire group through a series of affirmation exercises,[5] only our son was able to participate in these exercises fully. In the few years he had been in our family, he had learned well how to affirm both himself and others. The other students initially seemed embarrassed and uncomfortable with the process, as did many of the adults. By the end of the session, everyone commented upon how much they appreciated the activities and the feelings of self-esteem that surfaced during the activities. Since put-downs figure so prominently in the recent shootings in school and community settings throughout the United States and elsewhere, this is a skill worth teaching to all children, not just sons with special needs.

When one has been placed into a social service system for adoption, it is hard to communicate openly and honestly about needs, wants, hopes, and dreams. Such children are more likely to try to figure out what the social worker or potential adoptive family wants, rather than disclose what they want or need. Will they give the "right" answer? Will they still be loved and accepted if their answer is "wrong"? It becomes easier for such children to respond with "I don't know" or "I don't care." This is a necessary pattern for personal survival but can wreak havoc in family life, because when children claim they do not know what they want or need, parents cannot know either. It leaves both guessing. Feelings among such children, especially negative feelings such as anger and resentment, are more likely to be acted out rather than expressed verbally. To counter such patterns, we included time to share feelings in the "Just Me" notebook as part of the weekly sharing sessions. We began by inviting the children to share their feelings about emotionally safe topics, and slowly built in the opportunity to share more sensitive topics.

Respect for racial and cultural differences was easy to both talk about and model, since our home represented a mini–United Nations, with a total of sixteen nationalities represented among our five children and ourselves. More difficult was teaching respect for different learning styles and play patterns. When a ten-year-old is reading at the twelfth-grade level and an eleven-year-old can barely master a first-grade reader, this makes for a complicated family dynamic. Several of our sons were aggressive, competitive athletes. Several enjoyed imaginative activities either alone or with friends. Each wanted his skills and interests valued. We struggled to find ways to affirm all the ways each child was different, with varying levels of success. One tactic that worked was to invite each child to plan an activity for the family sharing time or an outing of the week. In this way, our sons had an opportunity to have their own needs met and also learned to plan activities that met the interests and skill levels of each other.

Gender differences, too, proved challenging due to the prevalence of gender stereotyping in the larger culture. We tried to blend feminist values with our peacemaking work. My husband and I shared in the tasks of nurturing, parenting, homemaking, and yard and car maintenance. Still, we often found ourselves falling into patterns made easy by a culture that trained us well for gender-specific roles. It took great vigilance to avoid such pitfalls, vigilance that was sometimes lacking due to the other demands on our energy. Our children saw that both of us held respected professional roles in our community, but I was the one working out of the home while Dan taught at a local college. Dan brought in a larger monthly paycheck than did I. And in home and family care, I was the one home with the children, while Dan commuted sixty miles each way for his work. While Dan and the boys did most of the cooking and much of the cleaning, the "invisible" tasks of planning, managing, and overseeing the care of the children and household activities fell squarely on my shoulders.

Language, too, in the music at church, in the text of books and newspapers, and in daily speech, all came under scrutiny. For children who already experience themselves as different—because of their adoptive status, race, ability level, or having an assortment of other "different" siblings—having parents stand up for gender equality, as well as for cooperative play and a world of peace with justice, and asking them to speak up and stand out in support of gender and other issues seemed way too much. In small and large ways, as they each reached their high school years, they rebelled; with their friends they refused to use inclusive or gender-neutral language, play games cooperatively, or participate in some of our more visible peace and justice work.

Children who have been physically or sexually abused find it difficult to accept nurturing touch. Our daughter was diagnosed with tactile defensiveness as a result of the abuse she experienced. We had to find a way to touch her as part of her daily routines, such as bathing and dressing, and do so in a manner that communicated to her that she was safe. Our sons, too, who had been sexually abused, needed to experience safe, respectful, nurturing touch. This posed greater challenges because the culture itself and peer pressure have boys turning away from demonstrative contact with both fathers and mothers as they go through the stages of preadolescence and adolescence. Wrestling and other contact sports seemed the only acceptable ways to obtain touch, and these activities were usually far from nurturing.

Our sons, like so many sons in contemporary culture, have been socialized to compete in games, sports, education, and work. Efforts to promote a cooperative way of playing and working together to achieve a common team or family goal proved challenging. We had some small successes: they enjoyed the intergenerational games I led at peace events and community gatherings; they cooperated with the weekly family sharing sessions, taking turns helping each other and planning sessions themselves; they also joined together to save money for special trips, to help with major household tasks, and to plan special events. Today, while each still enjoys competitive games—as players, spectators, or coaches—each of them also espouses teamwork in the schools or business settings where they work and, to varying degrees, they share homemaking tasks with those with whom they live.

Resolving conflicts peacefully and nonviolently posed the greatest challenge of all to each member of our family. Past family histories—mine, Dan's, and our children's—all played a part in what we viewed as conflict, how we viewed conflict, and how we thought a conflict should be resolved. Family meetings provided time to practice our family's conflict resolution model,[6] with varying degrees of success. When we took the time to identify a conflict, brainstorm alone and together effective ways to resolve the conflict, and choose one way that all could agree upon, we were usually successful. However, in the heat of an emotional uprising, we did not always use the skills and tools available to us. Instead, I would revert to my psychiatric training mode and embrace our children in what they came to call the CATC hold.[7] At times, we shouted, ranted, and even raged. Once, while preparing for a workshop I was to lead for parents on the topic of peace and the family, our then ten-year-old son looked me square in the eye and said "And you teach peace!" in his most sarcastic voice. I had just scolded him in a not-so-peaceful manner. Today, Dan and I are familiar with the work of Jack Lee Rosenberg and Beverly Kitaen-Morse, *The Intimate Couple* (1996), and can draw upon their insights regarding issues of abandonment and inundation to examine our own responses to a potential conflict situation and gain greater insight into potential conflicts involving any of our children. Twenty-five years ago we did not have this information, and our past histories sometimes took over. Forgiveness and reconciliation within the family are truly blessings which have helped all of us to overcome an assortment of parental and child missteps.

A culture immersed in consumerism and militarism wreaks havoc on any family's commitment to live simply in order to show respect for the needs of others who share life with us in our global village.[8] While we urged simplicity and used resale shops for clothing items, furniture, and games, our children's friends and classmates were wearing alligators on their clothing and touting the latest in computer games. Our car was an old model on a street where a new car every few years was the norm. Children who came into our family having so little felt different and insecure when their friends had so much. In a home without guns—toy or otherwise—all our children found creative ways to use Tinkertoys, pencils, Legos, and even fingers to make the necessary war toys. And in a culture that glorifies war, it was hard for our children to speak out against military aggression, especially after their cousin was taken hostage during the Iran hostage crisis.

An area of greatest pain occurred over issues regarding the military. While our three adopted sons showed no interest in serving in the military, the son born to us begged us to allow him to enlist before he turned eighteen so he could "protect people" in one or more of the countries then experiencing internal conflict, something we would not support.

Lastly, in our home, prayer and spiritual values were important. Our family attended church services regularly, and we often incorporated prayer services for special events in our home: Advent candles, Christmas Eve family vigil, Lent, and Easter. Our children all seemed to appreciate the richness of these rituals, both at home and at church and community celebrations. However, two had no experience with prayer and church service before joining our family, and another had lived in a number of foster homes where he was exposed to both Jewish and Christian religious experiences. Our family attended a Catholic church for regular services, but we also attended interfaith and ecumenical services with people of other faiths for special occasions, so they had a rich sense of the importance of religion in our own and others' personal lives. We also encouraged their participation in community service projects to help them see the connection between religion, spirituality, and serving others in need. Throughout the year, each child took turns planning a worship experience for Advent, Lent, and other special events.

Together these experiences helped shape our children and our family, as together we attempted to create a family.

Conclusion

Our first son was born to us in 1973. Our special needs adopted sons and our daughter joined our family between 1976 and 1979. In the intervening decades we have provided love and nurturing care for these five young people. They have filled our home and our lives with love and laughter as well as tears as we worked to create a family. Together we have experienced the joys and tribulations shared by most families everywhere. These young people have delighted audiences with their song and dance in school and community theatre; participated in soccer, baseball, and swim meets; and taken part in debate clubs, church, synagogue, and community service programs. There have been struggles, too: normal teenage rebellion, plus instances of drugs and alcohol use, and even an encounter with the criminal justice system. Together, with the support of family, friends, and helpful professionals, we have each survived these challenges and grown through them.

Today all five of these children are young adults. Each has made a special mark on life. Our youngest son now works as a computer programmer for a major financial institution and participates in team-building activities in his workplace. Another son works as an assistant at a local veterinary clinic, showing affection to animals and respect for their owners. Another son directs an alternative school program where students at risk are learning new skills and a sense of respect for themselves and others. Our oldest son team-teaches math to middle school students in a large public school system. Along the way, his students are also learning to respect each other and cooperate on common tasks. All four sons are involved in various ways in community volunteer work, and several coach youth sports teams at school or in the community. Our daughter works part-time with community groups serving children and the elderly. She delights people everywhere with her quick smile and eager offers to help however she can. When needed, each of her brothers will reach out to help care for her. Like young people everywhere, each of our sons has fallen into and out of love. Three are now parents themselves. In their own ways, all of these young people are actively involved with family and community and have participated in one way or another in the fullness of life. How we made "family" out of this mix, one where members of the family still seem to like each other, at least most of the time, continues to amaze me.

Peacemaking values can be integrated into a home with special needs sons. First parents must understand their own family histories and parenting practices. Then they must have knowledge of the special needs of each son or daughter, and how best, with the help of professionals, to meet those needs. Next they must be aware of and choose to integrate peacemaking values, attitudes, skills, and practices into their family's daily life experiences. Lastly they must find creative ways to link the issues pertinent to special needs sons with the values, skills, and tools essential to peaceful parenting. With care and patience, parents can help build peaceful homes for and with their special needs sons.

NOTES

1. The Adult Children of Alcoholic and Dysfunctional Families literature and movement dates to the publication of Claudia Black's *It Will Never Happen to Me* (Denver: Medical Administration Co., 1982).

2. Terry Orlick from Canada has written a number of cooperative sports and games books which promote the win-win model. These include *The Cooperative Sports and Games Book* (1976), *Every Kid Can Win* (1977), and *More Cooperative Sports and Games* (1985), all published by Pantheon Press, New York.

3. Descriptions for adapting these and other children's and family board games can be found in Jacqueline Haessly's books: *Peacemaking: Family Activities for Justice and Peace* (1980) and *Learning to Live Together* (1989).

4. These stages have been identified by Jophie Braden, social worker for families who were members of the Open Door Society in Wisconsin, an adoption network for families who adopted children with special needs.

5. See Haessly (1980) and Prutzman and Stern (1987) for affirmation activity suggestions.

6. One model for family meetings can be found in Haessly 1989. James and Kathleen McGinnis also have a model for family meetings in their *Parenting for Peace and Justice* book.

7. Several of our children named this body hold restraining technique, which I had first learned while working as a psychiatric nurse in the late 1950s, after the Child and Adolescent Treatment Center programs in Milwaukee that treated several of our children for emotional problems over a period of several years.

8. This topic is also addressed by Judith Arcana, *Every Mother's Son* (Seattle: Seal Publishing, 1986) and by Beverly McPhail.

WORKS CITED

Arcana, Judith. *Every Mother's Son*. Seattle: Seal Publishing Co., 1986.

Black, Claudia. *It Will Never Happen to Me*. Denver: Medical Adminstration Co., 1982.

Cannon, Nona. "Family Life Education for Peace." Unpublished papers, International Family Life Education for Peace Conferences. Costa Rica: University for Peace, 1987, 1992.

Haessly, Jacqueline. *Peacemaking: Family Activities for Justice and Peace*. Manwah, NJ: Paulist Press, 1980.

———. *Learning to Live Together*. San Jose: Resource Publications, 1989.

———. "From Violence to Peace: Families Confront Challenges and Embrace Possibilities," in *Mothering Teens*, Ed. by Miriam Kaufman, M.D. Prince Edward Island: Gynergy Press, 1997.

Judson, Stephanie. *Manual on Children and Nonviolence*. San Jose: New Society Press, 1984.

McGinnis, James and Kathleen. *Parenting for Peace and Justice*. New York: Orbis Press, 1981.

———. *Parenting for Peace and Justice: Ten Years Later*. New York: Orbis Press, 1990.

McPhail, Beverly. "Raising Feminist Sons: Notes from the Field." Paper presented at the International Conference on Mothers and Sons. York University, September 1998.

Myers-Walls, Judith. "Families as Educators for Global Citizenship." Unpublished paper, International Conference. Budapest, 1994.

Orlick, Terry. *The Cooperative Sports and Games Book*. New York: Pantheon Press, 1976.

———. *Every Kid Can Win*. New York: Pantheon Press, 1977.

———. *More Cooperative Sports and Games*. New York: Pantheon Press, 1985.

Prutzman, Priscilla. *Children's Creative Response to Conflict Program*. New York: Quaker Project on Nonviolence, 1974.

Prutzman, Priscilla, and Lee Stern. *A Friendly Classroom for a Small Planet*. San Jose: New Society Publishers, 1987.

Rosenberg, Jack Lee, and Beverly Kitaen-Morse. *The Intimate Couple*. Atlanta: Turner Publishing Co., 1996.

3

MASCULINITY, MATRIARCHY, AND MYTH

A BLACK FEMINIST PERSPECTIVE

Claudette Lee
and Ethel Hill Williams

Introduction

Recent statistics indicate that nearly one-third of the African-American male population is under some form of criminal justice supervision—through incarceration, probation, or parole (Mauer and Hauling). These conditions, combined with differences associated with the African-American culture, conditions associated with class and racism, have necessitated that black women take a different approach to both feminism and the parental relationship with their sons. Myths about the black family promulgated by scholars, political analysts, and the media compound this situation. The myth that is most dominant is still that of the black matriarchal family structure famously perpetuated by D. Patrick Moynihan in 1965. These are all challenges to the black feminist mother.

The major challenge, however, to a black mother raising sons today remains the same as that of yesterday—survival. The settings and techniques may have changed, but the challenge remains the same. Racism, discrimination, and oppression define the childhood of an African-American male. Mothering for an African-American woman is defined by fear for her male child. Therefore her approach and relationship with her son must be different.

This research proceeds to ask the question: Do black mothers rear their sons in a manner different from their daughters and from white mothers? And if so, what accounts for the differences? Is it the need for their black sons to survive in a world that devalues them and negates their being? Are the differences accounted for based on feminism, culture, or some other approach? Through a review of the literature and a number of interviews, this research explores some of the challenges associated with the mothering of black males, delineates a new feminist approach and, we hope, debunks many of the myths associated with African-American mothering.

History of Black Culture in America

"The family is one of the strongest and most important traditions in the black community" (Franklin, 5). Loyalty to family defied the efforts of slave owners to promote a casual attitude among blacks toward this all-important institution. In the face of tremendous odds, African slaves, despite the brutality they suffered and the separations forced on them by cruel slave owners, managed to keep family attachments and relationships alive. At the end of the Civil War, freemen searched frantically for family members separated by slavery. Many were successful and some were not. Since many slaves had been married by the mere consent of their owners, most freed slaves sought to make their marriages legal and their children legitimate in the eyes of the state.

Family stability in the black community survived Reconstruction. In the 1880s most rural and urban southern blacks lived in husband- or father-present households and subfamilies. Long marriages continued to be common among both rural and urban southern blacks. The great migration of blacks to the urban North during World War I and subsequent years did not adversely affect the stability of the black family to any significant degree. In 1925, for example, six of seven black households included either a husband or father (Gutman).

The strong cultural tradition of family among African Americans has survived slavery, segregation, discrimination, and enforced poverty. All of this has been done without the support of a racially hostile government that has upheld racist societal practices, policies, and attitudes. Patrick Moynihan's 1965 thesis on the black family suggested that the

African-American family was falling apart because of black matriarchy and that black women exploited black men. This opinion was treated as fact and became what has been referred to as the myth of black matriarchy. The suggestion that the overachievement of black women *rather than* the forced underachievement of black men caused the major problems in black families, promotes racism and blames black women for the problems of black families (Giddings). As Joyce Ladner notes, "No other racial, ethnic or religious group of females in the United States has undergone as much degradation, stereotyping and actual punishment as black women" (Ladner, 3).

Black Mothering

Black parents, like parents in every society, socialize their children to become self-sufficient, competent adults as defined by the society in which they live. For black families in the United States, socialization occurs within the ambiguities of a cultural heritage that is both African-American and European-American, and a social system that espouses both democratic equality for all citizens and castelike status for its black citizens (Peters). Peters describes the discipline of black parents as more direct and physical than the psychologically oriented approach preferred by mainstream families in the Euro-American culture (withdrawal of love, approval contingent on behavior or accomplishment). She asserts that the no-nonsense discipline of black parents is "functional, appropriate discipline administered by caring parents" (Peters; Peters and Massey 1997; Young 1970).

The socialization of black children in the United States prepares them to survive in an environment that is hostile, racist, and discriminatory against blacks (Bernard). Oppressive environmental forces influence how black families live and raise their children (Peters). Rearing children in a white-dominated society places special pressures on the black parent. Black mothers want their children to be comfortable with their blackness, to be secure, to be proud, and to be able to love. They want them to be at home in the world in which they live (Harrison-Ross and Wyden). According to Marie Peters and G. C. Massey, "Black parents have internally developed patterns of coping with racial oppression, strategies proven to be effective in the past that are incorporated into their own socialization process" (Peters and Massey, 3).

"In her study of Black mothers of young children, Richardson (1981) found that most of the parents believed this society places more limitations on the life chances and opportunities of blacks than any other group of people within the society because of racism. They [parents] agree that being black in a country full of anti-black feelings and/or actions presents real problems" (Peters and Massey 1997, 178). A person's own experiences influence their decisions about how they will raise their children. In preparation for expected encounters with racism, the mothers in Richardson's study felt that it was necessary to develop high self-esteem and self-confidence in their children. Other studies of black parenting have also reported the high priority black parents give to developing their children's self-esteem (Peters and Massey).

A number of black parents decide not to discuss racism or discrimination with their children because they do not want them to feel bitter, resentful, or prejudiced against others (Lewis). These parents expect that their children will discover institutional or individual racism someday and they are prepared to help their children cope with this reality as necessary (Peters). Therefore these black parents attempt to provide a buffer for the negative messages that may be transmitted to their children by a society that perpetuates stereotypical images of black people (Ogbu; Scanzoni).

Research on black families overwhelmingly shows that the behaviors and lifestyles of black people are different from those of whites. The lives of black parents and their child-rearing approaches are embedded in the racial, cultural, and economic situation of blacks in the United States. Some child-rearing practices are linked directly to a past that involves slavery and oppression. Many black families emphasize obedience in their child-rearing. It is an important issue and is not viewed negatively. It is reinforced throughout black culture and religion. In the past and in the present, the obedience of a black child could be a matter of life and death.

Social scientists have viewed the adaptation of black families to their circumstances of poverty and discrimination and those cultural aspects that reflect African heritage as "a problem" when they differ from the living patterns of whites. Consequently there has always been pressure to conform to the values and behavior of mainstream white America.

Racism, Criminal Justice, and the Black Male

One of the most crucial challenges facing the African-American family is the racial bias in the criminal justice system. The National Association of Criminal Defense Lawyers in the report *Racism in the Criminal Justice System* stated the following: "African Americans make up 12 percent of the U.S.

population but account for 45 percent of all arrests and over half of America's rapidly growing prison population." A 1990 report by the Sentencing Project, a Washington, D.C.–based think tank, found that one in four African-American males ages twenty to twenty-nine was under some form of criminal justice supervision in prison or jail, on probation, or on parole. In 1995, the Sentencing Project's *Young Black Americans and the Criminal Justice System: Five Years Later* revealed that the figure had grown to nearly one in three. Although the most reliable studies indicate that African Americans constitute about 13 percent of monthly drug users, they make up 35 percent of arrests for drug possession, 55 percent of convictions, and 75 percent of prison sentences. This racially disparate treatment threatens to disintegrate America's minority communities, depopulating them of wage earners and infecting them with ever-greater levels of alienation and anger. These factors impact the African-American mother's approach to mothering. They necessitate that primary emphasis be placed on teaching black males to survive above everything else.

In *The State of Black America*, published by the National Urban League, Inc. in 1993, Jeff P. Howard stated that the mortality rate for black males between the ages of fifteen and twenty-five is 3.25 times that for black women. The main cause of death is gunfire by a member of his own race. If an African-American mother manages to take very good care of her male child, tutors him, mentors him, and shows him how to survive, she still worries and prays about those circumstances out of her control. African-American mothers know that their sons live in a hostile social environment and that teaching them to navigate the rough waters of racism is the greatest challenge they have. Does a feminist approach to mothering assist black mothers in their efforts to secure their sons' survival? The following sections explore feminism from a definitional point of view.

Understanding the Feminist Perspective

There is a great deal of debate about the definition of feminism. As Ula Taylor put it: "As a theoretical construct, feminism presently has more raps than Queen Latifah" (234). Carmen Vasquez asserts: "We can't even agree on what a feminist is, never mind what she would believe in and how she defines the principles that constitute honor among us" (11). According to bell hooks: "Most people in the United States think of feminism, or the more commonly used term 'women's lib,' as a movement that aims to make women the social equals of men" (hooks 1984, 18). Pearl

Cleage, black feminist activist and scholar, uses a simple definition for the term. She explains feminism as: "the belief that women are full human beings, capable of participation and leadership in the full range of human activities—intellectual, political, social, sexual, spiritual, and economic" (28). It can also be viewed as a political movement whose foremost objective is the elimination of sexist oppression and all acts resulting from sexism.

Feminism as understood by most Western white women leads to the eradication of all forms of male supremacy. They commonly espouse that it should be the central agenda, globally, for all females. Ideologically, this focus enables Western white women, especially those who are privileged, to suggest that racism and class exploitation are merely the offspring of the parent system—patriarchy (hooks 1989).

Caraway reports that the media in the United States portrays feminism as a "for-whites-only" movement. It is viewed by both blacks and whites as the cultural property of middle-class white women. A number of writers on the topic see this version of feminism as a false universalism that generalizes the experiences of women. It ignores the specifications of race, religion, class, or sexuality (hooks 1984; Taylor; Collins 1996). Despite the removal of black women from the feminist struggle by the media, many African Americans have struggled against this exclusionary feminism and have participated in what appears to be a white-only feminist activity.

Black Feminism versus White Feminism

In response to exclusion from the broader feminist movement, black women have taken a feminist approach that is different from that of white feminism. It is a process of self-conscious struggle that empowers African-American women *and* men to actualize a humanist vision of community (Collins 1990, 30). It emerged in response to feminist theories and white women's movements that omitted serious examination of racism and the general concerns of black women and other women of color (Hamer and Neville). hooks has written, "Often the history of our struggle as black people is synonymous with the efforts of black males to have patriarchal power and privilege in order to redeem black manhood" (hooks 1989). Collins supports this argument. She writes: "Inserting the adjective 'black' challenges the assumed whiteness of feminism and disrupts the false universal of this term for both black and white women." Black feminism disrupts the racism inherent in presenting feminism as a for-whites-only ideology and political movement. This term positions black women to examine how particular issues affecting black women in the United States are part of women's emancipation struggles globally (Collins 1996, 5–6).

African-American women who use the term black feminism attach varying interpretations. Some perspectives emphasize the interaction between race, class, and gender oppressions. Each of these factors contributes equally to the plight of African-American women. Other perspectives focus on the importance of understanding black women's oppression as an ideology that emanates from a patriarchal culture—a position similar to that underlying white feminism (Hamer and Neville, 3). Collins, as summarized by Ula Taylor, contends that the diversity of black feminism can be summarized into four core themes:

- Black women empower themselves by creating self-valuations that enable them to create positive images of black womanhood.
- Black women confront and dismantle the structure of domination in terms of race, class, and gender oppression.
- Black women intertwine intellectual thought and political activism.
- Black women recognize a distinct cultural heritage that gives them the energy and skills to resist and transform daily discrimination (Taylor, 2).

Feminism versus the Concept of Womanism

Beyond the theoretical and ideological perspectives surrounding black feminism, black women are at a decision point that in many ways mirrors the struggle of all African Americans. The feminist consciousness of African-American women cannot be understood and explained adequately apart from the historical context in which black women have found themselves. McCray contends that it is critical to consider black women's African heritage, their strong religious beliefs, the caring roles they have been placed in through socioeconomic circumstances, and their need for mutual aid to survive a hostile environment. This environment impacts the black feminist perspective. Elmer Martin and Joanne Mitchell Martin assert, "As cruel and dehumanizing as slavery was, it ironically equalized the black man and the black woman."(192). This, again, sets black women apart from white women in their struggle for recognition and respect.

A number of difficulties surround the use of the term "feminism." Patricia Collins describes them as:

1. Attempts to express the genuine concerns of black women are compromised by pressures to absorb and recast issues within the white feminist framework.

2. The association of feminism with lesbianism brings black feminism into direct conflict with selected elements of the black religious experience. While individual African-American women may be accepting of gays, lesbians, and bisexuals as individuals, collectively they have distanced themselves from social movements perceived as *requiring* acceptance of homosexuality.

3. Many black women see black feminism as being "exclusively for black women only and rejecting black men" (Collins 1996, 6–7). This puts them at odds with black culture and the black experience that defines that culture.

Alice Walker presents a different concept, womanism, that takes into consideration all of the concerns posed by the concepts of feminism originally used by American white women and subsequently adopted into black feminism. Instead, white women, and men, are seen as part of the problems experienced by black people. Womanism provides an avenue to foster stronger relationships between black women and black men, committing its proponents to the survival and wholeness of an entire people, male and female. As an interpretive principle, the black womanist tradition provides the incentive to chip away at the oppressive structures, bit by bit (Cannon, 47–56). It serves as a means of addressing gender oppression without attacking black men (Collins 1996, 4). According to William VanDeburg, this is a pluralist version of black empowerment in which retaining black cultural distinctiveness allows group integration rather than individual assimilation. It is a theme seen in the teaching and nurturing of African-American women (Cannon; Collins 1990, 1996).

Womanism focuses on the need for racial solidarity and survival of the race. This perspective removes its followers from broader or more global women's issues. Black feminism's connection to existing women's struggles fosters a clearer agenda regarding gender; however, its associations with whiteness fosters its rejection by the very constituency it aims to serve.

Currently no term exists that adequately represents the substance of what diverse groups of black women alternately call womanism and black feminism. Collins suggests that the time has come to go beyond naming by applying the main ideas contributed by both womanists and black feminists to analyzing the centrality of gender in shaping a range of relationships within African-American communities. She suggests that, historically, African-American mothers have combined both approaches in raising their children. The issue of rearing male children to respect the talents and valuable input of women into society is important; however, equally—if not more—important is the necessity of raising their sons to survive in a racist and oppressive society (Collins 1996).

African-American mothering differs in its need to impose a sense of awareness of a racially oppressive society, and how to survive physically, mentally, and emotionally in an environment often hostile to the existence of blacks, especially black males. For African-American mothers this need extends not only to their sons but to *all* of the men in their lives. These are the efforts that have been labeled as matriarchal and domineering. They have been misunderstood by the dominant white culture and sometimes by black men.

The centrality of black women in "black family networks should not be confused with matriarchal or female-dominated family units. The conceptual assumption of the matriarchal thesis is that someone must 'rule' the household in order for it to function effectively. Neither black men nor black women rule black networks. Rather, African Americans' relationship to the slave political economy, and the resultant racially oppressive system, makes it unlikely that either patriarchal or matriarchal domination can take root" (Davis; Burnam, 198). This denounces the images created by others, either the "white-male created 'matriarch,' or black-male perpetuated 'super strong black mother'" (Collins 1990, 117).

This is the context of mothering on which this study is based. It assumes that African-American women combine both the feminist and the womanist approaches as a means of preparing their sons for, and protecting them from, the society in which they live. The following analysis surveys mothers from diverse backgrounds to determine the factors perceived to be most important to mothering.

The Impact of Feminist Thought on Mothering

The assumptions of the authors, based on the previous research, was that the universal approach described by Collins, combining both the appropriate tenets of feminism and the more black-oriented womanist approach, would be exercised by African-American mothers in rearing their sons. Black mothers, and perhaps other mothers of color, would place their priority in parenting on survival issues. They would stress the issues of safety, general protection, and the need to provide skills that would help their sons combat racism and the effect it has on the physical, mental, and emotional aspects of black survival. Mothering would not be in an overwhelmingly controlling or "matriarchal" mode, as is often attributed to African-American women, but would permit and encourage masculinity. The difference in parenting boys versus girls would be in issues stressing safety and protection while maintaining self-esteem. The important issues in rearing black girls, in addition to the basic questions of survival, center on protection from patriarchy and "mis-use" by all men. The approach and the focus is still somewhat different from the focus of white feminists with their daughters.

White mothers view their primary role as encouraging their children (sons and daughters) to make their individual contributions to humanity. Their feminist beliefs are manifested in rearing their sons to become aware of "femaleness." This emphasis includes guiding their sons in some way to an understanding of the importance of women to the universe, and pointing out to their sons that there is a need to explore a mode of thinking outside the patriarchal model. The difference in parenting daughters would be in nurturing the girls' awareness of self and the importance of becoming contributing members of society, while encouraging them to "march to the beat of a different drum" in a male-dominated society.

This study uses data collected from twenty-two personal interviews. The interviews were held in a one-on-one format to get a clear picture of each mother's motivating issues and to prevent one person from swaying the thoughts of another. The process of selection was random but not scientific. Interviewees included coworkers, friends, acquaintances, and those referred by others. There was an attempt to diversify the population as much as possible in terms of race/ethnicity, age, and other socioeconomic factors. Because the selection process was not scientific, many participants were from the same age group, and many had similar educational and income levels across ethnic/racial cohorts. There were eleven black, ten white, and two Hispanic mothers.

Interview questions were designed to obtain the mothers' views of their major responsibility as a parent generally, then their perceived responsibility as mothers of sons, including how their relationships changed as their sons reached different ages. The interviews revealed the following information.

Perceived Major Responsibility in Raising Sons

The responses to these questions had some similarities across the groups. Rearing sons (and daughters) to be good citizens and respectful adults was important to all of the mothers. These issues varied in order of importance by racial/ethnic groups. It was the major priority for Caucasian mothers. They emphasized the importance of raising their sons to be moral/ethical individuals and secure adults. Specific responses included: My most important role is to "love him"; "teach him right from wrong"; "teach him honesty, integrity, and the work ethic"; "teach him to have a faithful, loving and generous spirit"; and "encourage him to make goals and accomplish them."

The two Hispanic mothers emphasized "being compassionate, loving, and understanding" parents and "teaching their sons the way of the Lord" (religious training) as their first priorities. This was followed by teaching them good citizenship.

African-American mothers stressed grounding their sons with an understanding of the necessity of obtaining a good education, encouraging high self-esteem, and preparing them to deal with the everyday demands of life as the most important maternal function. Providing all of their children with a strong spiritual base was second on the list of priorities, followed by teaching them to be responsible and productive human beings.

The Mother-Son Relationship

White mothers consistently talked about discipline problems during the teen years, but they emphasized "reestablishing" close relationships once their sons moved into their adult years. Basic problems stemmed from the adult/adolescent power struggles that emerged in their sons' quest for independence between the ages of twelve and the early twenties. Issues such as ignoring curfews and all parental instruction appeared to be common. Mothers with younger sons emphasized enjoying a loving, friendly relationship that encouraged nurturing and warmth. Overwhelmingly these mothers discussed allowing their sons to develop a sense of independence. As conflict arose during the adolescent years, Caucasian mothers spoke of providing "guidance and advice" but allowing their sons to find their own way.

The Latino mothers described close, friendly relationships with their sons (even during adolescence). The ages described as problem years by white mothers were discussed by Hispanic mothers in terms of "testing the boundaries" but not affecting the parent/child relationship. Establishing and reestablishing relationships, as discussed by white mothers, was never mentioned.

Black mothers responded in a manner similar to Hispanic mothers. They spoke of their sons challenging parental authority rather than getting into trouble outside of the home. The African-American mothers emphasized strong parental supervision (at all ages) rather than the use of a guidance- and-advice approach as their sons became older.

Special Considerations, Precautions, and Activities Necessary in Parenting Sons

These questions were designed to be the most useful in addressing feminist and/or womanist issues in parenting. They asked about whether the mothers took special safety precautions with their sons as opposed to their daughters, or if there were certain activities or special considerations given to their male children. The Caucasian and Latino responses were very similar. The majority of mothers said they took no special gender-related precautions with their sons. The answers that varied from this response were related to concerns about pedophiles and stranger abductions. One white mother was very adamant about the warnings she gave her son. She stated, "I constantly alerted him because he is a blue-eyed blonde and much more likely to be preyed upon."

The discussion of special considerations and activities almost immediately brought out efforts by white mothers, to teach their sons to respect females. One mother declared, "Because he is a white male, I don't want him to be a 'male-chauvinist pig.'"

Both Hispanic mothers said they took no special gender-related precautions. One of the two explained that she taught her son about bigotry and "how to understand people's ignorance regarding Hispanics," but added that it was not a topic she dwelled on.

The questions on special considerations and precautions pointed out the greatest amount of variance between the black and white interviewees. Black mothers discussed instructing their sons "to be extra careful and not to do anything that would cause them to be stopped by the police" (this was due to the perception the larger society has of black males). Several mothers discussed the close bond they had with their sons. When asked which was stronger, the mother/son relationship or the mother/daughter relationship, the majority agreed that they were closer to their sons. They offered no reasons why this was so. Most of the African-American mothers spoke of the importance of helping their sons understand the necessity of treating all people with respect; one mother added, "including women." This statement was made in a matter-of-fact manner, not as something on which she placed great emphasis.

Conclusion

The findings of this study are consistent with the literature. Many of the ideas surrounding parenting were unique to the cultural experiences of each group. Mothering for white women centered around the need to nurture and care for their children. Their relationships with their sons were not very different from the relationships they had with their daughters (except when individual personalities warranted closer or more distant bonds). Those concerned with feminist issues took special care to provide their sons with the knowledge and introduce them to the activities that would foster respect for women as well as acknowledge the particular contributions made by women to society and the world.

Black mothers "attempted to instill a sense of self-acceptance strong enough to counteract the negative messages of the larger society. They raised their children to be assertive, emotionally expressive, and independent," just as the literature specified (McGoldrick, 189). Although they did not necessarily prefer sons, they tended to have a closer relationship with them than with their daughters, they feared more for their safety, and they took many more precautions to shield them from a racially hostile environment.

Do black mothers rear their sons in a manner different from their daughters and from white mothers? The answer is a resounding yes! It is difficult to determine whether the parenting differences found in this study resulted from a feminist/womanist approach, or whether the dissimilarities are more closely related to cultural and historical differences between blacks and whites. What can be said is that the "matriarchal" assumptions surrounding black female attitudes and actions are false. African Americans approach motherhood and day-to-day existence on the basis of helping a people to survive a hostile environment. The history of blacks in America certainly cannot be ignored or downplayed in any life circumstances. Parenting, as well as other black/white issues, warrants more extensive study.

WORKS CITED

Bernard, J. *Marriage and Family Among Negroes*. Englewood Cliffs, NJ: Prentice Hall, 1966.

Burnam, Margaret A. "An Impossible Marriage: Slave Law and Family Law." *Law and Inequality 5* (1987): 187–225.

Cannon, Katie G. *Black Womanist Ethics*. Atlanta, GA: Scholars Press, 1988.

Caraway, Nancie. *Segregated Sisterhood* . Knoxville, TN: University of Tennessee Press, 1991.

Cleage, Pearl. *Deals with the Devil and Other Reasons to Riot*. New York: Ballantine Books, 1983.

Collins, Patricia Hill. "A Comparison of Two Works on Black Family Life." *Signs* 14.4 (1989) 875–884.

———. *Black Feminist Thought: Knowledge, Consciousness, and the Politics of Empowerment*. New York: Routledge, Chapman and Hall, 1990.

———. "What's in a Name? Womanism, Black Feminism, and Beyond." *Black Scholar* 26.1 (1996).

Davis, Angela. *Women, Culture, and Politics*. New York: Random House, 1989.

Franklin, John Hope. "African American Families: A Historical Note." In *Black Families*, 3rd ed., edited by Harriette P. McAdoo. Thousand Oaks, CA: Sage Publications, 1997.

Giddings, P. *When and Where I Enter: The Impact of Black Women on Race and Sex in America*. New York: Bantam Books, 1985.

Gutman, Herbert G. *The Black Family in Slavery and Freedom, 1750–1925*. New York: Vintage, 1977.

Hamer, Jennifer, and Helen Neville. "Revolutionary Black Feminism: Toward a Theory of Unity and Liberation." *Black Scholar* 28.3/4 (1998): 22–30.

Harrison-Ross, P., and B. Wyden. *The Black Child: A Parents' Guide*. New York: Peter H. Wyden, 1973.

hooks, bell. *Feminist Theory: From Margin to Center*. Boston, MA: South End Press, 1984.

———. *Talking Back: Thinking Feminist, Thinking Black*. Boston, MA: South End Press, 1989.

Howard, Jeff, ed. *State of Black America*. National Urban League, 1993.

Ladner, Joyce. "Foreword." In *The Black Woman in America*, edited by Robert Staples. Chicago: Nelson Hall, 1973.

Lewis, H. *Blackways of Kent*. Chapel Hill, NC: University of North Carolina Press, 1955.

Martin, Elmer, and Joanne Mitchell Martin. "The Black Woman: Perspectives on Her Role in the Family." *Ethnicity and Women* 5 (1986): 184–205.

Mauer, Marc, and Tracy Hauling. *Young Black Americans and the Criminal Justice System: Five Years Later*. Washington, DC: The Sentencing Project, 1995.

McCray, R. "One-Child Families and Atypical Sex Ratios in an Elite Black Community." In *The Black Family: Essays and Studies*, edited by Robert Staples. San Francisco: University of California Press, 1980, 177–181.

McGoldrick, Monica, et al., eds. *Women in Families: A Framework for Family Therapy*. New York: Norton Publishers, 1991.

Moynihan, Daniel P. *The Negro Family: The Case for National Action*. Washington, DC: U.S. Department of Labor, Office of Policy Planning and Research, 1965.

National Association of Criminal Defense Lawyers. *Racism in the Criminal Justice System*.

Ogbu, J. *Minority Education and Caste: The American System in Cross-Cultural Perspective*. New York: Academic Press, 1978.

Peters, M. F. "Nine Black Families: A Study of Household Management and Childrearing in Black Families with Working Mothers." Ph.D. dissertation. Harvard University, 1976.

Peters, M. F., and G. C. Massey. "Chronic vs. Mundane Stress in Family Stress Theories: The Case of Black Families in White America." Unpublished manuscript. 1988.

———. "Parenting of Young Children in Black Families." In *Black Families*, 3rd ed., edited by Harriette Pipes McAdoo. Thousand Oaks, CA: Sage Publications, 1997.

Richardson, B. B. "Racism and Child-Rearing: A Study of Black Mothers." Ph.D. dissertation. Claremont Graduate School, 1981.

Scanzoni, J. *The Black Family in Modern Society*. Boston, MA: Allyn and Bacon, 1971.

Taylor, Ula. "The Historical Evolution of Black Feminist Theory and Praxis." *Black Scholar* 29.2 (1998): 234–253.

VanDeburg, William. *New Day in Babylon: The Black Power Movement and American Culture, 1965–1975*. Chicago, IL: University of Chicago Press, 1992.

Vasquez, Carmen. "Toward a Revolutionary Ethics." *Coming Up* (January 1983): 11.

Young, V. "Family and Childhood in a Southern Negro Community." *American Anthropologist* 72. (April 1970): 269–288.

4

MOTHERS, SONS,

===

AND THE ART OF PEACEBUILDING

Linda Rennie Forcey

I

My early work on mothers of sons suggested that the mother-son relationship is not all it could be. It seems that mothers tread cautiously with sons; in fact, one could argue ironically, there is too much of a certain kind of peacekeeping. When, as part of an oral history project, I asked women in mid-life what they currently talk about with their children, those with both sons and daughters recalled in detail only conversations with the latter (Forcey 1987, 81–101). There was generally with daughters an ongoing dialogue, a sharing of experiences and emotions, with empathy and support for one another. This was not, generally, true for sons. The conversations mothers recalled usually focused on their sons' worlds of school, work, or relationships, all on a markedly more superficial, safer level. As Adrienne Rich has pointed out, there is a "fear of 'alienating' a male child from 'his' culture" which still runs deep among women (205).

Patterns of communication between mothers and sons have been conditioned by the way the historical subordination of women in the public sphere has been combined with their temporary dominance over nurturing relationships with children in the private sphere, in the home. Such patterns also have been conditioned by the questioning by both women and men of a contemporary gender system with its private and public gendered spheres of activity. It should come as no surprise that these patterns are ambiguously characterized by such affectivities as peacekeeping and peacemaking, the mother traditionally regarded as both "the angel in the house" (Woolf, 285) and "the powerless appeaser . . . innocent of the real world" (Ruddick, 137).

These reflections are based on feminist research of stories from mothers with sons who are adolescents or older, peace research, and my own experiences as a feminist academic, peace activist, and a mother to six children (two of whom are stepchildren and three of whom are sons). I argue first, that for mothers of sons to be able to appreciate peacebuilding as an art, they, and all women and men, must come to understand the awesomeness of the contemporary responsibility placed upon mothers of sons. Second, I support the notion that mothers and sons must learn to share and care with a fuller knowledge of the human frailties and vulnerabilities of each other and of other women and men in all their diversity. Third, I maintain that peacebuilding requires that we all learn to appreciate better a strategy for change that seeks to implement standards of justice, nonviolent social institutions, and inclusive social norms for all sons and daughters, not just for our own. Questions like: What has gone wrong with the socialization of men in the United States? and: "Who should be in charge of the bringing up of our children? become issues not just for mothers but for everyone to ponder. This means that the private lives of mothers and sons must connect with all of our public lives, that we cannot remain unconnected from each other.

After thinking about mother-son relationships on both public and private levels for a good number of years now, I have concluded that many mothers see themselves as peacekeepers and peacemakers on the familial level, especially between sons and their fathers. They seldom see themselves as peacebuilders—that is, in a larger, public sense. Women often define peace in the family as merely the absence of conflict, and this is one of the reasons their communication with sons becomes limited to the noncontroversial. They often feel impelled to sweep their differences with sons under the carpet. They tend to take a "peace at any price" approach, thus making for severe limitations on the sharing of experiences (Forcey 1987). Thus even their roles as peacekeepers and makers come at great cost to their own self-esteem, growth, and peace of mind.

I argue, therefore, that as long as the mothering assignment includes having the sole responsibility for the well-being of sons, there will be little opportunity for genuine peacebuilding on the familial and larger public levels. Of course children have certain "demands" that must be met. Infants must be fed, diapered, cuddled, played with, talked to, cared for, and loved. Children's lives must be preserved and their growth must be fostered.[1] In fact, it is clear that human beings of whatever age need far more nurturing than they usually get. What remains in dispute, however, is who should be responsible for the raising, caring, and socialization of our sons and daughters.

II

I came to this topic of mothers and sons and the art of peacebuilding via several paths. One was theoretical and academic (a major focus of my dissertation and teaching in the field of women's studies); another, highly personal (the search for meaning in the suicide of a close friend); and another, familial and sometimes tortuous, at times contradictory, and not wholly coherent (that is, making sense of my own experiences as a mother of sons). I first began to reflect seriously about the mother-son relationship in 1971 when I returned to graduate school after childbearing and raising for more than a decade. My Ph.D. dissertation, entitled "Personality in Politics: The Commitment of a Suicide," examined the life of one young man, Robert Starobin, who killed himself at the age of thirty-one.

Bob had been a "red diaper baby," a prominent political activist of the 1960s, a respected historian, and a personal friend of mine. Through an analysis of his letters, personal papers, and diaries, and by open-ended interviews with his friends, fellow activists, colleagues, lovers, and family, particularly his mother, I attempted to tell from many different perspectives the story of the complicated interplay between one man's personal life and his political/socioeconomic environment. As I worked on the project I found myself becoming increasingly focused on Bob's mother, so much so that in my mind, she, as much as her son, was a victim. Before I and others who knew Bob had even met the woman, we had wondered about her and her relationship with her son. So did she, I later learned, for the suicide of a child becomes in the mind of the mother the ultimate violent failure of mothering. My developing feminist consciousness and my own children's emergence into adolescence were enhancing my empathy for all mothers. I found myself wanting to understand better that particular mother whose son, my friend, had killed himself. I found myself wanting to understand better the relationships of all mothers to sons, my own three included.

The dissertation could be considered the genesis of my book, *Mothers of Sons: Toward an Understanding of Responsibility*. The book was based on oral histories of one hundred mothers from a wide variety of socioeconomic backgrounds who had sons aged sixteen and older. I argued that mothers of sons had been placed in a catch-22 situation. In the eyes of our social commentators, they had been damned if they did and damned if they didn't. While Freud, practically every biographer of famous men, most social scientists, and many literary figures tell us that behind every conqueror, every hero, is *the* responsible mother, they usually describe her as overinvolved, overwhelming, and smothering. Alternately, we are told that behind every vain, hypersensitive, invidious, violent, sexually deviant, mentally ill, or merely unfulfilled male of whatever age there is that same responsible mother.

The peacebuilding theme emerged, somewhat surprisingly and serendipitously, from my reflections on the awesomeness of the mothering responsibility. On the familial level, I concluded from my analysis of the interviews that peacekeeping and peacemaking, rather than positive peacebuilding, was a central theme of many women's perceptions of their roles as mothers to sons. And, from their perspectives, these were ambiguous roles. Many mothers seem to believe that built into their responsibility assignment are some rigid communication rules about peacekeeping and peacemaking. To be a loving, caring mother of sons is 1) to teach sons to identify with their fathers; 2) to keep the peace between fathers and sons; 3) to be nonconfrontational with sons; and 4) to protect sons from "the truth" about painful, personal issues such as marital problems, divorce, illness, and even boredom. Many mothers, I concluded, withheld their opinions, did not speak their minds, avoided expressions of feelings and emotions, and, as often as not, suppressed much anger. In the line of duty, as they defined it, they opted for a much more limited honesty and openness—one that hid the self and precluded intimacy and thus genuine peacebuilding.

On the public level, most feminist peace researchers and I have found that the record as to mothers' support of national wars has been similar to that of men. Women as well as men are committed to what they regard as "the national interest." In my *Mothers of Sons* study, however, I spoke with many women who, while they encouraged their sons to join the military, did so not out of patriotism. Rather, they viewed the military as the only or best available means of shifting elsewhere the mothering responsibility—be it psychological, social, or economic—from themselves alone to a larger institution. Similarly, Barbara Omolade has pointed out that African-American women have a legacy of support for war because the military represents economic opportunity and social status for their sons and, incidentally, for their daughters too. "Few black women," Omolade tells us, "can live outside the dilemmas posed by this predicament. Which war zone does she protect her son from: The military or the street?" (184).

The *Mothers of Sons* book challenged the notion that women by virtue of their mothering capabilities are naturally more peace-loving than men or than other women. I argued that only when we can put to rest the all-powerful-mother stereotype and begin to see them as people with their own uniqueness, struggling with conflicting values at a particular historical moment, can we begin to understand. One mother I interviewed put it this way:

> I think we mothers of sons often just fall into the social expectations of the relationship rather than letting our relationships be unique in what they are. As women we live out others' expectations—what we should do, shouldn't do. That is all we seem to be able to act on. We simply have to speak out so that we can break through all of that. If we break through to what is really right or true or best for us then we can have this fundamental sense of being there for our sons and also being free. And our sons can have that same sense of being there for us and also being free. (149)

III

Many women find it difficult to examine critically this assignment of responsibility. There is a dearth of feminist analysis of the mother-son relationship together with the socialization of aggressive boys in the United States.[2] There are several reasons. One relates to a popular, deeply held perception about women's nature, another, to assumptions about the ways in which children grow and develop, and a third, to the ill-defined standards by which we measure "good" mothering. First, with respect to women's nature, mothers have generally been considered to be the nicer, kinder, gentler sex, innately able to provide unconditional love as the very definition of WOMAN. Not always, however. In what has been referred to as stage one of the contemporary feminist movement, for example, "the angel in the house" was, if not squashed, at least repressed. That is to say, the peaceful nature of women and their motherwork was not the focus. Building on the work of Simone de Beauvoir in the late forties and Betty

Friedan in the early sixties, feminists began to see the glorification of mothering as an instrument of women's oppression.

By the mid-seventies, however, a number of feminist scholars had begun to argue that the first wave of feminist theorizing invalidated ways of knowing that seemed characteristically womanly.[3] The second wave of feminist theorizing took a posture that sought to discover and validate women's lives in the concrete labors of their daily experiences. This standpoint (often labelled "essentialist") assumes a separate female world, one in which women are essentially different from men—more caring, more cooperative, more peaceful.

We should note that while this long-term debate still rages,[4] this assumption that women and men have essential natures (with women being nicer, kinder, gentler) has been challenged by many feminist theorists writing in the late eighties and nineties. These writers are extremely skeptical of any universalist ideas that downplay thinking about how distinct and different all people are. They believe that claims of difference can easily be read as a biologically essentialist claim compatible with conservative discourse as to the proper roles for women and men.

Women have also found this assignment difficult to question because the responsibility of mothers to children is predicated on certain accepted but questionable assumptions about the ways in which children grow and develop, which reflect the dominant cultural and psychological thought of any given historical period. In post-Freudian Western societies the presuppositions for healthy childhood development include an appreciation of the primacy of infancy, the need for early bonding with the mother, unconditional mother love, and the prolongation of infancy to adolescence and frequently far beyond. Childhood has become a forever stage, so that we now have our responsible mothers to blame forever. For boys, there are additional problematic assumptions about development that mothers are required to understand and do something about. These include recognition of the incestuous desires of sons to possess mothers, the need for sons to learn to repress these desires, acknowledgment of the inevitable rivalry between fathers and sons, an appreciation of the inevitable struggle for separation from mothers, and the need for sons ultimately to identify with fathers in order to become "normal," heterosexual, productive men.

As Philippe Aries reminds us, however, assumptions about childhood change over time. Mothers' roles in the lives of their children were not always as we now know them. As myriad contemporary feminists of color also remind the white, middle-class women of the United States, assumptions about childhood are not always as the dominant culture portrays them.[5] And, beyond the scope of this paper but important for all of us to consider, a number of leading developmental psychologists have recently rallied around a new hypothesis from grandmother Judith Rich Harris. She argues that what is important is not what children learn from their parents but what they learn outside the home. Put bluntly, peers matter more than parents (Gladwell, 54–64).

The third reason why this responsibility concept is as confusing as it is awesome is the lack of meaningful definition of what it takes to fulfill one's responsibility—what it takes to be a "good" mother. For mothers who have been attacked as vipers and held responsible for most of the problems of society, there is not too much to go on. The literature of the social sciences on mothers of sons explores the relationship primarily within a post-Freudian context that argues for the centrality of mothers to sons. It generally assumes a particular tension in the relationship, often explained in terms of an absent father who has left the wife as much in need of a husband as the son is of a father (Bibring).

The consequences for sons of women's dominance in the family, as social historian Christopher Lasch saw it, are positively awful. "Their unconscious impressions of the mother are so overblown and so heavily influenced by aggressive impulses and the quality of her care so little attuned to the child's needs, that she appears in the child's fantasies as a devouring bird, a vagina full of teeth" (217). Is it any wonder most women avoid questioning the meaning or the wisdom of the assignment? Is it any wonder that many mothers of sons choose to be, at any price, mere peacemakers and peacekeepers?

IV

Here we must realize the subtle distinctions that peace educators make among the terms *peacekeeping, peacemaking,* and *peacebuilding.* These will clarify how mother-son relationships can find a new focus with the art of peacebuilding.[6] By *peacekeeping* the educators refer to violence-prevention activities to create an orderly environment for our children. Peace researchers call this a "negative peace" approach. For example, in schools with high levels of physical violence there are often daily weapons searches, frequent detentions and expulsions, and the use of such devices as metal detectors. While many peacekeeping activities are essential for the well-being of children, they are limited in that they merely mirror a generally punitive criminal justice system, with a disproportionate number of African-American and Latino/Latina students becoming the subjects of peacekeeping exhortations.[7]

On the familial level, some mothers rely frequently on their own authority, a peace-through-strength approach, to educate their children, particularly their sons, about the consequences of violent behavior. They enforce rules that they believe will help deter self-destructive and cruel behavior in order to make a safer environment for their children. It must be noted here that mothers' experiences as peacekeepers, as all mothering experiences, must be viewed in the social, political, and economic contexts in which they emerge. As Patricia Hill Collins points out, motherwork for women of color: "reflects the tensions inherent in trying to foster a meaningful racial identity in children within a society that denigrates people of color. . . . White children are socialized into their rightful place in systems of racial privilege. Racially ethnic women have no such guarantees for their children; their children must first be taught to survive in systems that oppress them" (57).

In my own research I discovered there are layers and layers of struggles that are part of most mothers' total situation. Some mothers are too tired to deal with the day-to-day problems of their sons and are more than willing to delegate peacekeeping activities to the schools. This is how one overwhelmed mother described an encounter with the high school principal:

> We had a principal who called me on the telephone and told me to get down to the school because my sons wouldn't get on the school bus at the snap of a hat and he told me they were hoodlums. I don't go for this telephoning and I told him that if they do anything wrong I give my permission for him to pick up a ruler or use his fist—punch them one. But, I said, don't ever call me again because my husband is real sick and I am working so hard and I am tired and I don't want any more phone calls. Well, I know he didn't believe how sick my husband was and how bad things was around here and he kept on calling me and then my husband upped and died and this principal finally realized what I meant. I hope he's still thinking about it. (Forcey 1987: 69)

Proponents of *peacemaking* strategies tend to look beyond the prevention of disorder to a more proactive achievement of positive outcomes. In schools, educators use conflict resolution techniques to foster both positive growth and institutional change. The underlying assumption for peacemaking advocates is that when conflict resolution principles and processes are learned and utilized by every member of a school community, they bring peaceable schools. Conscious planning leads to noncoercive school and classroom management practices. Schools move away from competitive ideals toward the valuing of cooperation. Educators in peaceable schools try to involve parents, fathers as well as mothers, in building respect for conflict resolution processes, if only because it is clear that efforts to model cooperative behavior in classrooms can be undermined by coercive home discipline (Crawford and Bodine, 39–47).

While few mothers of sons are conversant with such principles of conflict resolution and management, many are sympathetic to their goals. However, most school conflict resolution programs make certain presuppositions about the equality of all parties involved in a conflict that clearly cannot work easily in the family setting. Philosopher Sara Ruddick argues that maternal thinking articulates an opposed and superior conception of conflict resolution "rooted in a maternal view of relationships." From mothers' perspectives, "it is not necessary to be equal to resist violence. Most mothers try to teach their children when self-respect demands a fight. Their own peacemaking—their attempt to create conditions of peace—includes training for active, engaged nonviolent fighting. Rather than depending on an illusory state of equality, they aim to fight as they live, within communities that attend to and survive shifting differences in power" (180).

My own research has shown, however, that mothers of sons often express ambivalence and sometimes downright anger regarding their identities as mediators and peacemakers. This is particularly so when interventions between sons and their fathers are involved. "You know, you get tired of being this intermediary. Being the sponge for everyone else's pain, being the only shoulder there is to cry on, being the only one for whom they can utterly fail," says Betty, a forty-five-year-old mother of two sons. "I tell myself over and over again that I must allow Lee and his father to meet on their terms and to let what happens happen. But after all these years of being in the middle it is very very hard for me" (Forcey 1987: 87).

Although conflict resolution strategies are becoming increasingly popular among educators and parents alike, there are concerns about the promise of conflict resolution programs. This is particularly so for elementary and secondary school programs that rely solely on peer mediation processes without making them an integral part of a larger school conflict resolution effort that attempts to get at the root causes of conflict. Some fear that strategies like peer mediation may tend to promote social control rather than social change. In the past, in truth, issues of social justice have rarely been part of the field. The point is that conflict resolution programs are not a panacea for ridding societies of violence.[8] Nor, in my view, are peacemaking strategies a panacea for solving problems of dysfunction in families; nor even enough for "good enough" parenting.[9]

The term *peacebuilding*, as used by peace educators, builds on the goals of peacekeeping and peacemaking as just defined, but tries to move farther. Nonviolence is the key assumption as well as a fundamental orientation of a peacebuilding approach. Nonviolence, as exemplified by its leading twentieth-century advocates, Mohandas K. Gandhi and Martin Luther King Jr., has three guiding principles: 1) to state explicitly one's intentions to conduct and resolve conflict without violence; 2) to adopt provisions to demonstrate and carry out one's intention; and 3) to avoid all killing or imposing of suffering on others while holding fast to one's own truths (Woito, 154–73). Nonviolence is a philosophy of life that focuses on how people treat themselves and others and a strategy for change that seeks to implement standards of justice, nonviolent social institutions, and inclusive social norms.

The goal of a peacebuilding approach, therefore, is not just to stop violence, either directly or indirectly, but rather to create in people's minds the conditions for what might be called positive peace. On the familial level, peacebuilding entails everyday experiences of mothers of sons. Summer, a divorced woman in her mid-forties with five sons, has an exquisite sense of the humorous reality and complexity of this. She explains:

> I'm quite a different mother now. I keep thinking I'm getting better and better at it. Maybe I'm not, but I surely have a different sense of motherhood. In the beginning I wanted my boys to be poets, writers, musicians. This is the only way I could picture them because these are the things I love. I made them take ballet lessons and forced them to read for one hour a day. I just expected them to love what I love to do.

She laughingly recalls the following incident reflecting the mood of her household:

> I remember one Saturday morning. Before [their] going off to play I insisted that each one find a room or quiet corner of the house to

either read or practice on a musical instrument for one hour. The previous evening I had read to them a speech Winston Churchill had delivered to the graduating class at Harrow. Pounding his fists on the podium, he had said, "Never, never, never give up." Now on this particular Saturday morning the boys were being extraordinarily subversive, just full of beans. Some were reading with their books upside down, others were playing their songs backwards. I was becoming more and more angry, and the situation was getting out of hand. Finally, in utter frustration, I announced I was giving up and they could all go to pot. With that declaration I stamped into my study, slamming the door behind me. Moments later a little white piece of paper emerged from under the closed door. The note said, "Never, never, never give up."

Summer says she never has given up, or, as she puts it, "to be more accurate, I have never given up on what I now see is the most important gift I could give my sons—respect for their freedom." She is comfortable with the knowledge that they will not be poets, philosophers, musicians; that they prefer parachuting, motorcycles, and computers:

> This process of awareness was extremely slow but now as I look back I see that as I became aware of my own struggle to be free, to gain my sense of self, they too became freer. (Forcey 1987: 78–79)

It is here on the familial level that mothers (and fathers) as peacebuilders sometimes play a unique role in fostering in their sons (and daughters) a love of freedom, a consciousness and tolerance of worldviews, a global vision, a sensitivity to issues of gender, race, and class oppression. They dare to reflect aloud with their sons as they themselves humbly and unabashedly struggle to find coherence and meaning in the complex processes of social change around them.

On the public level, as has already been noted, the peacebuilding record for mothers, for women in general, is not so good. While historians have demonstrated that women, guided by both feminist principles and political strategies, have played a central peacebuilding role in peace movement history,[10] most feminists readily acknowledge that women nonetheless often support wars enthusiastically and vigorously. The experiences of many women and their children involuntarily involved in conflict throughout the world illustrate the fact that the force of what women as nurturers do on the interpersonal level is painfully powerless in the global arena.

V

A part of me, my former essentialist, pre-postmodernist, pre-grandmother self, would have been tempted in this concluding section to exhort all mothers of sons to dedicate themselves to the pursuit of truth and light, where there can be no sexual oppression, no injustice of any kind. The life of political activism they would be urged to adopt would add to their already enormous responsibility for the caring and nurturing of their children. And it would be placing more blame on those women fighting for their own survival and that of children. This I can no longer do. It is with great wisdom that postmodern feminists have cautioned against any unified representation of the world's women that is constructed from any Western-centered approach.[11] Who am I to say how to do the right thing for all mothers of sons?

Nevertheless, I do not feel so humble that I cannot try to speak about mothers and their relationships with sons. As Rosemary Tong points out, "Feminists need a home in which everyone has a room of her own, but one in which the walls are thin enough to permit a conversation" (7). Continued feminist inability to speak out for women from a variety of cultures "only further reinforces the voices of those who have constructed approaches . . . out of the experiences of men," J. Ann Ticknor argues (17). The trick, it seems to me, is to honor the differences, but also to acknowledge at the outset what Edward Said calls "the massively knotted and complex histories of special but nevertheless overlapping and interconnected experiences—of women, of Westerners, of Blacks, of national states, and of cultures" (32). In granting each and every one a separate identity, Said argues, we need not lose the essence of the human community of which we as women and men are a part. It is, therefore, to this human community, not specifically to mothers of sons, that I address my own call to action.

This activity requires a sense of humility, a sense of humor, and a willingness to open our hearts and our pocketbooks to embrace a community considerably larger than the nuclear family by which we who are mothers define our responsibilities. There are four components: 1) resisting the dichotomization of women and men that implies women are nicer, kinder, gentler; 2) deconstructing the ideology of the all-powerful mother with the impossible responsibility; 3) appreciating the diversity of women's and men's lives as mothers and fathers, sons and daughters, throughout the world and over time; and 4) envisioning a more just and peaceful world.

I. Resisting the dichotomization of women and men

When it comes to peace in the family, feminist theorists as well as mothers of sons often, as suggested, see themselves as symbolizing peace, the preserver of life, the angel in the house. Feminist theorists like Sara Ruddick, Nancy Chodorow, Carol Gilligan, and Jean Baker Miller, to name but a few, have written that because of maternal practices women have developed an ethic of care quite different from men's. "If the world itself seems under siege, and if that siege holds any community and all children hostage, the effort of world protection may come to seem a 'natural' extension of maternal work," writes Ruddick (81). It is a way of thinking that, actually and not just theoretically, should socialize each new generation to nonviolent behavior and to a peaceful world order. But are these special peacekeeping and peacemaking skills contributing to the development of more peaceful sons and a more peaceful, more just world order? I think that would be lovely, but I think that is not presently a reality of women's lives.

British feminist Lynne Segal, striking her central theme about the inadequacy of polarized thinking about men and women, writes: "This has meant a minimal interest in conflicts and contradictions as they are experienced within feminine identity, a false universalizing of our own gender categories and a disregard for other social practices (outside mother-daughter bonding) as they impinge upon gender identity." Segal points out that: "the weight of one's own children can mean a contradiction of social vision, an envy and resentment of the welfare of others. . . . While it may be true that women are more concerned about peace and a better world . . . this does not necessarily mean that women are any less nationalistic, racist, or committed to class privilege than men" (1987, 6, 148).

2. Deconstructing the ideology of the all-powerful mother

The art of peacebuilding requires the deconstruction of the ideology of the all-powerful, all-responsible mother. Clearly, women's search for a balance of selfhood and caring in both the workplace and the home are contributing to the shattering of the myth. Joyous celebrations and recounting of warmly humorous anecdotes of daily living with sons are interspersed throughout my interviews (along with the painful, complaining ones). They illustrate ways in which mothers and sons were learning to support and understand one another once they had learned to accept those things they could not change. These upbeat stories were generally from women who had returned to school to continue their graduate studies or were employed outside the home. Rosalind C. Barnett and Caryl Rivers, two working mothers themselves, confirm my findings of the advantages for families of women working, in a four-year study of six hundred subjects (middle- and working-class married couples) conducted at Wellesley College and funded by the National Institute of Mental Health.

This is all well and good, you readers may be saying to yourself, but who, then, is going to be responsible? I believe that feminists were right to identify the importance of men's involvement in child care and nurturing as a crucial factor (albeit not the only one) in the elimination of gender oppression. It really must be part of the ideological struggle to break down the dichotomy between men and women.

This business of shared parenting is not always easy for mothers of sons. I will give you a personal example. Although I believe that I had, and have, a wholesome relationship with my youngest son, who was born shortly before I returned to graduate school and is truly a product of "shared parenting," I had lapses concerning my redefined mothering identity from time to time. One such lapse was the time he, at age ten, had an emergency appendectomy. On this particular day I had called from work to "check on things," only to discover that my husband had taken our son to the hospital. I dashed from work to the hospital in time to see him being wheeled off to surgery, his hand tightly clutching his father's. After the (successful) operation, my husband, who is prone to insomnia and late evening hours anyway, said he wanted to stay in our son's room for the night in case he awoke frightened or in pain. This certainly seemed like a sensible decision and I, prone to getting my eight hours, scampered home to bed.

But I could not sleep. Something was wrong. I felt extremely anxious. Surely our son would be expecting me, his mother, to be by his bedside when he awoke, I thought to myself. Not stopping for breakfast I dashed back to the hospital at the crack of dawn, theoretically to relieve my husband, but in reality to be "the essential one" for our son.

When I arrived, three big tears rolled down our son's cheeks, and he said, "Daddy, don't go. I felt so safe with you all night by my side." My body stiffened. For a moment I felt almost an uncontrollable rage toward the child. I wanted to shake his poor sore little form and scream, "I am your mother and you feel safe with only me alone." The irony of it all! Here before my very eyes had been the most beautiful proof that the mother does not have to be the only essential one, and I almost go berserk.

Many other women and I are beginning to understand the price that is paid by both mothers and sons (and fathers) when only the mother is the essential one. The responsibility assignment is beginning to be questioned. With a daring openness women are reflecting on what it means to fail at a task that is so defined that no one can succeed. They are also talking about the futility of their guilt, their lack of control, their feelings of ambivalence, their anger at the injustice of their situation, and the joy they and their sons are finding as they learn to free themselves of it. As Lynne Segal has written: "We need to break down the barriers between the private and the public, to fashion a society in which collective provision for individual needs ensures the maximum choices for those caring and those being cared for alike. . . . Women too *could* have the best of both worlds: but for that to happen the two worlds—the public world of paid work and the 'private' world of the home—would have no longer to be seen as unconnected" (Segal 1990: 58, 59).

3. Appreciating the diversity of women's and men's lives throughout the world and over time

One of the hallmarks of contemporary feminism has been to encourage women's consciousness of their common ground. The implication was that women as an oppressed group had a special understanding of all women. Thanks in large part to the contributions of both women of color around the globe and postmodernists, most feminists now see the need for the deconstruction of this myth of women's exclusive consciousness of women as women. In retrospect, in fact, it now seems inevitable that an end would come for feminism's day of an exclusionary solidarity that universalized woman as woman.[12] The challenge for women, as I see it, is to take seriously the dilemmas inherent in the feminist debate about difference. It is to recognize both the power of universalizing women as women in the name of solidarity for social change and the elimination of women's oppression, as well as the danger of denying or suppressing acknowledgment of differences among women.

Patricia Hill Collins points out that: "for women of color, the subjective experience of mothering/motherhood is inextricably linked to the socio-cultural concern of racial ethnic communities—one does not exist without the other. . . . This type of motherwork [for sons and for daughters in different ways] recognizes that individual survival, empowerment, and identity require group survival, empowerment, and identity" (47). Physical survival, Collins argues, "is assumed for children who are white and middle-class. The choice to thus examine their psychic and emotional well being and that of their mothers appears rational. The children of women of color, many of whom are physically starving, have no such choices however" (49).

Black feminists have been especially vocal and explicit about the importance of distinguishing state violence from male violence. They argue that white, Western feminists have been blind to this distinction, mouthing the significance of race and class but focusing only on white patriarchy as the source of all oppression. Kum-Kum Bhavnani, for example, rejects the idea that violence is "essentially masculine." Such a belief, she argues, negates black people's historical memory of and resistance to white women's support of racism, not only in the streets of South Africa but around the world. The ideology of the nicer, kinder, gentler woman, Bhavnani argues, is offensive to black women and to the many other women who have fought against racism and oppression. "Non-violence" and "peace," she argues, "end up being meaningless terms unless given tactical accuracy and political definition" (264, 268). Clearly, as Collins, Bhavnani, and other women of color have convincingly shown, peacebuilding requires that women include, but also get beyond, gender analysis.

4. Envisioning a more just and peaceful world

Lately the private/public distinction has taken on new meaning as the world witnessed President Clinton "sidling his way toward contrition" during the Monica Lewinsky scandal. Journalist Gary Wills writes that this separation: "bespeaks a certain derangement of identity if that is one's attitude toward one's own life. Is the private life, the deepest self, unconnected with public performance, both of them sealed off from each other, alternate masks one puts over one's face? Is there a self to *be* hidden?" (11).

The challenge for mothers of sons, and for all women and men, is to understand that what we do as citizens matters as much as what we do in the home. For women, this means we must acknowledge the tension between needing to act as women who value mothering and caring and needing an identity not overly determined by gender. It is about resisting claims that some categories (like mothering) are natural and inevitable. "What guarantees we have [for a more peaceful and just future]," Segal argues, "come from women's and men's engagement in a whole variety of political campaigns against militarism and arms production, and more" (1987: 201).

The challenge, to put it another way, is to be ever-vigilant of the age-old trap of oversimplifying the notion of mothers of sons, denying their differences with other mothers and other women, exaggerating their differences with men, and thereby lessening their power. And, most importantly for me as a feminist peace activist and educator, the challenge is to continue to reflect upon, value, and question the feminist assumptions, theories, and strategies that can best mobilize all mothers and fathers, women and men for a more peaceful and just world.

NOTES

1. Sara Ruddick provides an excellent portrayal of the daily practices of mothering.
2. One exception is Myriam Miedzian's groundbreaking exploration of how and why U.S. males turn to violence, and what we as a society can do about it, in *Boys Will Be Boys.*
3. See, for example, the works of Nancy Chodorow, Carol Gilligan, and Sara Ruddick.
4. This debate is summarized in Diana Johnson; Linda Forcey 1996.
5. See, for example, the essays in Evelyn Nakano Glenn, Grace Chang, and Linda Forcey (1994). Note especially Patricia Hill Collins, "Shifting the Center: Race, Class, and Feminist Theorizing about Motherhood."
6. See Marvin Berlowitz; Ian M. Harris; and Linda Forcey and Ian M. Harris.
7. See Kenneth Meier, James Stewart, and Robert England.
8. This point is central to the conflict resolution theory of John Burton, and to the practical suggestions of Linda Lantieri and Janet Patti.
9. D. W. Winnicott, the British child psychiatrist, says that "good enough" mothering is all we can expect from mothers, and is done by those with natural self-reliance who are not afraid of their great responsibility.
10. See, for example, the works of Barbara Jean Steinson, Harriet Alonso, Amy Swerdlow, Jill Liddington, and Sandi E.Cooper.
11. See, for example, V. Spike Peterson and Ann S. Runyon.
12. The deconstruction of this myth is discussed thoroughly in Elizabeth Frazer and Nancy Lacey.

WORKS CITED

Alonso, Harriet. *Peace as a Women's Issue: A History of the U.S. Movement for World Peace and Women's Rights*. Syracuse: Syracuse University. 1993.

Aries, Philippe. *Centuries of Childhood*. New York: Knopf, 1963.

Barnett, Rosalind C., and Caryl Rivers. *She Works, He Works: How Two-Income Families Are Happier, Healthier, and Better-Off*. San Francisco: Harper, 1995.

Berlowitz, Marvin. "Urban Educational Reform: Focusing on Peace Education." *Education and Urban Society* 27, no. 1 (1994): 82–95.

Bhavnani, Kum Kum. "Turning the World Upside Down." *Charting the Journey*. London: Sheba, 1987, 264, 268.

Bibring, Grete. "On the 'Passing of the Oedipus Complex' in a Matriarchal Family Setting." In *Drives, Affects, and Behavior: Essays in Honor of Marie Bonapart*, edited by R. M. Lowenstein. New York: International Universities Press, 1953.

Burton, John W. *Resolving Deep-Rooted Conflict: A Handbook*. Lanham, MD: University Press of America, 1987.

Chodorow, Nancy. *The Reproduction of Mothering*. Berkeley: University of California, 1978.

Collins, Patricia Hill. "Shifting the Center: Race, Class, and Feminist Theorizing about Motherhood." In *Mothering: Ideology, Experience, and Agency*, edited by Evelyn Nakano Glenn, Grace Chang, and Linda Rennie Forcey. New York: Routledge, 1994.

Cooper, Sandi E. *Patriotic Pacifism: Waging War on War in Europe, 1815–1914*. New York: Oxford University Press, 1991.

Crawford, Donna, and Richard Bodine. *Conflict Resolution Education: A Guide to Implementing Programs in Schools, Youth-Serving Organizations, and Community and Juvenile Justice Settings*. Office of Juvenile Justice and Delinquency Prevention and Office of Elementary and Secondary Education, U.S. Department of Education, 1996, 39–47.

de Beauvoir, Simone. *The Second Sex*. New York: Random House, 1974.

Forcey, Linda Rennie. "The Future of Feminist Discourse." *Peace & Change*, vol. 21, no. 1 (January 1996): 78–83.

———. *Mothers of Sons: Toward an Understanding of Responsibility*. New York: Praeger, 1987.

———. "Personality in Politics: The Commitment of a Suicide." Ph.D. dissertation. State University of New York at Binghamton, 1978.

Forcey, Linda Rennie, and Ian M. Harris, eds. *Peacebuilding for Adolescents: Strategies for Educators and Community Leaders*. New York: Peter Lang, 1999.

Frazer, Elizabeth, and Nancy Lacey. *The Politics of Community: A Feminist Critique of the Liberal Communitarian Debate*. Toronto: University of Toronto Press, 1993.

Friedan, Betty. *The Feminine Mystique*. New York: Dell, 1963.

Gilligan, Carol. *In a Different Voice.* Cambridge: Harvard University Press, 1982.

Gladwell, Malcolm. "Do Parents Matter?" *New Yorker* (August 17, 1998): 54–64.

Harris, Ian M. "From World Peace to Peace in the Hood: Peace Education in a Post-modern World." *Journal for a Just and Caring Education* 2, no. 4 (October 1996): 378–95.

Johnson, Diane. "What Do Women Want?" *New York Review of Books* (November 28, 1996): 22–27.

Lantieri, Linda, and Janet Patti. *Waging Peace in Our Schools.* Boston: Beacon, 1996.

Lasch, Christopher. *Haven in a Heartless World.* New York: Basic Books, 1977.

Liddington, Jill. *The Long Road to Greenham: Feminism and Anti-Militarism in Britain since 1820.* London: Virago Press, 1989.

Meier, Kenneth, James Stewart, and Robert England. *Race, Class, and Education: The Politics of Second Generation Discrimination.* Madison: University of Wisconsin Press, 1989.

Miedzian, Myriam. *Boys Will Be Boys: Breaking the Link between Masculinity and Violence.* New York: Doubleday, 1991.

Nakano Glenn, Evelyn, Grace Chang, and Linda Rennie Forcey, eds. *Mothering: Ideology, Experience, and Agency.* New York: Routledge, 1994.

Omolade, Barbara. "We Speak for the Planet." In *Rocking the Ship of State: Toward a Feminist Peace Politics,* edited by Adrienne Harris and Ynestra Kings. New York: Random House, 1990.

Peterson, V. Spike, and Anne Sisson Runyan. *Global Gender Issues.* Boulder: Westview Press, 1993.

Rich, Adrienne. *Of Woman Born.* New York: W.W. Norton, 1976.

Ruddick, Sara. *Maternal Thinking: Toward a Politics of Peace.* New York: Ballantine Books, 1989.

Said, Edward W. *Culture and Imperialism.* New York: Alfred A. Knopf, 1993, 32.

Segal, Lynne. *Is the Future Female?* London: Virago, 1987, 6, 148.

———. *Slow Motion.* New Brunswick, NJ: Rutgers University Press, 1990.

Steinson, Barbara Jean. "Female Activism in World War I: The American Women's Peace, Suffrage, Preparedness and Relief Movements, 1914–1919." Vols. 1–2. Ph.D. Diss., University of Michigan, 1977. New York: Garland Publishing, 1982.

Swerdlow, Amy. *Women's Strike for Peace: Traditional Motherhood and Radical Politics in the 1960s.* Chicago: University of Chicago Press, 1993.

Ticknor, J. Ann. *Gender in International Relations.* New York: Columbia University Press, 1992.

Tong, Rosemary. *Feminist Thought: A Comprehensive Introduction.* Boulder: Westview, 1989.

Wills, Gary. "Private Life, Public Destiny." *New York Times* (September 6, 1998): WK 11.

Winnicott, D.W. *The Child, the Family, and the Outside World.* Middlesex, England: Harmondsworth, 1961.

Woito, Robert. "Nonviolence, Principled." In *Protest, Power, and Change: An Encyclopedia of Nonviolent Action from ACT-UP to Women's Suffrage,* edited by Roger S. Powers and William B. Vogele. New York: Garland, 1997, 154–173.

Woolf, Virginia. "Professions for Women." In *Collected Essays.* London: Hogarth Press, 1966.

5

IN BLACK AND WHITE

ANGLO-AMERICAN AND AFRICAN-AMERICAN PERSPECTIVES ON MOTHERS AND SONS

Andrea O'Reilly

In "Man Child: A Black Lesbian Feminist's Response," African-American poet and essayist Audre Lorde asks us to "consider the two western classic myth/models of mother/son relationships: Jocasta/Oedipus, the son who fucks his mother, and Clytemnestra/Orestes, the son who kills his mother" (76). These ancient myths are continually retold and reenacted in Western culture and function, in Louis Althusser's terms, as ideological apparatuses that interpolate mothers and sons into specific relationship positions that are most fully dramatized in the narratives of Clytemnestra and Jocasta. The sanction against mother-son closeness and connection is signified and achieved by the incest taboo, while the enforcement of mother-son separation is represented and enforced by the murder of Clytemnestra. Both patriarchal narratives are enacted through the denial and displacement of the maternal presence.

I open this chapter referencing the above narratives because it is my contention that maternal erasure and disconnection are central not only to patriarchal thinking on mothers and sons but also to Anglo-American *feminist* thought on mothers and sons as well. This chapter will, through a close reading of three early, classic, Anglo-American, feminist texts on mothers and sons, examine how the early Anglo-American perspective on mothers and sons scripted mother-son attachment in terms of these hegemonic narratives of maternal erasure and disavowal. Next, the chapter will consider how recent Anglo-American feminist writings on mothers and sons call into question this patriarchal and early feminist view of maternal displacement to emphasize mother-son connection. Finally, the chapter will review recent African-American feminist theory on mothers and sons to explore both its emphasis on maternal presence (as opposed to maternal erasure) and its specific, racially determined mode of rearing sons.

Patriarchal Narratives

The story of Oedipus and his mother Jocasta was first told by the playwright Sophocles, but is known to us today through Freud's psychological theory of the Oedipal complex. The son's first love object, according to Freud, is the mother, but the son renounces this love upon the realization that this desire is forbidden and will result in his castration by the father. In the story of Clytemnestra and her son Orestes, the mother, as most accounts tell it, kills her husband Agamemnon upon his return from Troy to avenge his sacrificial killing of their daughter, Iphigenia, and because he has brought home with him a concubine. In retaliation against his father's death, Orestes kills his mother, which he defends as just vengeance for the death of his father. The Furies, the female chorus who are judge and jury, excuse the mother's crime because "the man she killed was not of her own blood." The son retorts: "Am I of my mother's blood?" to which they respond: "She nourished you in the womb . . . do you disown your mother's blood?" Apollo, called in to settle the dispute, states that: "the mother is not the parent of the child which is called hers. She is the nurse who tends the growth of the young seed planted by its true parent, the male." Finally Athena, a female goddess born from the head of Zeus, is asked to decide the verdict and rules: "No mother gave me birth. Therefore, the father's claim and male supremacy in all things wins my whole heart's loyalty." With her vote the son is pardoned, and the Furies, the last representatives of the mother right of ancient goddess times, are banished. These myths narrate the consolidation of patriarchal power through the son's identification with the patrilineal line and script mother-son separation as the precondition of manhood.

These ancient myths, functioning as ideological apparatuses, are continually reenacted and retold in our contemporary culture. A cursory review of
twentieth-century popular culture reveals many and diverse manifestations
of the ancient patriarchal narratives of forbidden Jocasta/emasculated
Oedipus and triumphant Orestes/defeated Clytemnestra. Philip Wylie in
his immensely popular 1942 *Generation of Vipers* coined the term
"momism": "Our land," writes Wylie, "subjectively mapped, would have
more silver cords and apron strings crisscrossing it than railroads and tele-
phone wires. She is everywhere and everything. . . . Disguised as good old
mom, dear old mom, sweet old mom . . . she is the bride at every funeral
and the corpse at every wedding" (185). In the 1960s the Moynihan report
was released and advanced the now infamous black matriarchy thesis that
described the black family as dysfunctional and argued that mothers were
to blame for the pathologies of the race. "In essence," wrote Moynihan,
"the Negro community has . . . a matriarchal structure which . . . seriously
retards the progress of the group as a whole"(75). Or as African-American
writer/critic Michelle Wallace puts it: "The Moynihan Report said that the
black man was not so much a victim of white institutional racism as he was
of an abnormal family structure, its main feature being an employed black
woman" (12). The 1980s gave us Robert Bly, the father of the men's mythopoetic movement and author of the best-selling *Iron John*, the notorious
thesis which suggests the American man has grown up with too much
mothering and not enough fathering; they suffer from what Bly diagnosed
as "father hunger." "[The modern man] is not happy," laments Bly, "he is
life-preserving but not life-giving, he is full of anguish and grief" (2–4).
Men have discovered their "feminine side" but have left unexplored their
true essential masculine identity. For Bly, healing occurs only when the son
"cut[s] his soul away from his mother-bound soul" and moves, again in
Bly's words, "from the mother's realm to the father's realm" (ix).

Feminism has long critiqued Wylie's momism, Moynihan's black matriarchy, and Bly's father hunger for their blatant misogyny and virulent
mother blame. From a sociohistorical perspective they are clearly backlash
texts. *Vipers*, popular after World War II when women were being repro-
grammed from workers back into mothers, articulates the culture's
uneasiness with what Miriam Johnson has called the white, middle-class
matrifocality of the 1950s. The minimal involvement of fathers in those
postwar years meant that the home was a maternal dominion where sons
grew to manhood under the mother's influence with little or no involvement from the father. The matrifocality of the home in the 1950s is what is

said to have caused, according to many social commentators, the "feminine" men of the 1960s; how Alan Alda came to replace John Wayne as the ideal identity of manhood. The Moynihan report was written in the 1960s, the decade that witnessed the civil rights movement and the beginnings of the feminist movement. *Iron John* takes as its cultural context the 1980s that witnessed increased economic independence for women, skyrocketing divorce rates, and, significantly, the beginning of the father's rights movement.[1]

Early Anglo-American Feminist Theory on the Mother-Son Relationship

The purpose of this chapter, however, is not to detail the patriarchal script of maternal displacement and denial. Rather, I am interested in exploring how this displacement and denial are represented, recast, and resisted in *feminist* theory on mothers and sons. The first and longest section of this chapter offers a close and detailed reading of three classic Anglo-American texts on the mother-son relation, Judith Arcana's *Every Mother's Son: The Role of Mothers in the Making of Men* (1983), Linda Forcey's *Mothers of Sons: Toward an Understanding of Responsibility* (1987), and Babette Smith's *Mothers and Sons: The Truth about Mother-Son Relationships* (1995)[2], in order to examine how this literature mimicked, albeit unintentionally, the patriarchal dictate of maternal displacement and denial. The three books, though spanning fifteen years, can be grouped together as a representative writing of the earlier Anglo-American feminist perspective on mothers and sons.

Judith Arcana's *Every Mother's Son* (1983)

In the prologue to *Every Mother's Son* Arcana asserts that: "mothers need to understand that we are creating and nurturing the agents of our own oppression; once we make them, their education as men in this misogynist society will pull them from our arms, set them above us, and make them the source of our degradation" (3). She goes on to argue that: "we would prevent this if we could, and to do so we must enter into conscious struggle with our sons, actively seeking to change what is currently defined as male and female behavior" (34). This book, developed from sixty interviews with mothers and with sons and from Arcana's own personal reflections on raising her son Daniel during his first ten years, explores how current practices of masculine socialization give rise to expectations of entitlement as boys grow into men and result in the disavowal of all things feminine in the adult male psyche.

Over the course of her interviews with mothers and sons, Arcana discovered that most mothers reject traditional definitions of masculinity. However, the sons of these same women had assumed, for the most part, a conventional gender identity, or were aware that such was expected of them. What accounts for this disparity between intent and consequence? A small number of sons in Arcana's study reported that their mothers consciously and enthusiastically socialized them to be masculine, while another small group said that while their mothers did not engage in overt gender socialization, it was done unconsciously and indirectly. However, the majority of sons in Arcana's study stated that they could not recall any incident in which their mother had explicitly or implicitly directed them to be "men." The disparity, Arcana argues, may be attributed to three factors of masculine socialization.

The first is that mothers, for the most part, are lesser agents in the socialization of sons. Many of the sons identified "culture" or "the father" as where they learned patriarchal masculinity. "Basic sex-role conditioning," as Arcana observes, "is not in mothers' hands, but in the hands of men who've made this culture" (120). Secondly, mothers raise children but they do not determine the material or ideological conditions of their mothering. Women, as Adrienne Rich reminds us, mother in motherhood, the latter being a patriarchal institution which is male-defined and -controlled. Mothers raise boys but they don't make men, because, as Arcana explains, mothers are "contractors rather than architects, following specifications not of our design" (115). Women, Arcana continues, "are relatively powerless in this culture, and though we raise the children we bear, almost none of us are free to bear and raise them *if or when we choose,* much less *as we choose*" (115).

Finally, while mothers may not initiate or enforce the gender socialization of their sons, they do accommodate it. A central and constitutive demand of mothering, as Sara Ruddick explains in *Maternal Thinking,* is "training children in the behavior acceptable to their social and cultural group" (110). Thus while mothers may reject patriarchy and its constructions of masculinity, they realize, consciously or otherwise, that their sons must take their place in that world. "The fear of alienating a male child from 'his' culture," writes Adrienne Rich, "seems to go deep, even among women who reject that culture for themselves every day of their lives" (205). Rich goes on to ask: "What do we fear? That our sons will accuse us of making them into misfits and outsiders? That they will suffer as we have suffered from patriarchal reprisals? Do we fear they will somehow lose their male status and privilege, even as we are seeking to abolish that inequality?" (205). "As mothers in this time," Arcana writes, "we are faced with a dilemma: we see that the old ways are not good; we wish to raise our children differently—but we fear they'll suffer ostracism, alienation, and loneliness in a society that has by no means given up its old definitions and restrictions" (1).

Another explanation Arcana offers to account for this discrepancy between aim and consequence centers on maternal practice itself. Mothering is about caring for and catering to the needs of children and nurturing self-esteem so that children see themselves as special and deserving; what Ruddick defines as the second demand of maternal practice, "to foster growth . . . sponsor or nurture a child's unfolding, expanding material spirit" (83). However, with sons this nurturance may be, according to Arcana, interpreted as privilege and entitlement: "Though children of both sexes put their mothers in the positions of servants . . . mothers of sons are, whether we feel it in the moment or not, inadvertently reinforcing the sexist premise that women exist to serve men. . . . Men learn from infancy to expect and solicit selfishness and cherishing care at the hands of women" (101, 102). While "[d]aughters learn from our mothers to *be mothers*, to give in that disastrously self-destructive way that has been honored by men as true motherhood; sons learn *to expect such treatment from women*" (102). Women in patriarchal culture are expected to devote their time and attention to children and men; sons thus, as Arcana identifies, derive double benefits from these patriarchal imperatives as both men and children. Given that women's secondary status is enforced in both the gender arena (service to men) and in the maternal realm (service to children), mothers must, if they hope to raise nonsexist men who reject traditional masculinity, challenge both patriarchal imperatives. Women, Arcana writes, "need to live out of ourselves. We wrong ourselves and our children if we subordinate our lives to theirs" (235). Mothers must, Arcana continues, "reject [the] traditional mother role [and] . . . accept . . . our sons into our daily lives" (247). In so doing the mother will enable her boy child to see her outside and beyond her maternal identity that positions her as secondary to, and in service to, children and men. Coming to know their mothers outside motherhood, sons learn to view and appreciate their mothers as, in Arcana's words, "whole people."

According to Arcana, mothers must, therefore, reject traditional motherhood if they hope to raise nontraditional sons; that is, men who have renounced patriarchal masculinity and the entitlement and privilege that such accords. No longer can mothers be, or be seen as, "the primary source of praise, encouragement, and selfless service" (280). However, as mothers reject this role of selfless service to sons, traditional male socialization, as Arcana explains, teaches boys "that they are to be the beneficiaries of a male culture: they will grow up to power, status, and the admiration and support of women. . . . When [a mother] moves to change that pattern with her son, he understands that she wants him to give up power. . . . [A] boy has to begin by *losing*" (280). In other words to become more human, he must become less male. This, then, is the second paradox of feminist male child rearing: sons gain by losing, and mothers are better mothers by "being less of a mother." This, in Arcana's view, is both the challenge and contradiction of feminist mothering of sons.

Arcana maintains that the patriarchal institution of motherhood oppresses women, impedes mother-son equality, and fosters both sexism and patriarchal masculinity. Women thus must reject traditional motherhood and become, in Rich's words, "outlaws from the institution of motherhood" in order to effect the gender transformations they wish for themselves and their sons, for women and men. Arcana perceptively identifies the many ways traditional motherhood oppresses women and perpetuates traditional masculinity. However, less clear in this critique is a distinction between motherhood and mothering. In *Of Woman Born* Rich distinguishes between two meanings of motherhood: "the *potential relationship* of any woman to her powers of reproduction and to children; and the *institution*, which aims at ensuring that that potential—and all women— shall remain under male control" (13). Motherhood refers to the institution of motherhood, which is male-defined and -controlled, and mothering refers to experiences of mothers which are female-defined and -centered. Across cultures and throughout history most women mother in the institution of motherhood. Patriarchal motherhood, however, does not negate the possibility and potentiality of gynocentric mothering. Mothers have always mothered against, beyond, and outside patriarchal motherhood. In dismissing motherhood, Arcana, I would suggest, loses sight of the radical potentiality of mothering; if you will, she throws the baby out with the bathwater.

Arcana also finds problematic the way mothering places mothers in service to children and in particular to sons. However, I would argue that maternal practice, as Ruddick argues, is by necessity concerned with meeting the physical, psychological, and social needs of children. "These three demands—for preservation, growth, and social acceptance," writes Ruddick, "constitute maternal work; to be a mother is to be committed to meeting these demands by works of preservative love, nurturance and training" (17). Service, the word Arcana uses to describe such work, is what one (a woman or man) must do when one engages in maternal practice; however "service" does not necessarily require the subordination and enslavement of the mother. Morever, care of children does not preclude care of self, nor does service equal servitude or require self-erasure. However, because service becomes confused in Arcana with servitude, as does the distinction between mothering and motherhood, motherhood is represented as an essentially oppressive state and hence rejected. This in turn results in the displacement and disparagement of the maternal.

Linda Forcey's *Mothers of Sons: Toward an Understanding of Responsibility* (1987)

The teaching of antisexism and the undermining of masculine socialization are, according to Arcana, the explicit goals of feminist mothering of sons. This is to be achieved by challenging both traditional practices of male socialization *and* traditional ways of mothering. Linda Forcey's *Mothers of Sons: Toward an Understanding of Responsibility*, the second book-length feminist work on mothers and sons, considers, as the title suggests, the issue of responsibility. The position advanced in her 1987 book differs significantly from Forcey's current thinking on mothers and sons. Thus the following exposé and critique of Forcey's responsibility thesis is pertinent only to this early work—as it laid the foundation for contemporary thinking about motherhood—and not to Forcey's subsequent research.

Mothers of Sons, based on the oral histories of one hundred women from various socioeconomic backgrounds, examines, in Forcey's words, "how mothers perceive their relationships with their sons. That is, what do they have to tell us about the relationship, and their responsibility to and for it?" (3). Her book opens with a review of early feminist thought on motherhood—the writings of deBeauvoir, Friedan, Bernard—and argues that these early feminist texts question "the sagacity of the assignment of solitary responsibility for 'mothering' to mothers [and] find it harmful to children of both sexes but especially sons" (32). Forcey recognizes that children must be nurtured; this is, in her words, "beyond dispute." However, Forcey goes on to argue that "what is not beyond dispute . . . is who should be responsible for seeing that the requisite nurturing gets done, and precisely what constitutes effective nurturing in order to promote this preservation and growth" (42). Traditional "malestream" mother-blaming thought, as feminists have rightly argued, is preoccupied with the so-called failures of mothers to fulfill their maternal responsibilities. However, Forcey maintains that this perspective informs *feminist* thinking on mothering as well; it too operates as a regulatory discourse, reinscribing mothers in the traditional ideological matrix of responsibility and blame:

> The differences between the traditional and the recently revised feminist approach to the mother-son relationship center on the reasons why mothers mother the way they do, and what it means to be a "good" mother. For these feminists, the "good" mother is she who, in spite of her oppression, assumes the responsibility for raising sons who are physically, emotionally, and socially well-adjusted and who do not separate from her, do not identify with their fathers, and do not assume the traditional masculine values. . . . As with the conventional wisdom on mothers of sons, this recent feminist scholarship implicitly assumes that mothers are all powerful. It calls on women to assume their rightful responsibility for their children's welfare in order to affect a nonpatriarchal society. (46, 47)

Feminists, in Forcey's view, have merely redefined the meaning of "good mothering" and have left unquestioned the "wisdom of the responsibility assignment itself" (46). As well they have failed to challenge the patriarchal premise that assumes "[that women] are more relational than men [and thus] should be assigned the primary responsibility for the care of children" (59).

Recent feminist writings, notably Nancy Chodorow's feminine relationality argument and the different voice theory advanced by Carol Gilligan, work to reconstitute women, Forcey maintains, as natural mothers, while in the feminist instance it is psychology and not wombs that predispose women to nurturance. The challenge of feminism should not be to determine how women may fulfill their responsibility as feminist mothers, Forcey argues, but rather to question the responsibility assignment itself. "No person," Forcey writes, "can successfully be responsible for the meaning of another's being. Not even mothers of sons" (59). Such a view,

Forcey continues, "is personally and politically damaging for both mothers and sons, women and men" (59).

Most of the women in Forcey's study "perceived themselves to have the primary responsibility for the well-being of their sons, a responsibility they find to be enormous and never-ending" (47). Nevertheless, women experience their identity and work as mothers as "responsibility" because such a role accords women a purpose and power not available to them otherwise in a patriarchal culture. Forcey explains: "Many women, particularly those in mid-life, do express their satisfaction in life in terms of how they view the results of their years as mothers as measured by the happiness of their sons. For many women being the 'essential' one in the family is a hard role to give up" (59). However, mothers must, Forcey argues, for the good of their sons *and* themselves, reject this maternal self-definition and come to define themselves outside and beyond their maternal identity as well as learn to share the work of child rearing with others.

In her final chapter, appropriately entitled "Jocasta Unbound," Forcey argues, in a manner similar to Arcana, that women must develop identities outside their maternal role; the three locations she identifies are school, work, and women's friendship. When women balance "caring and selfhood" they are less likely to define their identity and worth in the context of the responsibility assignment that, Forcey argues, is damaging to both mothers and sons. It is important to note that Forcey calls for the "unboundness" from motherhood in order to free *mothers* from the matrix of blame and responsibility, while Arcana champions unboundness, or in her words, rejection of traditional motherhood, so that *sons* do not see women exclusively in service to children and secondary to men. However, both agree that mothering must be shared; as Forcey concludes her book: "When the sons of tomorrow are the responsibility of the many instead of the one they will grow freer, stronger, and more caring, as will their mothers" (151). Thus both Arcana and Forcey advocate "less mothering" in order to effect the desired transformations in gender relations/roles for both men (Arcana) and women (Forcey).

Forcey maintains, as examined above, that the traditional and revised feminist view of the responsibility of mothers for sons "is personally and politically damaging to mothers and sons, women and men" (59). She exhorts mothers to renounce the exclusive and essentialist responsibility role through the formation of self-identities other than that of mother and by sharing the task of child rearing. The task of responsibility is, no doubt, "enormous" and "never-ending," as Forcey argues. However, I would suggest that the problem rests not so much with responsibility as with the way motherhood becomes defined in the dominant Anglo-American culture. A therapist interviewed by Forcey and who worked with poor and "struggling" mothers observed that "[such mothers] are just too busy. Their whole lives cannot be wrapped up in their sons. . . . If you are very, very busy, she argues, you don't put quite the same emotional burden on the child."(67). "The major difference between middle-class and working-class mothers of sons," she speculates, "was that in the case of the latter the mother was not the central person in the son's life and sons were not the central people in the mothers' lives" (67).

It would seem that the problem is not responsibility per se but rather that motherhood, as it is defined in Anglo-American culture, assigns this task exclusively to mothers. Furthermore, the work of mothering is assumed to preclude or take precedence over any other work and is defined solely as nurturance; paid employment is not seen as an aspect of mothering but rather as something that prevents women from mothering. Forcey apparently recognizes this, as suggested by her insistence upon the need for both shared child rearing and nonmaternal work and identities. Nonetheless her book, as its subtitle suggests, focuses on the responsibility assignment rather than on the way motherhood is organized in Anglo-American culture. Moreover, in Anglo-American culture mothers are assigned the responsibility but given no power—and accorded no real status—for the maternal work they do. Mothers do not make the rules, they simply enforce them. Again, it would seem that motherhood becomes oppressive to women not because of the responsibility assignment, as Forcey would argue, but rather because this responsibility comes with little or no power and prestige and because maternal responsibility—defined exclusively as care rather than work in Anglo-American culture—confines mothering and mothers to the home. Finally, as discussed earlier, mothering does, and must, mean being responsible for the children in your care; those who engage in maternal practice assume this task upon the arrival of the child, by birth or adoption. However, because Forcey in her early work identifies the responsibility assignment as the problem, her argument, as does Arcana's, advances "less mothering" as the solution and partakes in the displacement and disparagement of the maternal.

Babette Smith's *Mothers and Sons: The Truth about Mother-Son Relationships* (1995)

The final book on the mother-son relationship under consideration is Babette Smith's *Mothers and Sons: The Truth about Mother-Son Relationships.* Smith's research, developed from a comparative study of postwar and post-1960s mothers and sons, explores how mothers' and sons' perceptions of one another and their relationship have changed over the last fifty years. This study focuses on two interrelated questions: How do mothers perceive masculinity? And how do sons, in turn, perceive their mothers and their mothering? Of interest to us here in the discussion of the way motherhood is represented in feminist thought on the mother-son relation is Smith's second concern, sons' perceptions of maternal practice.

The postwar sons' reflections on their mothers and mothering was both startling and sad. These sons, Smith writes, "were struggling to love where they had little respect, to believe they *were* loved when they remembered no affection, to justify their love by saying their mother was *not typical*" (33). While the ideology of "the Good Mother," particularly as it was represented in the 1950s, demanded that mothers be selfless, moral, pleasing, passive, and subservient to their husbands, and led mothers to believe that they would be honored and appreciated for this, the views expressed by the now-middle-aged sons interviewed by Smith reveal the contrary; the mothers were neither admired nor respected for their maternal devotion. As one son commented: "The worst thing I think was the way she made herself a martyr to what everyone else wanted" (34). The few sons who spoke or wrote favorably about their relationship with their mothers remembered their mothers as "female people rather than [just] 'mothers'"(50). The memories of these sons "reveal that these women had also developed wide-ranging interests beyond the home, 'artistic and intellectual curiosity,' 'stories from work,' 'has published a book'" (50). They felt their mothers were "adaptable," or they had "broadness of outlook and knowledge," qualities which their sons celebrated (50).

In contrast, the post-1960s sons genuinely liked their mothers and enjoyed being in their company. Smith writes:

> The male experience of the mother-son relationship changed substantially. The consensus which emerged from these younger sons' opinions was a reversal of the past. The percentage which once ran 70:30 negatively about a man's mother, had turned right around to run approximately 70:30 positively. Most sons of this age group spoke

enthusiastically about their mothers, the percentage as well as the tone of the assessment, holding good among those who explored the subject in some depth and those who answered a briefer question-naire. These sons loved their mothers, as their fathers had loved theirs, but the younger generation also liked them. (175)

The reason, the interviews would suggest, is: a) the mothers of these sons were less invested in the ideology of the Good Mother; b) as a result of increased education, work, and travel opportunities for women, these mothers had more in common with their sons; and c) the familial, eco-nomic, and cultural changes occasioned by feminism gave women more confidence and clout. As well, and of particular significance to the discus-sion at hand, for the post-1960s son, according to Smith, "it was noticeably easier for [him] to agree that he admired or respected his mother when he did not have to pass judgement on her parenting at the same time . . . [in contrast], [1950s] sons had no choice but to evaluate their mothers in her maternal role" (182). Smith elaborates:

> [When they could,] sons of all ages nominated their mothers' achievements outside the home. Younger men who had this option more often were more readily admiring. They could avoid the ambivalence caused by passing judgement on the women's parental success in their own lives and external yardsticks, such as occupation, income, or title, were concrete evidence that society endorsed their personal opinion. This was the benefit which a woman's outside work could bring to the mother-son relationship—not as a role model, as it was for daughters (although these young sons did not automatically exclude their mothers as a role model), but by providing the boys with something about their mother which was understood and val-ued in their male world. (182)

Mothers who exhibited attributes valued in male culture and/or achieved what was deemed success from the masculine standpoint were more readily respected and admired by their sons. As one schoolteacher observed of the sons in the class: "Boys identify with mothers who are inde-pendent, freethinking, nice people, not only for security and emotional reasons, but also because they happen to like their mothers as people. These are mothers who actually present themselves to their sons as people *without overt 'being Mother'* " (185, italics added). And while Smith argues that the variable is not so much paid employment as self-confidence, she nonetheless concludes that women's work outside the home benefited the mother-son relationship because it, as noted above, "[provided] the boys with something about their mother which was understood and valued in their male world" (182). Male respect and admiration for mothers, Smith goes on to argue, is essential "because, without those elements, there is no basis for equality between them" (185).

Though not always explicitly acknowledged or addressed, the "beyond motherhood" thesis, if you will, of Arcana, Forcey, and Smith begins with the recognition that motherhood in patriarchal culture is neither valued nor respected and that mothers do not acquire any real or substantive power, status, or agency—economic, cultural, or otherwise—for the work they do as mothers. Thus, as a mother, the woman is not able to secure the respect of her son. Though this is a concern for all three, it is of particular importance for Smith because her theoretical platform for improving gender relations hinges upon sons respecting and admiring their mothers.

The problem, according to Smith, is "[how do] sons . . . hold their own mothers dear in a society which has little regard for mothers" (180). Smith argues, as we saw earlier, that this problem may be remedied through mothers fashioning an identity and role "beyond motherhood" in the public, male realm of work so as to, in Smith's words "provid[e] [their sons] with something about their mother which [is] understood and valued in their male world" (182). Smith's argument here resonates with earlier liberal feminist thinking on motherhood. Smith recognizes that motherhood is devalued in our culture but instead of addressing this larger problem, she exhorts women, as did much of earlier liberal feminist theory, to abandon the private realm of motherhood and obtain personhood, power, and prestige by entering the public arena of (paid) work. Smith's argument thus reinscribes, as did much of 1970s liberal feminism, the hierarchal gender opposition that privileges masculine values over those that are associated with the feminine, and in so doing both mimics and perpetuates the patriarchal disparagement and displacement of the maternal.

As Smith's argument seeks to distance mothers from motherhood and downplay their maternal role and identity, it also calls for the abdication of maternal authority and power. Smith argues that post-1960s mother-and-son relationships are more successful because they are based on equality and that this equality is what makes possible the respect Smith deems essential for a successful mother-and-son relation. While equality in relationships is generally understood to be a good and desired thing, in the mother-child relationship such equality is problematic because it denies the mother the power and authority that is rightly hers as the mother of the child. "There are," as Sara Ruddick observes, "many external constraints on [a mother's] capacity to name, feel, and act. But in the daily conflict of wills, at least with her children, a mother has the upper hand. . . . *If a mother didn't have this control, her life would be unbearable*" (35, italics added). The mode of mothering advocated by Smith is what Valerie Walkerdine and Helen Lucey define in their book, *Democracy in the Kitchen,* as "sensitive mothering": "[A defining characteristic] of the sensitive mother is the way she regulates her children. Essentially there should be no overt regulation; regulation should go underground; no power battles, no insensitive sanctions as these would interfere with the child's illusion that she is the source of her wishes, that she had 'free will'" (23, 24). Sensitive mothering is child-centered, characterized by flexibility, spontaneity, affection, nurturance, playfulness, and most importantly democracy, and is contrasted to the stern, rigid, authoritative, "child should be seen and not heard" variety of parenting. While sensitive mothering may make possible the mother-son equality so valued by Smith, it centers and depends upon the abdication of maternal power and authority.[3]

Smith argues, as did Forcey and Arcana ten years earlier, that the less a mother relates to her son as "mother," the greater the chances will be of raising nonsexist, nonmasculine (as it is traditionally defined) boys and improving relations between mothers and sons and men and women generally. This will allow sons to see their mothers as other than secondary and subservient to men and children, according to Arcana, will undercut the responsibility assignment, according to Forcey, and will enable boys to respect and admire their mothers, according to Smith. Each downplays, denies, and in some instances disparages the responsibility, authority, and power of mothers as mothers of sons, while according the same to women as women. In so doing Smith, Arcana, and Forcey script mother-and-son relation, albeit subtly and no doubt inadvertently, in terms of the patriarchal imperatives of maternal erasure and displacement as enacted in the narratives of Clytemnestra and Jocasta.

New Anglo-American Feminist Perspectives on the Mother-Son Relationship

Feminist theory on mothers and sons has been informed by and has developed in the context of feminist thinking on mothering and motherhood over the last thirty years. More specifically, Anglo-American feminist theory on mothers and sons mirrors and reenacts the theoretical trajectory of

Anglo-American feminist thought on the mother-daughter relationship. In the 1970s the received view—or what Toni Morrison calls, in another context, the master narrative—of mothers and daughters was that this relationship, particularly in the daughter's adolescent years, was one of antagonism and animosity. The daughter must differentiate herself from the mother if she is to assume an autonomous identity as an adult. The mother, in turn, is perceived and understood only in terms of her maternal identity. The mother represents for the daughter, according to the received narrative, the epitome of patriarchal oppression that she seeks to transcend as she comes to womanhood; and the daughter's failings, as interpreted by herself and the culture at large, are said to be the fault of the mother. This is the patriarchal narrative of the mother-daughter relationship. The lives of mothers and daughters are shaped by these cultural narratives even as mothers and daughters live lives different from, and in resistance to, these assigned roles. Feminist Anglo-American writers, most notably Nancy Chodorow, author of the influential *The Reproduction of Mothering*, and Nancy Friday, author of the best-selling *My Mother/My Self*, argue that mother-daughter identification is ultimately detrimental to the daughter's attainment of autonomy. For Chodorow, writing from a psychoanalytic perspective, this is because mother-daughter identification results in the daughter having weak "ego-boundaries"; with Friday, separation is required to enable the daughter to assume an adult sexual identity as a woman.

The 1970s feminist view that problematizes if not pathologizes mother-daughter identification has now fallen out of favor among Anglo-American feminist theorists. Indeed most Anglo-American feminists, since at least the mid–1980s, regard mother-daughter connection and closeness as essential for female empowerment. From the early 1980s feminists, both lay and academic, have increasingly linked female power to mother-daughter connection. Today Anglo-American feminist writers challenge the normative view of mother-daughter attachment that scripts estrangement as both natural and inevitable, and argue that identification empowers mothers and daughters alike, giving rise to the transformation of patriarchal culture. Drawing upon the ancient Elyeusis rites of Demeter and Persephone, recent feminist writings on the mother-daughter relation celebrate mother-daughter connection and explore how such is achieved and sustained through maternal narratives, the motherline, feminist socialization of daughters, and gynocentric mothering. To this end, feminist theorists identify and challenge the various cultural practices and assumptions that divide mothers and daughters and seek an alternative mother-daughter narrative scripted for empowerment as opposed to estrangement.[4]

A similar trajectory may be observed in Anglo-American feminist writing on the mother-son relation, with an approximate ten-year time lag. The texts examined above tend to downplay women's maternal role and identity. In contrast, the contemporary Anglo-American feminist view emphasizes mother-son connection and positions it as central to the reconfiguration of traditional masculinity. Similar to the new Anglo-American feminist literature on mothers and daughters that recasts connection as empowerment by referencing the mythic mother-daughter dyad Demeter and Persephone, the contemporary Anglo-American feminist emphasis on the mother-son connection is also frequently conveyed through a mythic mother-and-son relation, that of Thetis and Achilles.

"Thetis, according to the myth, dipped her son Achilles into the river Styx to render him immortal. However, fearing that he might be lost to the river, she held onto him by his ankle. Achilles, as the story goes, remains mortal and vulnerable to harm. Thetis would be forever blamed for her son's fatal flaw, his Achilles heel." However, contemporary feminist theorists reinterpret the traditional reading of this narrative to argue, as Nikki Fedele and Cate Dooley do in their chapter in this book, that "the holding place of vulnerability was not, as the myth would have us believe, a fatal liability to Achilles. It was the thing that kept him *human and real.* In fact, we consider it *Thetis' finest gift* to her son" (page 185, this volume). Fedele's and Dooley's research with mothers and sons, as discussed later in this volume, reveals that "boys with a secure maternal connection develop stronger interpersonal skills and enjoy healthier relationships as adults" (page 188, this volume). Mother-son connection, they conclude, is what makes possible the new masculinity we desire for our sons and men in general.

The Thetis and Achilles model of mother-son attachment advanced by Dooly and Fedele is examined fully in Olga Silverstein and Beth Rashbaum's 1994 book *The Courage to Raise Good Men.* The book opens with a poem about Thetis and Achilles that Silverstein wrote many years ago for her now middle-age son upon his birth. Presenting herself as Thetis, Silverstein worries that her love, like that of Thetis, might damage her son's manhood:

> Even Thetis, dipping her mortal boy
> In Styx, dreaming of armouring him

Against both worlds, gripping her joy
In fatal fingers, allowed the dim
Danger of her handhold on his heel [. . .]
If immortal mothers are to such folly prone,
How am I to guard against the thumbprints
On my own? (1)

As a young mother whose views on child rearing were very much shaped by the larger patriarchal culture of 1940s America, Silverstein believed, as do many mothers, that she, like Thetis, "might fail to let [her son] go, and the love [she] felt for him might in some way damage the armour of his manhood, rendering him as vulnerable as Achilles—who of course died of a wound to that very heel by which his mother had once clung to him" (1). "Hands (and thumbs off) is the warning to mothers of son," Silverstein notes, so that to mother a son is to engage in a continuous "process of pulling back" (1–2).

Silverstein challenges this received view of mother-son relation and argues, similar to Janet Sayers in her chapter in this volume, that the mandate of disconnection and the taboo against mother-son intimacy is the root cause of sons' difficulties as adults. The assumption is that boys, as scripted by the Freudian Oedipal scenario, gradually withdraw and distance themselves from their mothers as they grow into manhood. A close and caring relationship between a mother and a son is pathologized as aberrant, while a relationship structured upon separation is naturalized as the real and normal way to experience mother-son attachment. Silverstein explains: "[Our culture believes] that a male child must be removed from his mother's influence in order to escape the contamination of a close relationship with her. The love of a mother—both the son's love for her, and hers for him—is believed to 'feminize' a boy, to make him soft, weak, dependent, homebound. . . . [O]nly through renunciation of the loving mother, and identification with the aggressor father, does the . . . boy become a man"(11). In other words, the majority of us in Western culture see mother-son separation as both inevitable and desirable.

Silverstein challenges the central, organizing premise of patriarchally mandated mother-son separation, namely that this process is both natural, hence inevitable, and "good" for our sons. She emphasizes that what we interpret as a normal process is, in fact, a culturally scripted and orchestrated act. Moreover, she argues that it is mothers and not boys who both initiate and direct the separation. "By expecting our sons to cut off from us," she writes, "we make sure that they do" (159). The mother, aware that mother-son connection and closeness is disparaged and pathologized in our culture, is ever-vigilant that she not be "overclose" with her son. While her son nurses in her arms, she may worry about the intimacy and stiffen, pull back, or look away; so too when her eight-year-old scrambles onto her lap she will laugh proudly and nudge him off, saying that he is now a big boy and cannot fit in her lap; and when she is kissed by her teenage son, she will turn her cheek, tense her body, and mumble to hurry and not be late. The gestures of distancing are often subtle yet cumulative. A boy, Silverstein argues, "absorb[s] at an unconscious level that his mother is somehow uncomfortable with him, that she is pulling back from him, that their closeness is problematic" (31). "Soon, Silverstein continues, "he responds in kind, so that his mother, who wasn't aware that she herself was the original actor in this scenario of withdrawal, eventually assumes that the withdrawal was his not hers" (31). Once the son reaches adolescence, the mother, increasingly concerned about mother-son closeness and the damage such may inflict on her son's incipient manhood, may abruptly withdraw from her son; an act that the son may experience as abandonment. Confused and hurt by his mother's rejection of him, the son decisively breaks from his mother and forges an identity separate from her modeled upon the masculine values of self-sufficiency and autonomy, particularly as they pertain to emotional identity. Whether the son is fully aware of the mother's distancing, he nonetheless, Silverstein argues, experiences a deep and inexplicable loss that is seldom understood or articulated; a loss that profoundly scars the boy and causes him to grow into a psychologically wounded man. William Pollack, in his recent *Real Boys: Rescuing Our Sons from the Myths of Boyhood,* maintains that the force of such separation is "so hurtful to boys that it can only be called a trauma— an emotional blow of damaging proportions . . . [a] relational rapture [that] profoundly affects the psychology of most boys—and of most men— forever" (12, 27).

Demanding that young boys distance and differentiate themselves from their mothers, we require them to deny or repress the so-called feminine dimensions of their personalities. Silverstein argues that sons are deeply betrayed by their mothers' rejection of them and deeply wounded by the loss of the feminine in themselves occasioned by this separation. The result of this, she says, is: "lost boys, lonely men, lousy marriages, and midlife crises," or, as Pollack describes it, "a deep wellspring of grief and sadness that may last throughout [men's] lives" (12). Over the last decade, and particularly in the last few years, our culture has identified a crisis in masculinity. Though varied and diverse, the majority of commentators on this "crisis in masculinity"—from Robert Bly to feminist journalist Susan Faludi in her recent best-selling book *Stiffed: The Betrayal of the American Man*—agree that masculinity must be redefined and that such is to be achieved through a reconnection of father and son. Silverstein counters the received narrative to argue that "the real pain in men's lives stems from their estrangement from women" (225). Similarly, Pollack emphasizes that boys and men "[are] forever longing to return to [the mother], and to the 'holding' connection she once provided him, a connection he now feels he can never regain. If a boy had been allowed to separate at his own pace, that longing and sadness would not be there" (27). "As a culture we have to," as Silverstein concludes, "face up to the longing [of sons for mothers]—its power, its persistence throughout a man's life, its potential for destruction when unacknowledged" (225).

Early Anglo-American feminist theorists on mothers and sons believed that motherhood oppressed women, impeded mother-son equality, and fostered both sexism and patriarchal masculinity. This literature consequently downplayed, denied, and at times disparaged women's maternal identity and viewed as problematic women's responsibility and authority as mothers. A mother must rear her son outside/beyond motherhood, they argued, in order to raise a nonsexist, nonmasculine (as it is traditionally defined) boy and to improve relations between mothers and sons, and men and women generally.

In contrast, the "new" Anglo-American feminist theory argues that too little mothering, and, in particular, the absence of mother-son connection, is what engenders both sexism and traditional masculinity in men. Thus a mother must foreground her presence in the life of her son; she must establish and maintain a close and caring connection with her son throughout his life. The mother is, accordingly, afforded agency as a mother, and her maternal responsibility and authority are emphasized and affirmed. This perspective positions mothering as central to feminist politics in its insistence that true and lasting gender equality will occur only when boys are raised as the sons of mothers. As the early feminist script of mother-son connection required the denial of the mother's power and the displacement of her identity as mother, the new perspective affirms the maternal and celebrates mother-son connection. In this, it rewrites the patriarchal and early feminist narrative to give Jocasta and Cyltemnestra presence and voice and a central and definitive role in the lives of their sons.

African-American Feminist Theory on the
Mother and Son Relationship

Most of the writing by Afrisporic women has tended to focus on the mother-daughter relationship; little has been written on the mother-son relationship.[5] The notable exceptions are Joyce Elaine King's and Carolyn Ann Mitchell's *Black Mothers to Sons: Juxtaposing African American Literature with Social Practice* (1995) and *Saving Our Sons: Raising Black Children in a Turbulent World* (1995) by novelist Marita Golden.[6] In the introduction to their book King and Mitchell, explaining their research interest in mothers and sons, write: "Considering the particular vulnerability of black males in this society and the role that mothers typically play as primary nurturers, this focus on black mother-to-son parenting is long overdue" (2). The initial question King and Mitchell explored in selected African-American fiction and asked of their research participants was: "What have you done to protect your son(s) from society's hostile forces?" (6). In their study of African-American literature they found that protection was the primary aim of black mothering and manifested itself in two diametrically opposed modes of mothering: "mothers who whip their sons brutally 'for their own good' and mothers who love their sons to destruction through self-sacrifice and overindulgence" (9). The first strategy is sustained by the belief that "a black man-child duly 'chastened' or broken at home will pose less of a threat to a society already primed to destroy him" (10), while the latter seeks to shield the child from all that is deemed harsh and upsetting. Each position, they argue, psychologically maims the son; the first by breaking the child's spirit, the latter by thwarting the child's maturation to true selfhood. The conflicting demands of protection and nurturance first identified by Ruddick in *Maternal Thinking* become, in the instance of rearing black sons, an impasse, an irreconcilable contradiction. The women interviewed by King and Mitchell all spoke of this paradox in the mothering of black sons; while sons must go into the world to mature socially, psychologically, and otherwise, this same world threatens their very physical survival. The question black mothers ask in the raising of their sons is, in the authors' words: "How [can they] help sons develop the character, personality, and integrity a black man-child needs to transcend these forces?" (19).

Golden's book also assumes as its central theme the survival of black men and is dedicated to the black men who have died violently in Washington D.C. since 1988. Golden wrote this book, as she explains in her epilogue, "because at this moment there is no subject more necessary to confront, more imperative to imagine. Until I wrote about our sons, I could not speak or think or dream of anything else" (185). Homicide, Golden tells us, is the leading cause of death for young black men in America. The violence, drugs, crime, joblessness, and killing of black male youth mark, according to Golden, a new kind of Middle Passage. Her book narrates this crossing as it tells the story of her own son's journey into manhood; in this telling and testifying Golden lists possible causes, drafts solutions, and seeks to imagine what, in her words "we will look like, how will we sound, once we are spewed forth from the terrible hold of THIS ship" (9). As in King's and Mitchell's literary and sociological study, Golden recognizes that for blacks who have the financial means, retreat has become the strategy of choice; in the instance of her own life, Golden withdrew her son from public school in Washington D.C. and enrolled him in a private boarding school, as she and her husband had purchased a house in the suburbs. However, in saving your son this way, you remove him from the black community, the "sites of resistance"—family, community, history—that have traditionally nurtured and empowered African Americans by creating black-defined narratives and identities. The women of King's and Mitchell's study spoke of the "liberating, healing power of family lore, bloodlines, and family secrets" (37). "Knowing about ancestors," King and Mitchell write, "strengthens identification with family values that can help a son overcome anger and hopelessness. Such family lore can also develop a son's confidence in himself . . . it frees black males from the diminished definitions of their humanity and self-worth that society offers them" (38). Golden, too, recognizes that the double consciousness Du Bois eloquently wrote of more than a hundred years ago is, in her words, "draining and sometimes killing our spirits" (14). With integration came the loss of communities, traditions, beliefs, legends, narratives, and rituals, the "sites of resistance" that have long sustained and enriched black American culture. While suburbs and boarding schools may save black sons from the killing fields of the so-called American inner cities, they also result in the further disintegration of black communities, the very thing that holds the promise of salvation for African-Americans.

This again is the impasse of black mothers; one that is etched on the very bodies of black men, as Golden remarks of her own son: "The unscathed openness of Michael's demeanor was proof that he had been a protected, loved child. But this same quality was also suddenly a liability, ones that he has to mask" (95). Nurturing sons to be confident and proud,

mothers recognize that these same traits, because they may be miscon-
strued as insolence, obstinacy, and arrogance by other black youth, police,
or whites generally, put their sons at risk. Golden realizes, as do King and
Mitchell, that this paradox of mothering black sons necessitates a new
mode of mothering, one fashioned specifically for black male children.
And while King, Mitchell, the women of their research group, and Golden
have not designed a blueprint for such mothering, they all agree that sons
must be taught, in Golden's words, "that the first line of defense against
racism is to mold themselves into disciplined, self-respecting refutations of
its ability to destroy our souls or ourselves" (186). Or as James Baldwin
wrote in 1971: "It evolves upon the mother to invest the child, her man
child, with some kind of interior dignity which will protect him against
something he really can't be protected against, unless he has some kind of
interior thing within him to meet it" (as quoted by King and Mitchell, 39).
Audre Lorde wrote in "Man Child: A Black Lesbian Feminist's Response"
that: "for survival, Black children in America must be raised to be warriors.
For survival they must also be raised to recognize the enemy's many faces"
(75). She goes on to say:

> The strongest lesson I can teach my son is the same lesson I teach my
> daughter: how to be who he wishes to be for himself. And the best
> way I can do this is to be who I am and hope that he will learn from
> this not how to be me, which is not possible, but how to be himself.
> And this means how to move to that voice from within himself, rather
> than to those raucous, persuasive, or threatening voices from out-
> side, pressuring him to be what the world wants him to be. (77)

The aim of black mothering is thus to nurture and sustain the "singular
soul," "the voice from within," and the "interior thing" of black sons so that
they are able to transcend the maiming of racism and grow into manhood
whole and complete. Mothers of black sons, according to these writers,
must negotiate between the need to keep their sons physically safe while
simultaneously promoting their psychological maturation: this pull
between nurturance and protection is at the heart of raising the black
male child. This may be contrasted to the challenge and contradiction of
feminist mothering, according to early Anglo-American feminist thought,
which is to redefine loss as gain; boys must learn that in renouncing patriarchal masculinity they achieve humanity. Thus the mothering of sons,
according to Anglo-American thought, centers on the taking away of
power from sons, while for mothers of black men, it means bringing their

sons *to* power; to nurture and sustain that "soul," "voice from within," and "interior thing." For mothers of black sons this is achieved by grounding sons in their culture of origin, the black community. Anglo-American feminist mothering, in contrast, necessitates a challenge to the son's community of identification, the male peer group, or more generally patriarchal culture.

African-American feminist theory, as with the new Anglo-American feminist perspective, emphasizes women's agency, responsibility, and authority as mothers. The presence and involvement of the mother are recognized as crucial and essential to the son's maturation. African-American mothering of sons, however, is specifically racially determined in its emphasis on survival. "The major challenge . . . to a black mother raising sons today," as Claudette Lee and Ethel Williams explain in their chapter in this book, "[is] survival. . . . [:] Racism, discrimination, and oppression define the childhood of an African-American male. Mothering for an African-American woman is defined by fear for her male child. Therefore her approach and relationship with her son must be different" (56–7). In its focus on survival—what Ruddick defines "as the central constitutive, invariant aim of maternal practice" (19)—African-American mothering foregrounds, even more than the new Anglo-American perspective, the importance and centrality of the mother in the sons's life, for it is she who both provides protection and teaches her son how to protect himself, physically and otherwise. African-American feminist thought on mothers and sons, in its emphasis on maternal agency, responsibility, and authority, particularly as they pertain to ensuring the son's survival, recasts Jocasta and Clytemestra as pivotal characters in the mother-and-son drama.

Conclusion

Early Anglo-American feminist thought tended to downplay, devalue, and at times disparage motherhood. Arcana asked mothers to abandon traditional motherhood to allow sons to see their mothers in roles other than ones of service and subservience, Forcey championed the unbounding of motherhood to free women from the oppressiveness of the responsibility assignment, and Smith argued that only by relating to her son outside of motherhood could a mother hope to secure his respect so as to achieve a relationship based on equality. Sexism and patriarchal masculinity, they contended, are perpetuated and reinforced through maternal practice, by placing women in service to boys (Arcana), by making women responsible for sons (Forcey), and by preventing sons from respecting women (Smith). Maternal responsibility is censored by Forcey and, to a lesser degree, Arcana; maternal authority, in turn, is criticized by Smith. In each, the woman, as mother in both definition and act, is rendered absent and silent. In contrast, recent Anglo-American feminist thought focuses on maternal presence and argues that mother-son connection is what makes possible the new nonpatriarchal masculinity we desire for our sons, and for all men. The stress on maternal presence and involvement is underscored by an insistence on the significance of maternal responsibility, agency, and authority. Maternal presence and involvement are further emphasized in African-American feminist theory—as is the affirmation of the importance of maternal responsibility, agency, and authority. Presence and participation in the sons' lives are stressed in African-American feminist theory because black boys' lives are at risk. Black mothers must protect their sons to ensure their survival, both physically and psychologically, and teach them how to do the same for themselves.

The above developments in Anglo-American feminist thought on mothers and sons, along with the emergence of a distinct African-American feminist perspective, have recast the roles of mothers and sons and rewritten the patriarchal script of mother-son separation/maternal absence as they are enacted in the narratives of Jocasta and Oedipus, Clytemnestra and Orestes. In so doing, they give both voice and presence to the mother and make mother-son connection central to the redesign of both traditional masculinity and the larger patriarchal culture. This new perspective, I want to suggest, allows for real and lasting social change. Feminist positions that depend upon the marginalization of motherhood and a mitigation of maternal authority and agency, I argue, cannot effect change, because they reinscribe, albeit perhaps unknowingly and inadvertently, the valorization of the masculine and the degradation of all that is deemed feminine in our culture. The denial and disparagement of the maternal bespeaks a larger unease with, and aversion to, the feminine. The new feminist perspectives—Anglo-American and African-American—in highlighting maternal voice and presence, affirming maternal agency, authority, and responsibility, and foregrounding mother-son connection, have imagined and made possible a truly feminist narrative of mothers and sons. Indeed, a story to live by.

NOTES

1. The disparagement and erasure of the mother which these texts enact may also, as many feminist theorists have argued, be interpreted psychoanalytically as bespeaking both male fear of maternal power and the need to deny and repress the feminine in order to construct a masculine identity. Nancy Chodorow in *The Reproduction of Mothering* argues that the father's absence from the home in the sons' early years necessitates the son defining his masculinity by negation; that which his mother is, he is not. As well, for the infant son, the powers of the mother appear limitless. Our individual flesh-and-blood mother is also identified archetypally with the primordial Great Mother, who held very real life-and-death powers over mortal men. In our individual and collective unconsciousness we remember that time when we lived under the mother's power in the pre-Oedipal and prepatriarchal world. Dorothy Dinnerstein in *The Mermaid and the Minotaur* maintains that fear and hatred of women and mothers in particular originate from the infant's experiences of dependency and helplessness, which in turn come to structure adult consciousness.

2. *Mothers and Sons*, though written by the Australian writer Babette Smith, advances an Anglo-American view on feminism in general and the mother-son relation in particular.

3. For a detailed discussion of sensitive mothering, please see my article, "'Ain't That Love?': Antiracism and Racial Constructions of Motherhood" in *Everyday Acts Against Racism*, ed. Maureen Reddy (Seattle: Seal Press, 1996), 88–98.

4. This is examined at length in my two recent articles on Anglo-American feminist theory and the mother-daughter relation: "Across the Divide: Contemporary Anglo-American Feminist Theory on the Mother-Daughter Relationship" in *Redefining Motherhood: Changing Identities and Patterns*, ed. Sharon Abbey and Andrea O'Reilly (Toronto: Second Story Press, 1998), 69–91; and "Mothers, Daughters and Feminism Today: Empowerment, Agency, Narrative," in *Canadian Women's Studies* 18:2 & 3 (Summer/Fall 1998), 16–21. See also the introduction to *Mothers and Daughters: Connection, Empowerment, Transformation*, ed. Andrea O'Reilly and Sharon Abbey (New York: Rowman and Littlefield, 2000).

5. African-American motherhood has been examined in recent African-American feminist theory. See in particular Patricia Hill Collins, *Black Feminist Thought: Knowledge, Consciousness and the Politics of Empowerment* (New York: Unwin Hyman/Routledge, 1990); "The Meaning of Motherhood in Black Culture and Black Mother-Daughter Relationships" in *Double Stitch: Black Women Write about Mothers and Daughters*, ed. Patricia Bell-Scott and Beverly Guy-Sheftall(New York: HarperPerennial, 1993), 42–60; "Shifting the Center: Race, Class, and Feminist Theorizing about Motherhood" in *Mothering: Ideology, Experience, and Agency*, ed. Evelyn Nakano Glenn, Grace Chang, and Linda

Rennie Forcey (New York: Routledge, 1994), 45–65. See also my article, " 'I come from a long line of Uppity Irate Black Women': African-American Feminist Thought on Motherhood, the Motherline, and the Mother-Daughter Relationship" in *Mothers and Daughters: Connection, Empowerment, and Transformation*, ed. Andrea O'Reilly and Sharon Abbey (New York: Rowman and Littlefield, 2000), 143–159. See also the *Journal of the Association for Research on Mothering*, Vol. 2.2 on "Mothering in the African Diaspora."

6. This chapter will examine book-length studies of African-American mothers and sons as it did with Anglo-American feminist theory. Audre Lorde wrote the classic article, "Man Child: A Black Lesbian Feminist's Response" in *Sister Outsider* (Freedom, CA: The Crossing Press, 1993).

WORKS CITED

Althusser, Louis. "Ideology and Ideological State Apparatuses." In *Lenin and Philosophy and Other Essays*, translated by B. Brewster. New York: Monthly Review Press, 1971.

Arcana, Judith. *Every Mother's Son: The Role of Mothers in the Making of Men*. New York: Anchor Press/Doubleday, 1983.

Bly, Robert. *Iron John*. New York: Vintage, 1990.

Chodorow, Nancy. *The Reproduction of Mothering: Psychoanalysis and the Sociology of Gender*. Berkeley: University of California Press, 1978.

Collins, Patricia Hill. *Black Feminist Thought: Knowledge, Consciousness and the Politics of Empowerment*. New York: Unwin Hyman/Routledge, 1990.

———. "The Meaning of Motherhood in Black Culture and Black Mother-Daughter Relationships." In *Double Stitch: Black Women Write about Mothers and Daughters*, edited by Patricia Bell-Scott and Beverly Guy-Sheftall, New York: HarperPerennial, 1993. 42–60.

———. "Shifting the Center: Race, Class and Feminist Theorizing about Motherhood." In *Mothering: Ideology, Experience, and Agency*, edited by Evelyn Nakano Glenn, Grace Chang, and Linda Rennie Forcey. New York: Routledge, 1994. 45–65.

Dinnerstein, Dorothy. *The Mermaid and the Minotaur: Sexual Arrangements and Human Malaise*. New York: Harper & Row, 1977.

Forcey, Linda Rennie. *Mothers of Sons: Toward an Understanding of Responsibility*. New York: Praeger, 1987.

Friday, Nancy. *My Mother/My Self: The Daughter's Search for Identity*. New York: Delacorte Press, 1977.

Golden, Marita. *Saving Our Sons: Raising Black Children in a Turbulent World*. New York: Anchor Books/Doubleday, 1995.

King, Joyce Elaine, and Carolyn Ann Mitchell. *Black Mothers to Sons: Juxtaposing African American Literature with Social Practice.* New York: Peter Lang, 1995.

Lorde, Audre. "Man Child: A Black Lesbian Feminist's Response." In *Sister Outsider.* New York: Quality Paperback Book Club, 1993. 72–80.

Moynihan, Daniel P. *The Negro Family: The Case for National Action.* Washington, DC: U.S. Department of Labor, Office of Policy Planning and Research, 1965.

O'Reilly, Andrea. "Ain't That Love?': Antiracism and Racial Constructions of Mothering." In *Everyday Acts against Racism,* edited by Maureen Reddy. Seattle: Seal Press, 1996. 88–98.

———. "Across the Divide: Contemporary Anglo-American Feminist Theory on the Mother-Daughter Relationship." In *Redefining Motherhood: Changing Identities and Patterns,* edited by Sharon Abbey and Andrea O'Reilly. Toronto: Second Story Press, 1998. 69–91.

———. "Mothers, Daughters and Feminism Today: Empowerment, Agency, Narrative." *Canadian Women's Studies* 18:2&3 (Summer/Fall 1998): 16–21.

———. " 'I come from a long line of Uppity Irate Black Women': African-American Feminist Thought on Motherhood, the Motherline and the Mother-Daughter Relationship." In *Mothers and Daughters: Connection, Empowerment, and Transformation,* edited by Andrea O'Reilly and Sharon Abbey. New York: Rowman and Littlefield, 2000.

O'Reilly, Andrea, and Sharon Abbey, eds. *Mothers and Daughters: Connection, Empowerment, and Transformation.* New York: Rowman and Littlefield, 2000.

Pollack, William. *Real Boys: Rescuing Our Sons from the Myths of Boyhood.* New York: Random House, 1998.

Rich, Adrienne. *Of Woman Born: Motherhood as Experience and Institution.* New York: W.W. Norton, 1986.

Ruddick, Sara. *Maternal Thinking: Toward a Politics of Peace.* New York: Ballantine Books, 1989.

Silverstein, Olga, and Beth Rashbaum. *The Courage to Raise Good Men.* Viking: New York, 1994.

Smith, Babette. *Mothers and Sons: The Truth about Mother-Son Relationships.* Sydney: Allen & Unwin, 1995.

Walkerdine, Valerie, and Helen Lucey. *Democracy in the Kitchen: Regulating Mothers and Socializing Daughters.* London: Virago Press, 1989.

Wallace, Michele. *Black Macho and the Myth of the Superwoman.* New York: Verso, 1990 (1979).

Wylie, Philip. *A Generation of Vipers.* New York: Rienhart & Company, 1942.

II

MEN AND MASCULINITIES

6

SWIMMING AGAINST THE TIDE

FEMINISTS' ACCOUNTS
OF MOTHERING SONS

Alison M. Thomas

Introduction

Most academic definitions of socialization are based on the theme of adults preparing children to take their place in the society into which they have been born. In most cases this involves children learning how to act out adult roles by modeling the behavior of those around them, especially that of their parents or those most involved in their upbringing. This applies as much to children's acquisition of gendered behavior patterns as to any other learned behavior, and psychological theories concur in identifying the modeling of parental behavior as the primary way in which children learn the gendered roles considered appropriate in their society (Maccoby).

Such a process is obviously facilitated when models of both genders are readily available to children to observe and imitate, as in societies in which production, as well as reproduction, is carried out in or close to the home. However, in most "modern" industrialized societies[1] this is no longer the case, since adult work is generally performed away from the home and therefore typically removes one or both parents from the home for large portions of each working day.

Throughout most of the twentieth century, the ideology of the family wage and the definition of the father's role as that of "family breadwinner" meant that for most men the amount of time they were able to spend in the home with their children was restricted to a couple of hours in the evenings and time together on weekends (Beail and McGuire; Parke). As Julia Brannen and Peter Moss (1987) pointed out, this necessarily limited their chances of playing an active part in their children's upbringing, at least on a day-to-day basis. Joseph Pleck quotes a "breadwinner" father interviewed in a 1950s community study, lamenting his own lack of involvement with his family: "I'm a rotten Dad. If our children amount to anything it's their mother who'll get the credit. I'm so busy I don't see much of them and I don't know how to chum up with them when I do" (Pleck, 89). With "homemaker" mothers thus taking on primary responsibility for child rearing and fathers routinely absent from everyday activities in the home, Mirra Komarovsky (1953) was the first of many to observe that men often risked becoming marginal figures in their children's lives (see also Pleck; Parke). In contrast to this, however, children typically had far greater daily exposure to adult females and the activities they engaged in, whether this was via their mother or another woman—since throughout the twentieth century it continued to be the case that most alternative caregivers and the majority of elementary school teachers were female.

In other words, one of the important consequences of these twentieth-century work/family patterns was to restrict the opportunities that children had to interact with their father and model his behavior directly, in the way that the gender socialization theories stipulated. Instead, children of both sexes were for all intents and purposes raised and socialized primarily by their mothers in an everyday world populated predominantly by women.

Theorizing "Masculine" Socialization

Some versions of the standard socialization theories recognized the gender implications of this asymmetry of parenting and incorporated this into their accounts of gender identity development, arguing that because boys generally lacked the direct access to adult role models of their own sex that girls enjoyed, this necessarily made the process of gender identification more difficult for them (see Hartley; Lynn; and Greenson). According to this analysis, rather than developing an understanding of their adult gender role by modeling the behavior of their same-sex parent (as girls were able to do), boys would have to do a lot of their learning about how to be "masculine" indirectly, and primarily by learning how to differentiate themselves from their mother and other women—that is, in effect, by learning how *not* to be "feminine" (Maccoby and Jacklin).

This analysis, in highlighting the greater difficulties for boys of forming a gendered identity, thereby granted a "scientific" basis to many of the concerns of popular child-rearing books of the 1940s and 1950s (such as Wylie; Spock)[2]. These had focused on how boys deprived of sufficient exposure to their father (and at the same time at risk of "coddling" by their mothers) might be damaged by this: mothers were therefore exhorted to pay particular attention to ensuring that their sons did not grow up effeminate. Indeed, in the absence of the father, it was felt to be a mother's job to "interpret" him and his role in the family to her children—and especially to her sons (Farber; Blendis).[3] Even as recently as the 1980s, Jacqueline McGuire (1991) found that many mothers she interviewed reported making a deliberate effort to foster their son's relationship with his father, and justified this in terms of their belief that this father-son identification had a particular importance, even if it meant relinquishing their own closeness with their son. For according to Olga Silverstein and Beth Rashbaum, "Most women . . . fear that a mother's influence will ultimately be harmful to a male child, that it will weaken him, and that only the example of a man can lead a son into manhood" (9).

Many, however, have noted the distress that this separation process often risked causing, both to mothers and to their growing sons: as both tacitly acknowledged the unwritten rule requiring them to develop a gradual distance from each other, each was liable to misinterpret the other's stance as evidence of a withdrawal of affection (Silverstein and Rashbaum). There are, moreover, other negative consequences of this process of masculine self-differentiation. Insofar as it requires a boy to distance himself from his mother and reject "femininity," in favor of identifying with the often artificial extremes of "macho" masculinity depicted by the mass media, it has potentially damaging consequences in many areas of gender relations. It can, for example, manifest itself in the expression of misogynist attitudes and sexual harassment (Wood; Thomas 1997), as well as in aggressive behaviors toward other males (Ryan) and is thus, arguably, detrimental to society.[4]

The perpetuation of this masculine socialization process thus places limits on the possibility of bringing about any significant changes in the organization of adult gender roles, since it is clearly difficult to encourage men to be more nurturant and emotionally expressive (and thereby better able to share responsibility for child rearing, for example) when such qualities are widely regarded as "feminine" ones in modern Western societies, and the essence of "masculinity" is to repudiate all such traits. It follows that raising a son to be any of these things would necessitate taking the risk of making him "deviant," and since—as Silverstein and Rashbaum have observed—"The fear of what would befall an insufficiently 'masculinized' boy in this society is enormous," the majority of mothers have refrained from taking such a risk (5).

Until quite recently, then, even though mothers may have disliked many aspects of their son's passage into manhood, it seems clear that most nevertheless collaborated in this process and sought to ensure that their son grew up with an appropriately "masculine" identity by encouraging him to grow away from their influence.

The Impact of Social Change

However, over the last few decades we have seen significant changes in the gender-differentiated family patterns which characterized most of the twentieth century, as increasing numbers of women have entered the workforce and abandoned the full-time "homemaker" role.[5] The rapid growth of "dual-earner" families and the corresponding erosion of the former dominance of the single-earner "breadwinner" family have had a dual impact on the gender socialization process. First of all, it is now the case that the majority of children no longer have a "stay-at-home" mother to take charge of their early upbringing, thereby blurring what was previously the most salient distinction between mothers and fathers from their children's perspective. Second, given the changes to gender roles that have occurred in their own working lives, many parents are now questioning the appropriateness of continuing to bring up sons and daughters to expect to take on gender-differentiated roles in adulthood. The gender roles that were once viewed as "natural" are now problematized, and as a consequence we have become increasingly self-conscious about how we communicate the significance of gender to our children. As Ivan Illich observed, "How to choose, assume and transmit sex roles has become a major worry for many people" (82).

This concern is particularly relevant for mothers, since the changes that occurred as women moved into the workplace have exposed a notable lack of change in the home. By the mid-1980s there was growing concern that women were taking on paid work outside the home without relinquishing their "traditional" responsibility for domestic work within it—thus effectively taking on a "second shift" (Hochschild and Machung). Women had changed, but men, for the most part, had not. Over the past fifteen years this has therefore led to a renewed interest in reappraising and redefining traditional male roles, especially in the home, and from this it has indeed become apparent that while men's attitudes toward their role in the family may well be shifting, their behavior has been generally slow to change—especially amongst older generations.[6] It is for this reason that many women are now choosing to focus their efforts on the next generation and are trying to raise both sons and daughters to resist gender-differentiated roles, rather than see them perpetuate the same gendered asymmetries and inequalities in their own adult lives.

Once again, however, this is something that is easier for them to achieve with daughters than with sons. According to Ruth Hartley's claims (1959), girls should be able to develop a flexible idea of adult female roles by simply observing and modeling their mothers' behavior, and indeed, many feminist mothers have been successfully encouraging their daughters to grow up challenging conventional expectations of "femininity" through their own example. This is of course made easier by the fact that there are also obvious and tangible rewards for young women in resisting conventionally feminine roles (especially when this entails relinquishing some of the burden of responsibility in the home), since such roles are no longer accorded much status in contemporary society.

However, the situation is rather different for sons: for a start, there has been a general lack of antisexist men willing and able to act as unconventional role models for their sons (at least until recently), and this has again meant that mothers are the ones who are taking responsibility for directing their sons toward resisting traditional forms of masculinity. On top of this, it is clear that for young men the "costs" of challenging conventional masculine roles are much higher—given a society that still does attach considerable prestige to "masculinity"—and when this entails (for example) sharing domestic responsibilities with women, such "costs" are not clearly compensated by tangible benefits.

All of these factors have made the task of rearing antisexist sons a formidable one and have once more brought to the fore the concerns expressed some fifty years earlier regarding the risks to boys of being emasculated by their mothers. Many mothers indeed feel ambivalent about this, since, as Adrienne Rich (1977: 204) noted, "The fear of alienating a male child from 'his' culture seems to go deep, even among women who reject that culture for themselves every day of their lives."

Nevertheless, in recent years there have been growing numbers of women who have decided to defy traditional norms and ominous cautionary tales and who have set out to raise their sons to be different. Rather than encouraging them to follow the conventional path of gradual separation from themselves and their "feminine" influence in order to assume a "masculine" identification with their father or other adult males, these women have chosen to resist such a distancing and to encourage their sons to remain close to them. In the next section I report the experiences and insights of some of the many women who have attempted this—and who are thus "swimming against the tide."

Outline of Study

In 1994 Robyn Rowland and I launched a small-scale qualitative research study aimed at collecting feminist mothers' accounts of their experiences of raising sons(Rowland and Thomas).[7] Over a period of several months we wrote to forty-two women whom we knew to have one or more sons, and invited them to reflect on and write about their particular experiences *as feminists* of bringing up sons, either via responses to an open-ended questionnaire, or in the form of an independent personal account along the same thematic lines. Working in part from our own experiences as mothers of sons, we highlighted a number of themes for them to consider in their responses:

- What their initial reactions were on discovering the sex of their child(ren) (and how others had reacted, especially feminist friends)
- How they felt about their son(s) now
- What they felt had been the particular rewards and/or difficulties of having a son or sons
- How the experience of mothering their son(s) had altered as he/they grew older
- How their feminism had affected their experience of mothering their son(s)

- How having a son or sons had affected their feminist politics
- Any specific moments when they had been made aware of their gender differences as a barrier between them
- Their hopes for their son(s)
- Differences between mothering their son(s) and daughter(s)

The women to whom we wrote (mostly in the United Kingdom, Australia, Canada, and the United States) came from a variety of different class and ethnic backgrounds and covered a wide age range (as did their sons). For some their son was their only child, while others had more than one son, or daughters as well as sons. Some were bringing up their son(s) alone, others with a partner; of these, we took care to include those in both lesbian and heterosexual relationships.

In all, we received personal accounts from thirteen women, while a further seventeen women completed the questionnaire.[8] The sons of these thirty women ranged in age from five and one-half months to thirty-two years old. For eleven of the women, their son was their only child; eight had more than one son; and the remainder had one or more daughters as well as the son they wrote about. Seven of the women were (or had been) bringing up their son single-handedly; one had joint custody of her son with his father, from whom she was separated; one had raised her now-adult son in a collective household; four had raised sons with their woman partner, and the remaining seventeen with the boy's father or stepfather.

Findings

Elsewhere Robyn Rowland and I have highlighted a range of themes which emerged from the accounts and questionnaire responses of these feminist mothers of sons (Rowland and Thomas). Here I wish to focus on three of these themes in more detail: these are first, their efforts to encourage an alternative and more positive style of masculinity in their sons; second, the frustrations which these women expressed with regard to the everyday difficulties of bringing up their sons to resist masculine stereotypes in the context of immense pressures from elsewhere to conform to these; and third, the ambivalence many nevertheless expressed regarding the effects of their own active attempts to sabotage a conventional masculine identification in their sons.[9]

Theme 1: Envisioning a New Masculinity

Most feminist mothers see themselves as aiming to bring up their sons to be different from the masculine "norm" in various ways, and the women who participated in our study were no exception. Elsie Jay wrote of her conscious commitment to "creating a new man—sensitive, expressive, non-violent, respectful and loving of women" (Jay, 122), and this was a predominant theme, with most of the mothers describing their efforts to encourage nurturant behavior and emotional expressiveness in their sons and to discourage aggressive behavior of all kinds:

> I actively encourage affectionate, sensitive and emotional behaviour/conversation and deliberately never encourage "macho" or masculinist dress/behavior/language/violence. (Kate)

> I have sought to appreciate his emotional sensibilities and encouraged him to do so, even if this means not being "boyish." (Deborah)

> I've encouraged him to pursue "feminine" interests, like reading, and talking about feelings. I've discouraged macho pursuits like toy guns etc. (Susie)

Others also mentioned more practical concerns, such as wanting their sons to be competent in the domestic sphere:

> I actively sought to "enable" him to stand on his own feet as a human being; he can cook, wash, clean etc. and should never be a burden on another woman. (Celia)

Those with older sons referred to their often lengthy discussions with their sons about how they had tried to raise them, and to their efforts to point out to them the gender inequalities that they were liable to encounter as they grew up:

> I have been able to discuss with them how I have raised them and why, and discuss how they feel. (Connie)

Yet it was often difficult for them to feel confident of having achieved the right balance; as Arlene McLaren noted, "at one and the same time I worry about ramming feminist, anti-oppressive ideas down my son's throat and not doing it enough"(McLaren, 124). Yvonne reported that as her son got older she spent a lot of time discussing with him "the negative aspects of masculinity, violence, machismo" that they saw around them. Louise

Enders felt that it was important not only to influence the way her own sons behaved but also to make them aware and critical of the negative masculine traits they might encounter in others, including their own friends. She wrote:

> My sons can recognise patriarchal patterns in their friends' behaviour. I hope that I have equipped them with the knowledge to contribute to challenging and changing other men's phallocentric behaviour. (Enders, 128)

However, several mothers with older sons acknowledged that their sons had often responded by accusing them of making it harder for them to fit in with their peers:

> They both feel that relations with girls have been affected (because girls prefer more macho men) and accuse me of making them into wimps. (Connie)

One particularly poignant theme for many mothers in this context was how they felt about the risk of "losing" their sons to patriarchy. They had seen their sons enter the world innocent of the demands and expectations to be "masculine" that would soon be directed at them, and many expressed their fears and regrets at the perceived inevitability of the erosion of this innocence. Bev Thiele wrote of the challenge of preserving her six-month-old son and his "cheerful openness" in the face of the pressures she anticipated he would later face to "be tough," "to be a man" (Thiele, 101). Yvonne wrote of the joys of having known her son (now adult) "as a child unspoiled by socialisation into masculinity"; but also admitted that she had eventually come to accept that "other institutions have a far greater influence on learned masculine behavior than my home." This became a second major theme in women's accounts—that of the struggle to "swim against the tide" in mainstream male-dominated society.

Theme 2: Swimming against the Tide

This was a universal theme in women's accounts—the realization that feminist mothers attempting to raise their sons to be different are always "going against the grain of the dominant culture" (Connie). Where these mothers reported the struggle to be most intense was in relation to the expectations of the school system, peer group pressures, the mass media, and, for some, the influence of their son's father and other adult role models.

Several mothers reported having found themselves in conflict with the masculine ethos of their son's school, in which traditional values of manliness were promoted, and Connie acknowledged that this had sometimes created problems for her sons, who felt caught between two different value systems. Kate noted two stages in the socialization process that her son had encountered within the school system:

> There were two difficult times—when he first went to infant school and had to learn to be more like a "boy" by hiding/controlling his feelings, then at secondary school, where he "toughened up" further, including playing rugby and all that entails. (Kate)

Yvonne also identified the pernicious influence of the dominant cultural models of masculinity emanating from the mass media and competitive sports, to which her son was drawn. These, she felt, had been instrumental in socializing her son into a particular style of macho behavior which she felt promoted an identification of masculinity with aggression and "ruthless power," which again she deplored.

Deborah, a British Afro-Caribbean woman, had experienced the added complication of having to deal with covert racism at her son's school, where she felt he had been adversely affected by "white racist perceptions of black boys." However, at the same time as helping him to resist such stereotypes and find a positive identity for himself as a young black man, she had wanted to discourage him from identifying with some of the black male role models available to him via popular culture (such as rap), because of their blatant sexism.

In many cases, in fact, mothers reported that it was the combination of popular culture and peer group pressure, rather than the school system per se, which had the most influence over their son(s). Nancy wrote of the "machismo trip" each of her sons had embarked upon while disengaging from her and "trying on" various masculine traits in the years of middle childhood. Connie was so appalled at the behavior of some of her son's friends when they visited her home that she had made active efforts to work on them also, letting them know that even if *their* mothers cleared up after them, she would not!

While most mothers whose sons had reached school age mentioned similar experiences of trying to counter the pressures toward peer-group conformity, some had also had to tackle the influence of other older (adult) role models on their sons: Yvonne reported a number of "outright confrontations" over this while her son was in his late teens. For those raising their son alone after separating from his father, this was a particular problem. Zarina, having just split up with the father of her two-year-old son, was concerned at how sharing joint custody with her ex-husband was likely to limit the control she would have over her son's upbringing from now on. Zoe, also divorced, stated quite bluntly that her main problem with her son involved repairing the psychological damage done to him by his father, who in her view had "screwed him up."

Even among those women who were in continuing relationships with the father of their son, there were some who expressed reservations about the influence he had over him. Deborah, for instance, mentioned that she had to "block" some of the sexist expectations and values that her partner conveyed to their son. Connie expressed her disappointment that her efforts to rear her sons to resist traditional masculinity had been unsupported by her husband, and that she had failed in her hope of transforming him, too, into a "New Man" in the process.

Nevertheless, several other women made reference to the active, practical support they felt they had from their son's father for their aims: Bev Thiele found it helpful for her son to be growing up with a father who did not conform to dominant stereotypes of what a "man" should be. Arlene McLaren remarked upon the significance of the fact that when her son was young he was cared for primarily by his father during a period in which she was commuting long-distance to work. Such early experience of close care from fathers was seen by many as significant in influencing how their sons formed their own expectations of the gendering (or not) of adult roles.[10]

Clearly, having some support in the bid to raise a nonsexist son in a still-sexist society was recognized as an asset by those who had benefited from it. Yet all women wrote of their feelings of "swimming against the tide" and of finding it an exhausting struggle. While some expressed the hope that their efforts to "inoculate" their son(s) against patriarchy would succeed, at least in the longer term, others were less optimistic about this: as Zoe commented regarding her nineteen-year-old son: "No matter what we have said, the pressure of peers/friends/extended family/society generally to 'be a man' has been overwhelming."

Theme 3: The Risks in Sabotaging "Masculinity"

A particular difficulty expressed by many women in our survey was their recurrent anxiety as to whether what they were striving to do with their son was justified or whether they were—in Yvonne's words—"compromising his masculinity." Louise Enders admitted:

> I raised my son to be different to other males, often, I felt, at his expense. . . . In effect, my son was/is a social experiment. (Enders, 127–28)

For some of the feminist mothers in this study and in the special issue of *Feminism and Psychology*, 1996, their concern was indeed related to the perceived risk of making their son *too* "different" and thereby exposing him to potential ostracism from his peers. As Arlene McLaren explained:

> I want my son . . . to be able to socialise with his peers, to understand them, to find a place among them, and not to be so "other-worldly" and principled that "cultural reality" is too hard to bear. (McLaren, 125)

While all wanted their sons to resist the "warrior" models of macho masculinity promoted in popular culture, they were nonetheless wary of rendering them "too" sensitive and thereby vulnerable to being picked on and bullied for being different. Susie, in common with many, expressed her ambivalence in this regard:

> It's hard to encourage him to be sensitive and caring, whilst knowing his peers might then see him as a "softie" or a wimp.

Interestingly, amongst the mothers whose sons were now adult, several admitted to feeling relieved that their sons appeared to have emerged more or less unscathed by their own feminist influence upon their development, having achieved some kind of balance between their values and those of the dominant culture. As Judith confessed:

> Having secretly feared the impact of my feminism upon them, I think I have had an ever increasing sense of relief at their normality.

While concern for their sons' ability to relate to their peers was raised by many women, others also mentioned their fear of damaging their own relationship with their son by their constant criticism of the negative aspects of traditional masculine values. Another concern expressed by several women was that this kind of criticism might risk undermining their son's self-confidence. As Zoe explained:

> It has been difficult to challenge some aspects of his masculinity without making him so vulnerable that it is counter-productive.

For many women this therefore meant looking for as many opportunities as possible to find compensatory ways of being positive toward their son—though without overdoing this. Susie described herself as "trying to draw a line between encouraging his personal development and stopping him developing a macho type personality." Deborah had found the same difficulty in getting the balance right with her son:

> There is a constant tension between not reinforcing male expectations of women to look after them and "save them" and responding to his real emotional needs for nurturance, support and a place to be vulnerable.

She pointed out that given the added difficulties that sons of feminist mothers face in having to deal with two conflicting messages about being male, she felt that she owed it to her son to offer him extra support, while at the same time being wary of allowing him to take that support for granted. Here, then, as in so many other areas, we find yet more evidence of the contradictions faced by feminist mothers of sons and the feelings of ambivalence that these contradictions provoke in them.

Discussion: Finding a Role for Fathers?

A recurrent motif in all of these accounts is that of the struggle many mothers experience when they try to help their sons grow up in ways that defy traditional masculine stereotypes. Many women made it plain that their commitment to doing this stemmed from their commitment to feminism and indicated that they drew strength from their belief that it was important for their sons to learn "new ways of being men" (Rich, 210). Indeed, as Louise Enders observed, "Having sons is integral to my hope for the future of feminism" (129). However, as noted earlier, many also reported feeling a lack of support for their efforts, not merely from wider society (which was only what they expected) but also from those around them, and this made their self-appointed task seem all the more daunting.

Here, then, I want to focus on an aspect of their experiences that intersects in important ways with all three of the themes outlined in the previous section: that is, the question of men's role in supporting (or resisting) these women's efforts to raise a feminist son. To what extent do men share women's vision of a "new masculinity?" Are they prepared to swim against the tide of convention in encouraging their sons to be different?

And how do they appraise (and themselves cope with) the risks of sabotaging masculinity?

As noted earlier, it has long been the case that women have carried the main responsibility for child rearing. However, insofar as the mothers in this study are now seeking to teach their sons that being a man can (and should) involve participating on a more equal basis in child rearing, one might expect those of them living with the fathers of their sons to seek greater involvement in this project from them. Why, then, was so little mention made of them?

It is of course important to remember that in focusing specifically on women's personal involvement with their sons' upbringing, this research did not directly address the contribution of any co-parents. It may thus be that the absence of attention to fathers in women's responses merely reflects the absence of questions asked regarding their role. In fact, as we have seen, some women did make reference to the support received from their partners; nevertheless, the dominant impression gained from studying these accounts is that these mothers see themselves as fighting mostly single-handedly for their son's future. What can we infer from this? Are men still reluctant to participate in women's efforts to bring up their sons to resist hegemonic masculinity? Or are women wary of involving men in a cause to which they may doubt their commitment?

Although, as we have seen, fathers did not participate as much as mothers in their children's upbringing throughout most of the twentieth century, the prevalence today of dual-earner families has to a certain extent already begun to reduce the previous imbalance in parental involvement. However, there is at the same time considerable evidence to suggest that many mothers continue to feel a sense of ownership of responsibility for their children's upbringing (Thomas 1999). As one mother in this study commented wryly, "It is mothers who raise children—whatever men may think" (Harriet). Insofar as this is a legacy of women's traditional role within the family, it may thus be hard for many to concede any part of this traditional "territory" to men (McBride and Darragh). Moreover, given what we know of the present inequitable division of labor in most households (including those of many heterosexual feminists!), some women may have quite justifiable doubts as to the extent of their partner's commitment to their own vision of gender equality for their son, and so prefer not to relinquish their own influence over him.

Deborah, for example, noted that her son was more strongly attached to her than to his father, and admitted to having mixed feelings about this:

while her partner's "sexist values" made her want to keep her son under her influence, she nevertheless regretted that she was not able to feel comfortable letting him identify more closely with his father. This is something which Johnetta Cole has highlighted in questioning whether "a father can participate in raising a feminist son until the father deals with his own sense of masculinity" (Cole, 43). Harry Christian, in his research on antisexist men, claimed that many had learned to challenge and resist hegemonic masculinity not from their father, with whom they often had a rather distant relationship, but through having a close and warm relationship with their mother (Christian). Like Cole, he therefore claims that until men are able to be nurturant, nontraditional role models to their sons it is better for the sons *not* to identify with them.

This is of course welcome support for all those women who, like Zarina, Zoe, and Deborah, do not see their son's father as a desirable role model for the "New Man" they want their son to become. However, other women (such as Connie) clearly cherish hopes of making the rearing of an antisexist son a joint project with their son's father, with the idea that this might also serve to change *his* attitudes and behavior in the process; and a number of the women in this study and in the special issue of *Feminism and Psychology* (such as Livingstone, McLaren, Thiele, Thomas) indicated that their son's father was already playing an important part in this endeavor.

Although until recently it was evident that fewer men than women were making a conscious effort to raise antisexist sons, there are some signs that this may soon start to change. During the 1990s there was a surge of interest in the father-son relationship, much of it focusing on the "father-hunger" which many men reported feeling as a consequence of growing up with a remote and emotionally distant father.[11] Recent research with younger fathers suggests that many men wish to enjoy a closer relationship with their children than they had with their own father and are, accordingly, committed to greater involvement in their children's lives and a more nurturant father role.[12]

On the evidence of the psychological theory and research reviewed earlier, this would mark an important change in boys' gender socialization. As Hartley (1959) and Lynn (1966) observed, boys have frequently had to learn what it means to be male indirectly (whether from their mothers or from the mass media) rather than directly, from their own fathers, and this has been seen to have a number of undesirable consequences (Thomas 1997). However, the same theories indicate that the most straightforward way for boys to develop a healthy, flexible, and less artificial identification with their gender should be for them to have the opportunity to model themselves directly on a nurturant and fully involved father figure, just as girls have benefited from being able to observe and model the increasing flexibility in their mothers' adult roles as these have evolved over the past quarter century.

Research on families in which fathers are participating in "shared parenting" does indeed show that boys gain from having before them a positive model of nurturant fathering, which enables them to see practical alternatives to conventional masculine role models (Coltrane 1996). Coltrane, moreover, argues that his research indicates that there may in fact be benefits for all family members when shared parenting is practiced. For although the theories emphasize the developmental benefits for boys in particular, children of both sexes appear to prosper from increased contact with their fathers. Another obvious benefit that shared parenting offers is to women, as they are able to shed some of the burden of responsibility for child rearing. However, possibly the most significant outcome for the families in Coltrane's study was that the fathers' increased hands-on involvement in child care had the effect of making them more competent at parenting, more sensitive to the children's needs, and more nurturant. This was rewarding not only to the men themselves, but also to their partners; as Coltrane notes: "When fathers and mothers both perform routine child care and housework, it can promote mutual understanding and enhance marital solidarity" (78).

While studies such as Coltrane's thus provide strong support for the benefits of this kind of shared parenting, it is of course important to remind ourselves that—as seen here in the cases of Zoe and Zarina—there are many women who for good reasons may not wish to involve their son's father (or any other man) in his upbringing. However, for any woman who is raising her sons within a stable, nonabusive, heterosexual relationship, sharing child rearing with a partner who is, like her, committed to a new vision of a less gender-differentiated society must surely be the best way forward, benefiting mother, son, and father alike. As others have observed before me, if men are the problem, then they can also (and indeed should) be part of the solution.

Conclusion

In this chapter I have discussed the experiences of mothers who are raising their sons to resist traditional forms of masculine behavior, and I have reviewed evidence that suggests the potential benefits of encouraging more men to share in this endeavor. As we start to see signs that increasing numbers of men *are* choosing to become more actively involved in their children's daily lives—and with positive consequences—we can begin to hope that the tide may at last be starting to turn in our favor, and that as feminist mothers we will no longer have to swim against it.

NOTES

1. In this chapter I am confining myself to discussing the gender socialization of boys in modern industrialized societies, since it is there primarily—in societies such as those of North America, Western Europe, and Australia—that twentieth-century changes in gender roles have led to the problematizing of masculinity in the last quarter century.

2. Silverstein and Rashbaum (22) cite various other such books, including *Their Mothers' Sons* by Edward Strecker and David Levy's ominously titled *Maternal Overprotection*, both first published in 1943 and sufficiently popular to warrant reissue in the 1950s.

3. Farber (1962), for example, noted that mothers often referred to the values and expectations of the father in dealing with their children in his absence (e.g. "What would Daddy think/say?"), and by these means contrived to present him as a role model for their children.

4. According to Ryan, "Masculinity, then, can be viewed as a defensive construction, developed . . . out of a need to emphasise a difference, a separateness from the mother. In the extreme this is manifested by machismo behavior with its emphasis on competitiveness, strength, aggressiveness, contempt for women and emotional shallowness, all serving to keep the male secure in his separate identity" (Ryan, 26).

5. For a detailed historical account of the ways in which parental roles have been influenced by social and economic changes, see Demos (1982), and Pleck (1987).

6. See, for example, Charlie Lewis and Margaret O'Brien (1987), and Lynne Segal (1990).

7. No claims are made for the representativeness of this sample: our purpose in conducting this research was simply to explore some of the issues that had been faced by these self-identified feminist mothers in their efforts to bring their sons up to resist traditional forms of masculinity. While some of the concerns of these mothers may not apply to others, it is evident that many of the problems they reported facing are common to all parents as they contemplate their son's future in a changing world.

8. Thirteen of these individual accounts were published in the special feature on mothering sons, "Mothering Sons: A Crucial Feminist Challenge," in

Feminism and Psychology (Robyn Rowland and Alison M. Thomas), in which they are discussed along with responses from twelve women who completed questionnaires; a further five questionnaires were received after the publication of this feature but are included for discussion here.

9. In this section those women whose personal accounts were published in the special feature are cited by name with references to the page number in *Feminism and Psychology* (see note 8); those whose questionnaire responses are quoted here are identified by a pseudonym.

10. In my own case I remember being thrilled to hear my son, then aged six, declare that both mummies and daddies were "someone who looks after you." He too, was speaking from his own experience of being cared for as much by his father as his mother.

11. See for example Robert Bly (1990) and Steve Biddulph (1994).

12. See for example Charlie Lewis (1986); Kerry Daly, (1994); and Scott Coltrane (1996).

WORKS CITED

Beail, N., and J. McGuire. *Fathers: Psychological Perspectives*. London: Junction Books, 1982.

Biddulph, S. *Manhood: A Book about Setting Men Free*. Sydney: Finch Publishing, 1994.

Blendis, J. "Men's Experience of Their Own Fathers." In *Fathers: Psychological Perspectives*, edited by N. Beail and J. McGuire. London: Junction Books, 1982.

Bly, R. *Iron John*. Reading, MA: Addison-Wesley, 1990.

Brannen, J., and P. Moss. "Fathers in Dual-Earner Households through Mothers' Eyes." In *Reassessing Fatherhood*, edited by C. Lewis and M. O'Brien. London: Sage 1987.

Christian, H. *The Making of Anti-Sexist Men*. London: Routledge, 1994.

Cole, J. "Raising Sons" *Ms.* (Nov./Dec. 1993): 42–44.

Coltrane, S. *Family Man: Fatherhood, Housework and Gender Equity* New York: Oxford University Press, 1996.

Daly, K. "Uncertain Terms: The Social Construction of Fatherhood." In *Doing Everyday Life: Ethnography as Human Lived Experience*, edited by M. Dietz, R. Prus, and W. Shaffir. Toronto: Copp Clark Longman, 1994.

Demos, K. "The Changing Faces of Fatherhood: A New Exploration in American Family History." In *Father and Child: Developmental and Clinical Perspectives*, edited by S. Cath, C. Gurwitt, and J. Ross. Boston: Little, Brown, 1982.

Enders, L. "Feminism and Mothering of Sons." *Feminism and Psychology* 6 (1996): 127–128.

Farber, B. "Marital Integration as a Factor in Parent-Child Relations." *Child Development* 33 (1962): 1–14.

Greenson, R. "Disidentifying from the Mother: Its Special Importance for the Boy." *International Journal of Psychoanalysis* 49 (1968): 370–374.

Hartley, R. "Sex-Role Pressures and the Socialisation of the Male Child." *Psychological Reports* 5 (1959): 457–468.

Hochschild, A., and A. Machung. *The Second Shift: Working Parents and the Revolution at Home.* New York: Viking Press, 1989.

Illich, I. *Gender.* London: Marion Boyars, 1983.

Jay, E. "Birthdays. Gaydays." *Feminism and Psychology* 6 (1996): 121–123.

Komarovsky, M. *Women in the Modern World: Their Education and Their Dilemmas* Boston: Little, Brown, 1953.

Lewis, C. *Becoming a Father.* Buckingham: Open University Press, 1986.

Lewis, C., and M. O'Brien, eds. *Reassessing Fatherhood* London: Sage, 1987.

Livingstone, S. "Rethinking the Oedipal Complex: 'Why Can't I Have Babies Like Mummy?'" *Feminism and Psychology* 6 (1996): 111–113.

Lynn, D. "The Process of Learning Parental and Sex-Role Identification." *Journal of Marriage and the Family* 28 (1966): 466–470.

Maccoby, E., and C. Jacklin. *The Psychology of Sex Differences.* Stanford: Stanford University Press, 1974.

Maccoby E., ed. *The Development of Sex Differences.* Stanford: Stanford University Press, 1966.

McBride, B., and J. Darragh. "Interpreting the Data on Father Involvement: Implications for Parenting Programs for Men" *Families in Society* (1995): 490–497.

McGuire, J. "Sons and Daughters." In *Motherhood: Meanings, Practices and Ideologies,* edited by A. Phoenix, A. Woollett, and E. Lloyd. 1991.

McLaren, A. "Working with and against Male-Dominated Culture." *Feminism and Psychology* 6 (1996): 124–126.

Parke, R. *Fatherhood.* Cambridge, MA: Harvard University Press, 1996.

Pleck, J. "American Fathering in Historical Perspective." In *Changing Men: New Directions in Research on Men and Masculinity,* edited by M. Kimmel. Newbury Park: Sage, 1987.

Rich, A. *Of Woman Born: Motherhood as Experience and Institution.* London: Virago, 1977.

Rowland, R., and A. M. Thomas. "Mothering Sons: A Crucial Feminist Challenge." *Feminism and Psychology* 6 (1996): 93–154.

Ryan, T. "Roots of Masculinity." In *The Sexuality of Men,* edited by A. Metcalf and M. Humphries. London: Pluto Press, 1985.

Segal, L. *Slow Motion: Changing Masculinities, Changing Men.* London: Virago, 1990.

Silverstein, O., and B. Rashbaum. *The Courage to Raise Good Men.* London: Penguin, 1994.

Spock, B. *Baby and Child Care.* New York: Duell, Sloan and Pearce, 1945.

Thiele, B. "Ewan—It Means 'Heart and Mind' and Heart Comes First." *Feminism and Psychology* 6 (1996): 100–102.

Thomas, A. M. "'Boys Will Be Boys?' Resisting the Myth of 'Essential Masculinity'" *Feminism and Psychology* 6 (1996): 114–117.

———. "'Men Behaving Badly?' A Psychosocial Exploration of the Cultural Context of Sexual Harassment." In *Sexual Harassment: Contemporary Feminist Perspectives*, edited by A. M. Thomas and C. Kitzinger. Buckingham: Open University Press, 1997.

———. "Survival Strategies for Women in the Transition to Parenthood: Resisting the Myths of Motherhood." Paper presented at the Annual Conference of the Association for Research on Mothering, Brock University, St. Catharine's, Ontario, October 1999.

Wood, J. "Boys Will Be Boys." *New Socialist* (May/June 1982): 41–43.

Wylie, P. *Generation of Vipers*. New York: Rinehart, 1942.

7

FEMINIST ACADEMIC MOTHERS' INFLUENCES

ON THEIR SONS' MASCULINITY

Sharon Abbey

*Boys will be boys not because they were born that way
but because masculinity requires it of them.*
                                        —*Babette Smith*

Introduction

Several years ago I began to question the influence feminist academic mothers have on their children with two of my female colleagues at the university. Each of us had raised a young adult son and daughter while pursuing our careers as elementary school teachers and tenured faculty professors. Initially we were predominantly interested in how our professions had influenced the education of our daughters (Abbey, Castle, and Reynolds 1998; Castle, Abbey, and Reynolds 1998). At some point during this study with our daughters, our sons questioned why we were not interested in their experiences as well. Their queries and good-humored taunting encouraged us to undertake a second study addressing our responsibility as feminist mothers raising sons. At the time of this second study, one son was completing his fourth year of computer studies at university while the other two sons had recently completed their undergraduate degrees and were pursing very diverse careers as a police officer and a professional actor in classical theater. My colleagues' sons grew up in two-parent homes while my son was raised, for the most part, by a single mother.

This chapter will examine the predominant theme of masculine identity that emerged from this second study with our sons. The resulting dialogue forced us to consider how our interest in gender deconstruction discourse served to disrupt power relations with our sons and to encourage them to resist binary theories of their own masculinity. I begin this chapter with an overview of the diverse and complex range of images, messages, and myths about masculinity in relation to the identities our sons have constructed about themselves. Next, I address possibilities and dilemmas involved in the role of mothers who serve as advocates of gender restructuring. I question the forces that work against mothers as they seek ways of helping their sons become free, confident, and independent men who are capable of liking themselves, taking risks, forming close and authentic relationships with others, and facing the future with courage and optimism. Finally, I briefly consider strategies for revising how schools operate and what they value within this context of gender identity.

As a feminist mother assuming the role of emotional caretaker for my son, there are several reasons why I believe we ought to be concerned about the masculinity of our sons. First of all, our sons should be conscious of the social construction of masculinity and how their values are shaped by society and male role models, including their fathers. Secondly, although it is important that they are able to relate to their male peer group, they should also be comfortable with who they are and be committed to becoming advocates for accepting a broader repertoire of acceptable behavior patterns. Thirdly, by understanding feminist ideals of masculinity, it is more likely that our sons will effectively interact with strong, independent young women.

Traditionally, Western society celebrated the powerful connections that develop between mothers and sons. However, we have recently lost sight of much of this wisdom and, as a result, have closed off channels for its appropriate expression (Pollack). Consequently, there are surprisingly few cross-gender studies of mother-son relationships or of the crucial role such dyads play in socialization. In fact, according to Carol Tavris (1992), most of the literature offers a limited or mismeasured interpretation of mother-son relationship as it applies to the dominant framework of fathers, husbands, and sons. Even liberal feminist interpretations of this dyad

(Arcana; Caron; Forcey; and Smith) emphasize the oppression of mother-hood. In addition, most of the studies about understanding young men's lives have been written by men and exclusively address male relationships between fathers and sons set within a masculine hegemonic context (Gilbert and Gilbert). Often this literature infers a subordinate role for mothers as patriarchal conformists or compliant enforcers of the status quo (Hearn and Morgan).

Such predominantly narrow messages can result in mothers internalizing limited, androcentric, male descriptions of mother-son dyads as subtle interactions between letting go and clinging. Olga Silverstein and Beth Rashbaum (1994) point out that these interpretations may encourage a mother to fear "contaminating her adolescent son with her own femininity, [or] compromising his sexuality," thus effecting a very abrupt withdrawal of emotional support (108). Cutting a son loose in this fashion, they insist, "feels more like abandonment than liberation" to him (127). In fact, by encouraging their sons to separate from them and by placing such a high value on independence, mothers may be the agents of their own oppression, effectively supporting a society that pulls males from their mothers and sets them in a more highly valued place. This essentialist viewpoint also impedes mother-son interdependence in that it tends to discount and marginalize the responsibility, authority, and power of women to socialize their sons with respect to gender identity. As well, this type of discourse places unrealistic pressure on boys to pull away from helpful maternal support at a time when they are struggling to construct their understanding of themselves. If mothers are to assume a significant role in helping their sons develop a healthy sense of who they are, their maternal role must be valued and taken seriously by others.

Our Children's Views of Their Own Gender Identity

The topic of feminism was not consciously addressed in our first study with our daughters, and I am not sure why. Perhaps we assumed some common female understanding and familiarity with the daughters that we have already confronted and examined in our own lives as women. On the other hand, since we were not brought up in male cultures and don't have male bodies, we likely shared a need to clarify our sons' gendered standpoints with the sons. Although our children's views on what constitutes a feminist varied, it was obvious that they tended to believe that there were painful consequences and penalties associated with being perceived as a feminist. Our daughters tended to resist feminism because of the strong positions we have taken about gender equity and their perceptions of our radical groundbreaking work as difficult and unrewarding. Our sons, on the other hand, seemed more concerned about stereotypical impressions held by their peer group that might threaten their male identities and set them apart as different. They did not want to appear too closely identified with their mothers or thought of as a "sissy" or "momma's boy." My son was the only one who identified with a feminist construct. During one of our conversations he pointed out: "I see things from a feminist point of view that I don't think maybe other guys my age see. I think that results from growing up with my mother and sister in a single-parent home." Closely identifying with his mother and female family members did not seem to be the issue for him that Nancy Chodorow (1978) would have us believe in her object-relations theory.

As the conversation about gender identity intensified with our sons, we were even more surprised at how hesitant and insecure they were about defining their own masculinity. There was obviously a lot of emotional baggage attached to this term for them that we not previously had been aware of. They seemed apprehensive about exposing themselves to ridicule or criticism from each other and especially from their feminist moms. They also admitted feeling defensive and embarrassed about being white, middle-class males in North America and frustrated with a society that imposed such anxieties and inhibitions on them. It was obvious that they were unsure of what we expected them to say and whether we were deliberately trying to set them up. According to one son: "If we say the wrong thing we will have to answer for it! We are not proud to be males. Men are on the run. . . . There are a lot of guys that embarrass me by the way they treat others." My son shared a similar sentiment by stating: "Testosterone . . . is seen as a bad thing." Needless to say, we found their lack of confidence and confirmation about their masculinity very surprising and disturbing.

All three of our sons seemed almost speechless and tongue-tied, as well as apologetic, about endorsing possible stereotypical interpretations and old-fashioned archetypes of maleness that included "the fearless hero," "the lone ranger," and "the distant warrior." They spoke of maleness as avoidance of femininity, restricted emotionality, nonrelational attitudes toward sex, pursuit of achievement and status, self-reliance, strength and aggression, and, to a certain degree, homophobia. Their description of masculinity included very different concepts, exemplifying the multiplicity of the term. For example, one son endorsed an essentialist view of masculinity, associating it with control; the physical appearance of heavy, muscle-bound jocks who "hit on women"; powerful Greek mythology figures such as Zeus, Hercules, or Apollo; and figures such as Oedipus who viewed mothers as the problem from whom sons must escape. This fixed concept emphasized norms, standards, and modes of action in which men prove themselves, earn rewards, or rescue women. It supports an image of aggression, strength, and competition that includes "locker room" stories of sexual conquests and the defeat of opponents. It also leads to discounting "male advantage" in school if the male was on the receiving end. By rationalizing rewards as an earned privilege, such viewpoints ignore the cultural construction of gender. In comparison, another son defined masculinity in relational terms—as the antithesis of all that is considered feminine, such as "knowing too much about gourmet cooking or going to the theater." His definition included the fear of losing masculinity by doing something associated with females. In contrast, my son defined masculinity as "privilege and freedom of movement or power" and, for him, it brought to mind images such as "cigars, scotch, and football games." His concept involved relationships to other men and inferred the image of success.

Our sons' responses clearly revealed their confusion about masculine identities, lending support to Carol Tavris's observation that: "If men are rejecting the John Wayne model of masculinity, they seem less sure than women about what should replace it" (49). As a result of these conversations with our sons we began to ask ourselves some hard questions as mothers and educators: To what extent do our sons feel abandoned and betrayed? Why were we not more sensitive and attuned to our sons' identity struggles? What degree of responsibility should mothers take for gender identity difficulties and their possible solutions? In the end, we realized that we had given little prior thought to the complexities of male gender identity and, as a result, had a lot to learn about masculinity if we were to offer support to our sons. In this regard, I don't think we are alone!

For my part, as a single/divorced mother, I recognize that my son had few family role models for constructing his masculinity when he grew up. Both grandfathers, who were kind and sensitive men, died before he was born, and he spent a great deal of his youth surrounded by a devoted grandmother, a working mother, and an older sister. My son was certainly aware that I would have preferred that his father, who worked in a time-consuming, high-profile, competitive law career, had spent more time with his family. Years later, my son saw me marry a very different type of man, one who enjoyed staying home and participating in household and care-taking responsibilities. I now question the impact that my choice of partners had on my son's notions of masculinity. As William Pollack (1998) advises, "the real issue for the son of a single mother . . . is not the presence or absence of a man in the house but the mother's attitude toward men in general" (94). In the end, I hope that I presented a healthy attitude toward men and that Graham has gained some sense of certainty and satisfaction by realizing that a broad repertoire of relational skills and emotional rich-ness are also available to him. I also hope that he regains some of the lost esteem and pride associated with being a male.

Diverse Definitions of Masculinity

Many definitions of masculinity put forth by feminists tend to exaggerate the negative. For example, Gloria Steinem refers to masculinity as "a social construct that makes men shorten their own lives, distance themselves from children, punish women in their headlong effort to be not-women, and try to defeat each other" (Smith, 10). In response, current definitions put forth by men readily acknowledge the problematic nature of fixed con-ceptions of masculinity that are visages of social and historical constructions; they insist on the need for change and multifaceted defini-tions that move away from the notion of one fixed universal norm. Male researchers also credit the role feminism has played in leading the way toward a critical examination of assumptions about men and masculinities (Hearn and Morgan; Michael Kaufman). Frank Blye (1996) observes that the meaning of "masculinity" is in a constant state of flux and conflict, and Robert Connell (1995) points out that masculinity has recently shifted to fit the needs of the corporate world and knowledge-based industries rather than religion or frontier expansion. He explains that masculinity is now organized around technical knowledge, hierarchically organized work-places, advanced capitalism, and rationality. He identifies three simultaneous factors through which masculinity is negotiated, including "a place in gender relations, the practices through which men and women engage that place in gender, and the effects of these practices in bodily experience, personality and culture" (71). He states that: "masculinities are not only shaped by the process of empirical expansion, they are active in that process and help to shape it" (185). Consistent with these beliefs, Michael Kaufman (1994) concludes that: "redefining masculinity means we also must reshape our world to include equality, diversity, and shared strength between men and women" (4).

Current literature also reveals a darker side of masculinity. Although our sons learn that they are the beneficiaries of male power, from an early age they also pay a devastating price for this social status, according to Kaufman. He argues that male experience of power and privilege is contradictory and that men are often confused, wounded, and isolated. He explains that any confusion of terms relates to "the ways we define male power and privilege over thousands of years and has brought pain and insecurity along with power and control. This pain remained buried until the challenge of feminism left men feeling vulnerable, empty, and full of questions" (93). Although men may never fully learn to discard their "unmasculine" characteristics, Kaufman emphasizes that masculinity is stifling and forces men to suppress a range of human feelings and possibilities. Consequently, many of these emotions disappear because they are repressed and replaced with facades of strength, courage, and competence. Although the renewed interest by men in examining the place, the practices, and the effects of masculinity in our culture is certainly a step in the right direction, Judith Arcana (1983) reminds us that men might be constrained but women are still oppressed. While men might be constricted and suppressed and twisted out of shape, she argues that they still hold more power than women. Based on this type of feminist counterargument, Jeff Hearn and David Morgan (1995) urge male researchers to be aware of the controversy triggered by the limited institutionalization of recent studies on men and masculinities and the danger of these studies being used against the interests of women.

According to Kaufman, masculinity is "an idealized version of what it means to be male," "a collective hallucination" (25, 32). It is "a state of mind and a story of how to behave" (29). It is not a universal or a timeless absolute but instead is elusive and out of reach, depending on culture and class norms. It creates a mask, a shell, that protects against the fear of not being manly. He feels that the basic quest of manhood is the acquisition of power and control. It is important for mothers to understand that, realistically, ways of being male change over time and place, and there are a variety of diverse styles of masculinity rather than one single consensual model for boys to internalize. Adopting any one of these styles depending on circumstances and contexts can be complex, confusing, and pressure-laden for young males. Robert Gilbert and Pam Gilbert (1998) refer to "multiple masculinities" that open up many possibilities and expand, rather than restrain, the lives of men (49). Similarly, Connell suggests a multicultural image of gender that would validate a broad range of traits and attitudes for everyone. Judith Butler (1990) takes this notion one step further by considering gender as a performance—a reenactment of a series of behaviors already socially sanctioned—rather than as some underlying internal unity. Viewing masculinity as a performance also shifts the emphasis from biological roots to inequalities and power relations in everyday practices.

The current literature also emphasizes that masculinity often resides in the dichotomy between fulfilling internalized needs and meeting standards set mostly by other men and boys, so that authority and domination are merged into the systemic structuring of personality itself. There is general consensus that there appears to be a gap and often a great deal of tension between the collective public ideal and the actual lived private practice of male students, which may be compounded by the societal schisms pitting subservience against independence. As my son pointed out: "I loved to act, recite poetry and sing at a young age but I kept it hidden . . . I remember being in a school play and being just traumatized and mortified because I had to dance around in tights and I didn't want my friends to see me." He recognized that the male peer group would be quick to punish him for straying from the prescribed path.

By endorsing dualistic thinking, we confuse the difference between natural characteristics of biology and social creations of gender. This makes masculinity look natural. According to Kaufman, we look at the world through gender-colored glasses and are taught to see differences in gender even thought there may be more similarities. We come to expect differences and obscure the similarities. Moreover, the relative invisibility of men as an explicit focus in sociological research (Hearn and Morgan) may, in part, result in the unexamined belief in essentialist arguments that all men share core traits which define masculinity. These traits are defined in contrast to feminine characteristics and include such dichotomous terms as "more rational than emotional, more callous than empathetic, more competitive than co-operative, more aggressive than submissive, more individualistic than collectivist, etc." (Gilbert and Gilbert, 48). Although the invisibility of men may have served their interests at one time by keeping their activities apart from critical scrutiny, as Michael Kimmel (1987) claims, they may now give rise to the "crisis" rhetoric our sons believe in, which suggests that men are a homogenous group who are in danger of losing their shared biological identity. This "paradise lost" essentialist view of masculinity as superior to femininity easily leads to the conclusion that men need to break their early bonds with mothers in order to become men. If not, they may be discouraged from engaging in "masculine" activities and may lose their masculinity as a result. Gilbert and Gilbert point out that this essentialist perspective "can only narrow rather than expand men's opportunities to be human" and "denies their differences among men themselves, and the wide range of attributes which could simply be called human" (29). They also argue that reducing masculinity to a singular universal essence denies men "the capacity to re-create themselves in new, diverse and imaginative ways" (35). Masculine stereotypes are false and limiting. They hinder the ability of boys to function at their base and also the effectiveness of the mothers who are raising them. Part of the job of mothers raising sons must include liberating them to be able to manifest both an outer strength of character and an inner sensitivity and to combine positive masculine traits with a nurturing feminine spirit. Possibilities for taking action and making a difference will be discussed in the next section of the chapter.

Mothers as Agents of Gender Restructuring: Issues and Dilemmas

In this study my colleagues and I seemed to be committed to an ideal image of masculinity which includes an androgynous combination of traits: warm, gentle, sensitive, able to cry, faithful, both task-committed and family-oriented, respectful of women's autonomy, able to express emotion. We know the kind of sons we want to raise and this results in a struggle to reconcile that ideal image with what Pollack refers to as "the old Boy Code" (95). Arcana points out that tension is created when Anglo-American mothers reject traditional definitions of masculinity while their sons assume the conventional gender identity that they feel is expected of them. There are many other cultural forces working against this ideal as well. For example, Kaufman suggests that relational traits are difficult for men to acquire because they tend to remove themselves from the emotional work of child care. Essentialists such as Robert Bly (1990) also oppose this new-age image by insisting that defining masculinity in relation to women will develop a breed of "soft" men who are too domesticated and feminized and left without strong links to men and male mentors. By becoming aware of underlying oppositional forces, we can consciously develop strategies to resist them.

Ironically, mothers themselves also work against new images of masculinity. In her endorsement of Silverstein's and Rashbaum's book, *The Courage to Raise Good Men*, Gloria Steinem reminds us that "the first male-female bond is the one between mother and son, and breaking it has been a recipe for male dominance." It is perplexing to note that, on the one hand, mothers feel that fathers are generally lacking in certain emotional qualities, and on the other, mothers believe boys need to be with these men as models of male behavior when, in fact, they model roles women reject. In view of these tendencies, "if sons are to make new men of themselves," Arcana argues, "they must model what their mothers know as well as their fathers" (276). In addition, Arcana points out:

> We've neglected to tell [sons] the truth of our lives—so that they don't know who women are. We have encouraged in them a sense of entitlement, urged them to go off and conquer the world. We've put others before us, especially their fathers, demonstrating that we have little value and less self-esteem. We've assumed that our sons are inherently very different from us, and we have helped to strengthen and lengthen the list of those differences, while feeding the notion that what is different about them is better. (277)

We might ask, If mothers have bowed to the education of sons in male culture, have they also unwittingly colluded in cultural conditioning of their own sons? Have mothers allowed men to disrespect and blame them in the presence of their sons in such a way that their sons have learned to see their mothers as subservient, passive, powerless, dependent, compliant, silent, or victimized? As Arcana explains:

> We have been trapped with our sons, imprisoned in false ways of being, blocked into "feminine" and "masculine" by a culture whose very language turns mother into mocking profanity, son into demeaning insult. . . . [Men] have replaced their ancient respect for their mothers with a desperate and abusive need of women. When we recognize this has not always been so, we know that it need not always be so. (290–91)

Babette Smith (1995) also points out that feminism has failed the mothers of sons by perpetuating their ignorance of masculinity. There are various reasons for this. To begin with, women tend to view the opposite sex as outsiders, and this is often compounded with layers of cultural and religious rhetoric that presumes innate characteristics rather than social influences. In addition, from their subordinate position, women's views are often excluded or devalued, and they are pressured into maintaining the status quo. They also tend to idealize the differences between masculinity and femininity rather than seeking to understand commonalities. In order to begin the task of gender restructuring, Smith suggests that mothers must try to understand the masculine culture of which their sons are apart and help them talk openly about it. Inappropriate advice that encourages resisting the male status quo in order to adopt feminine traits is one of the greatest sources of sons' ambivalence, she points out, often affecting their development of respect, trust, and intimacy. Knowing when to support male bravado as well as when to suggest alternative relational models will help boys feel that their mothers' input is genuinely helpful. "Only when mothers understand the nature of the culture which opposes their hopes will they be able to play their part as agents of change," she argues (73).

On a more positive note, Pollack offers new hope that empowered mothers will create a new Boy Code and emphasizes that they are the key to helping boys mature into self-respecting men. "Much in the way that mothers led the way to paving new opportunities for their daughters," he explains, "it may be mothers who will show us the way to help boys feel freer as they grow into men" (108). In order to do so, Pollack insists, mothers must trust their own instincts to take the lead from their sons and to stay emotionally connected while at the same time resist the pressure from many sources to separate and to cut off their close interdependent relationships with sons.

Kaufman believes that mothers can also serve a vital role in encouraging men to support women's struggles by putting a face on those struggles in order to personalize and legitimize them. In the end, Kaufman advises, "whatever privileges and forms of power men stand to lose, there is a new world of connection, security, nurturance, eroticism, partnership, and redefined power that [men] have to gain" (274). Although the male bond is deeply grounded in a strong collective memory of fear and distrust, mothers must invite their sons to join women in reshaping their lives and their world and teach them that feminism is as much about their lives as men as it is about the lives of women. Kaufman believes that mothers can help their sons develop the capacity to listen to voices of women openly, to recognize inequities, and to understand their pain and anger. Admitting to limitations of the current definition of masculinity is the first step, as well as helping sons find a compromise between the old and the new, and

knowing when to resist and when to support. Trying to change sons in isolation is not the answer. Mothers must work to change the worldview of
masculinity as well.

"To survive the requirements of masculinity," Smith concludes that
"sons learn to split themselves in two" (69). One side becomes a defensive
facade that hides their real side. She believes that their social conditioning
is largely negative and that this limits the kind of person they can become.
Instead of making friends, boys often make allies, relating to their peers
for what they offer rather than for who they are. As a result of societal
encouragement for males to hide their emotions, Ann Caron (1994) concludes, men often cannot give their feelings a name or talk about their
own relational needs. Instead they may feel a tightness in the throat or
stomach and respond to these feelings with defence mechanisms and non-
verbal behaviors such as denial, violence, or distractions. By assuming that
sons' lack of demonstrative affection is innate, mothers unwittingly delight
in evidence of this "normal" masculine trait and willingly withhold necessary forms of emotional connectedness.

Smith points out that a mother's company can offer safe refuge from
the pressures of masculinity. Perhaps mothers can also serve important
roles to teach their sons to name their emotions, act upon them appropriately, and get on with things. Related to this role, Kaufman urges mothers
to help their sons reclaim the capacities and joys that they buried in their
quest for "an armour-plated manhood." Mothers can help sons develop
the ability to acknowledge and express their emotions constructively and
to rely on traits that will connect them with others. Sons must learn to
understand the difference between their reality and their facade in order
to validate their inner nature and differentiate between their maleness and
masculinity. In addition, mothers can encourage their sons to relate to
male friends in "feminine" ways by expressing their needs and emotions,
by caring and by trusting each other. Part of this endeavor includes con-
vincing sons to drop their mask of indifference or independence and
break through their facade of toughness and insensitivity in order to recognize and accept their own vulnerability.

For the sake of our sons, mothers must challenge hegemonic masculine
standpoints in order to expand the human possibilities for men as contributors of a fair and just world for everyone. Although Arcana agrees that
mothers must seek every opportunity to resist patriarchy and challenge its
assumptions, she identifies the dilemma felt by women as both mothers
and feminists. Not only do mothers see that old ways are not good but they

also fear that their sons will be penalized by changing the very power structures that currently privilege them. Somehow they still hope that their sons will be able to take advantage of "male privilege" with respect to employment opportunities. Pollack warns mothers that failing to give sons a consistent message may increase their confusion and sense of shame over their own masculinity if they find themselves "unable to live up to a mother's ambiguous messages about what a man should be" (95).

It is Adrienne Rich (1986), however, who names the maternal dilemma about alienating sons from "their'" culture most aptly: "What do we fear? That our sons will accuse us of making them into misfits and outsiders? That they will suffer as we have suffered from patriarchal reprisals? Do we fear they will somehow lose their male status and privilege, even as we are seeking to abolish that inequality? Must a woman see her child as 'the enemy' in order to teach him that he need not imitate a 'macho' style of maleness?" (205). As Arcana points out, while feminist mothers and daughters struggle for liberation together, these same women and their sons represent opposing forces in which mothers encourage their sons to give up power. In other words, for sons to develop strong relationships with their mothers, they are often expected to begin with a loss. She urges mothers to help their sons discard layers of masculinity by recognizing that traditional gender roles serve as a barrier against their search for spiritual and emotional connections with their mothers, with each other, and with themselves. Mothers cannot expect themselves to undertake such an enormous task alone. They must be strong advocates for heightened sensitivity related to gender issues in schools as well. The final section will conclude with a few implications for education.

Implications for Schooling

The typical definitions of masculinity espoused by our sons support Judith Arcana's notion that men continue to be socialized much as they have been for centuries in a patriarchal culture. As consumers of cultural myths, popular media, and marketing campaigns, boys are subtly influenced to see themselves as certain kinds of people and to make sense of their lives in specific ways within the discursive framework of their particular culture. However, their responses will always be selective and the expectations they set for themselves will be tentative, contingent, and even resistant. Educators as well as mothers need to be cognizant of these varied responses as well as the cultural influences encouraging them in order to confront effectively the patterns that produce nonnurturant, emotionally unresponsive, highly competitive, and materially oriented students.

Schools, Gilbert and Gilbert point out, "are thoroughly gendered in their own organization and practice" (114). Not only does a masculine style of management emphasize competitive grading and ranking, sports, and status consciousness, which influences the way teachers relate to students, but curriculum and epistemology also emphasize objectivity, rationalism, reductionism, and universalism as preferred ways of understanding the world. According to Judith Kaufman (1994), "Reason is associated with members of dominant groups, and emotion is associated with members of subordinate groups. . . . Students are not told that there is more than one way to construe the world . . . with both thought and feeling" (45). In order for girls and boys to be more aware of gender constructions and to be able to make behavioral choices from a broader base of options, mothers may need to become strong catalysts for change. Individually, mothers are in an ideal position to communicate with and to encourage their children's teachers to be self-reflective and willing to examine their own beliefs and practices about gender as well as their disciplinary strategies and willingness to encourage all students "to present themselves through whatever repertoire of behaviors, styles and forms of expression are most readily available to them and most appropriate to their context" (Gilbert and Gilbert, 235). Collectively, mothers also can form a strong force to influence school boards to develop gender policies and curricula that help students to understand how stereotyping and peer-group pressure develop and operate to advantage and marginalize; how masculinity constrains as well as advantages; how such practices are sustained; how a range of alternatives makes more sense than one rigid view of acceptable gender patterns; and how to interact with others and express emotion effectively.

Conclusion

While the research on masculinity is increasing our understanding of its complexity, there is still a lack of consensus about how we would like to see it change, as well as a reluctance to address these questions in any fundamental way. In this study, our sons have helped us to realize that their gender identities are just as emotionally loaded as their sisters' and that their defensiveness serves to silence them in ways that are still not well defined. We now appreciate that our sons, as well as our daughters, must be encouraged to express their emotions and misgivings about themselves, and that school and well as home must play a part in bringing about these changes in attitudes and practices. Redefining constructs of masculinity and identity consciousness-raising for both girls and boys must become valued priorities for education in order to recognize the pressure, limitations, and confinement imposed by each stereotypical role. Although gender identities are filled with emotional contradiction, it is important to reexamine beliefs about mother-son interdependence, separate valued traits that deserve to be honored from those that are obsolete and dysfunctional, and encourage the development of emotional intelligence.

As long as we willingly reward oppression or privilege, marginalizations, competition, and violence in our homes and schools, we are supporting the authorial voice of gender hegemony. As educators, illuminating issues related to mother-child relationships points to the need to develop courses where issues of gender are central and where critical and reflective discussion about gendered realities in school settings and across diverse racial and class populations can occur. In the end, mothers must also question their own reluctance to speak out against a school system that inhibits, restricts, diminishes, or denies diverse gendered needs and experiences. As my son points out: "I think it is important for men to communicate more than they do. My vision of an ideal masculinity includes more openness, more communication, no chauvinism, and no competition. I think heterosexual men have a lot to learn about caring."

WORKS CITED

Abbey, S., J. Castle, and C. Reynolds. "Comparing How Mothers Influence the Education of Daughters and Sons." In *Redefining Motherhood: Changing Identities and Patterns*, edited by S. Abbey and A. O'Reilly. Toronto, ON: Second Story Press, 1998. 29–58.

Arcana, J. *Every Mother's Son*. New York: Anchor Press, 1983.

Bly, J. *Iron John*. Reading, MA: Addison Wesley, 1990.

Blye, F. "Masculinities and Schooling: The Making of Men." In *Systemic Violence: How Schools Hurt Children*, edited by J. Epp and A. Watkinson. Washington, DC: The Falmer Press, 1996.

Butler, J. *Gender Trouble: Feminism and the Subversion of Identity*. New York: Routledge, 1990.

Caron, A. *Strong Mothers, Strong Sons: Raising the Next Generation of Men*. New York: HarperCollins, 1994.

Castle, J., S. Abbey, and C. Reynolds. "Mothers, Daughters and Education: Struggles between Conformity and Resistance." *Canadian Journal of Education*, 23 (1) (1998): 63–78.

Chodorow, N. *The Reproduction of Mothering*. Berkeley, CA: University of California Press, 1978.

Connell, R. *Masculinities*. Berkeley, CA: University of California Press, 1995.

Forcey, L. *Mothers of Sons: Toward an Understanding of Responsibility*. New York: Praeger, 1987.

Gilbert, R., and Gilbert, P. *Masculinity Goes to School*. New York: Routledge, 1998.

Hearn, J., and D. Morgan. "Contested Discourses on Men and Masculinities." In *Identity and Diversity: Gender and the Experience of Education*, edited by M. Blair and J. Holland. Philadelphia, PA: Open University Press, 1995. 173–185.

Kaufman, J. "The Wedge between Emotion and Cognition: Feminism, Knowledge, and Power." *Holistic Education Review*, 7 (4) (1994): 43–49.

Kaufman, M. *Theorizing Masculinities*. Thousand Oaks, CA: Sage, 1994.

Kimmel, M. *Changing Men: New Directions in Research on Men and Masculinity*. Newbury Park, CA: Sage, 1987.

Pollack, W. *Real Boys: Rescuing our Sons from the Myths of Boyhood*. New York: Random House, 1998.

Rich, A. *Of Woman Born: Motherhood as Experience and Institution*. New York: W.W. Norton and Company, 1986.

Silverstein, O., and B. Rashbaum. *The Courage to Raise Good Men*. New York: Penguin, 1994.

Smith, B. *Mothers and Sons*. St. Leonards, NSW: Allen & Unwin Ltd., 1995.

Tavris, C. *The Mismeasure of Woman*. New York: Simon and Schuster, 1992.

8

LESBIANS RAISING SONS

BRINGING UP
A NEW BREED OF MEN

Jess Wells

I would like to paint a social portrait of being a lesbian mother of a son. There are fourteen million people in lesbian households in America. The number surprised me: fourteen million. We struggle to love and nurture under conditions that I can honestly say no other group in America (except for the developmentally challenged) is forced to face. Until recently it was almost routine that out lesbians had their children taken away from them. Until recently we bore children in heterosexual marriages because we could not meld our desire for children and our need to be lesbians. What ensued was too frequently nasty, expensive, and debilitating court battles, struggles to maintain our dignity and our beliefs in the face of hostile ex-spouses who told our children we were sick and perverted—try maintaining discipline and respect with that on the other end of joint custody. At best, those situations have turned into parallel parenting, two sets of values, two sets of frequently opposing lifestyles. At worst, I am talking about kidnapping of children by ex-spouses. Lesbian mothers face the constant threat of reopened custody hearings. And it is not just "one weekend here, one there," which I personally think is damaging enough. It is custody hearings that deny all access to the mother. Or onerous arrangements where the children are allowed to visit as long as there are no other lesbians in the house. In the case of Sharon Bottoms, custody was granted to a woman who has proven herself even to the social worker to be unfit: the grandmother who allowed her daughter to be molested more than four hundred times by her boyfriend—she gained custody rather than keep a little boy in the house of his lesbian mother. In the case of another lesbian mother in the South, custody of her twelve-year-old daughter was lost to her ex-husband who had been in prison for killing his first wife—despite the testimony of another stepdaughter who said the father had repeatedly molested her. A molester and murderer gained custody so the daughter would not grow up in a lesbian household. To add to the tragedy, the lesbian mother died of a heart attack just weeks after the verdict.

These are the poster children of our community, if you will, the horrific cases that, as in any civil rights movement, are the frontispiece to the myriad injustices too subtle to gain national attention. For example, in situations where lesbian couples decide together to have children, their family units are still not being recognized, which means that in the case of death of the biological mother, children are being ripped from the women who are their parents and given into the custody of relatives who have not raised them.

Every single one of us has multiple closets to worry about: coming out at our children's school, to doctors, what to tell the kids themselves, how to equip the kids to tell their friends, how to handle Father's Day, how to keep internalized homophobia from creeping into our children's consciousness, and yet how to protect them in a hostile world. There is also the problem of what I call second-generation homophobia, where grandparents keep a skeptical eye on our parental abilities and prefer to visit the straight sister and her kids, regardless of how good or talented our child might be.

And we have a real void in the mothering role-model department. Coming from a culture that is just stepping its toe out of the closet, our mentors are lesbians without children or mothers who are in the closet. We are just starting a dialogue about parenting, and it is very difficult to have finesse about parenting when you are forging new ground.

Lesbian families are more apt to be multiracial, in part because our community has fairly good politics on race; partly because many of us cannot afford private adoption and so go through county agencies, which have a predominance of children of color. Or because we take part in adoptions from foreign countries. This provides a wonderful diversity.

We are also poorer as a community than many. Think of sixty cents on the dollar for women and then multiply by two. Reports are that 85 percent of lesbians in America earn less than $36,000 annually.

And we do not seem to be doing any better in the divorce department than heterosexuals. If the heterosexual divorce rate is 60 percent, ours if probably hovering around 75 percent, although the only hard evidence I have of that is the scars on my heart.

Now, I do not want to paint a bleak picture here, but consider the cultural portrait:

- A hostile legal system
- Borderline economic resources
- A high incidence of divorce
- The challenge of multiculturalism
- Relentless homophobia

But into that scenario has come a new generation of lesbian mothers: out lesbians, or at least lesbians who are not in heterosexual relationships, women who make the conscious choice to have children. In fact, one could say that nearly all children of lesbians are wanted, since we have no "oops" method of family planning. There are other positive mediating factors as well. Generalizations are double-edged swords, of course, but it can generally be said that new lesbian mothers are not in the group with extreme economic pressure. Since lesbians are famous for turning their ex-lovers into beloved family members, the high incidence of what one calls divorce is spawning a resurgence of the extended family and, I hope, challenging the idea that romantic love is the best foundation for family-making. And for all my description of the outside pressures, the actual parenting that goes on in a lesbian household is, honestly, pretty incredible. I mean, think about it, we are both women. As Rosanne Barr mimics on her TV shows: "Lesbians sound like this: it's my turn to be nurturing and supportive. You were nurturing and supportive yesterday."

Layered on top of this complex scenario is the issue of gender—especially for lesbians because we give birth predominantly to boys. At the beginning of the baby boom, in our community the odds were eighty-five to fifteen that you would have a boy. Now it is a bit more like sixty-five to thirty-five. You see, female sperm, or sperm carrying the double-X chromosomes, swim slower and live longer (note the longevity of the female right off the bat); while the male sperm swim faster but die off faster. So the nearer to your point of ovulation that you inseminate, the greater your chances of conceiving a boy. Lesbians tend to inseminate on the day of ovulation because, let's face it, that is a difficult thing to predict, even with those sticks. And because of the AIDS crisis, sperm are almost without exception frozen and quarantined, which means they live in the female body only one day, as opposed to fresh sperm, which can live for up to three. So, voila, the birth of boys.

For me personally, the announcement that I was to give birth to a boy was very upsetting. I thought that I had nothing to teach a boy; that I did not have a man in the house so my son would be without his clan; that he and I would really have nothing in common, as I do not do sports. I worried about my family of origin assuming I would turn him into a sissy. And wasn't I spawning a member of the oppressing class?

And so, being a writer, I set about to compile a book, now called *Lesbians Raising Sons*, recently a finalist for a Lambda Literary Award for nonfiction. It took me on a very personal and gratifying journey in which I started by believing I could be a good mother in spite of being a lesbian, and it took me to a place of believing that I could be a good mother to a son specifically because I was a lesbian.

Lesbians are particularly susceptible to the rules of the patriarchy which have convinced us all that women cannot make men—men make men, women make sissies. To be healthy, a boy must separate from his mother. So what happens in a household where there are no men? Grace Woodacre, in her piece in my book entitled "Back to the Village," says that everywhere she went as a lesbian mother, the first question she was asked was whether her child was a girl or a boy, and then whether there were any men in his life. She wanted a button for her lapel that said "I Have a Role Model: Buzz Off." The nuclear family teaches us that we are defective in some way if we do not have a man in the house (and certainly all single, divorced, or widowed women are tarred with that brush as well). There is anecdotal evidence from the National Center for Lesbian Rights, which spends 85 percent of its time on family law, that lesbians lose custody of their children more frequently when the children are boys, specifically because of the role-model issue. But as Woodacre points out, the role models in one's life are the football coach, funny Uncle Louis, the kid down the street who lets you into his fort. Your mother did not have sex with any one of them, so why is the role-model issue used against lesbians? When you realize that male role models do not have to live in your house or sleep in your bed, the world opens up, and we are back to the concept of a village being responsible for the well-being and instruction of children.

Every nascent political group starts by proclaiming "we're just like you," and the queer parenting community is no different. "We're parents like you," and that is essentially true, but it is a statement to combat the assumption that we are inherently inferior parents. A recent sociological study from England shows that, in fact, in many ways children from lesbian homes are happier, more content, and more able than those in other families to express their emotions (though less comfortable with combative or hostile situations). It was the first evidence I had ever seen that said we might be damn good parents.

In fact, we are different parents. Our children are different in subtle ways. The title of my chapter is lofty: bringing up a new breed of men. So how, exactly, are our children different? Many essays in this book touch on the ideas of mothering and feminism, and as I compiled my book, I was driven to ask the question again and again: How is lesbian parenting any different from feminist parenting? First let me describe how our sons are different from sons within patriarchal families. I think lesbians provide their sons with several tremendous gifts. The first would be a broadened spectrum of emotional expression. We understand that the prohibition against men expressing any emotion other than anger has ramifications for world and domestic peace. We all know that the world tells girls what they cannot do and boys what they cannot feel. Lesbian parents strive (like feminist parents everywhere) to encourage our sons to embrace all kinds of emotions.

We encourage them to develop nonviolent methods of negotiation. We teach our sons self-sufficiency in terms of domestic chores like cooking and sewing and picking up after themselves. We encourage them to be able to nurture, and if you have ever tried to buy a doll for your son in today's marketplace, that is no small feat. And it is not just to avoid the domestic servitude of another generation of women: self-sufficiency is, in itself, a tremendous gift.

Our sons are also the sons of outsiders, which breaks their entitlement to privilege even when they are white and middle-class. While the homophobia that makes this true is dreadful, it does allow our sons, regardless of their class, to be more empathetic to social underdogs.

Perhaps most important, though, is that we encourage—in fact actively work—to be sure that our sons understand that gender is not the underpinning of the world order. This is perhaps our most noticeable difference from all other social groups. Our sons have a broader color palette to dress in, fabrics to experience, beads and decoration, toenail polish. If you have been in a children's department for kids older than eight months, you may agree that it is very sad to witness how limited our boy's choices are. They can look like little jocks or little bankers and that is it. I generally do not tell people this, but my son has a dress of his own. His godfather, despite all his liberalism, wanted to know why, and my first reaction was to say: "Because I am not ever going to be the one who says 'boys don't do this.'" But I also bought the dress because I wanted my son to be able to experience textures and feelings with all of his body, not just his hands and his penis, as is usually reserved for men. We teach our sons that self-definition is not a box their bodies put them in but an entirely individual, infinitely mutable expression of their imaginations, their psyches, and their souls.

And our sons see women in a very different light: the person with the most power in the family is a woman. The person with slightly less power in the family is a woman, and those power positions are based on personality, not gender. The person with the tools is a woman. The person with the kitchen implements is a woman. Their understanding of what women can and cannot do is broader. There are several marvellous stories in my book about adult sons, one on the eve of his marriage, and how tender they are. These differences are so difficult to put your finger on, but there is a gentle respect that emanates from children of lesbians.

And of course it goes almost without saying that there are now fourteen million people in America who are much less apt to be homophobic. *Lesbians Raising Sons* contains a wide range of stories: tales of adoption, of birth, of transgendered kids and brave moms, of the pain of losing our children to the patriarchy, of the joy and humor of loving our children and guiding them as best as we can. It is a new era for us when Melissa Ethridge makes lesbian parenting a mainstream event, when our community is changing forever as a result of the entrance of our sons into the world. It is a wonderful era when we are questioning and deeply valuing the root of manliness and the bond between mother and son. I am blessed to be a mother, and I am honored to have been associated in some way with these stories.

WORK CITED

Wells, Jess., ed. *Lesbians Raising Sons: An Anthology.* Los Angeles, CA: Alyson Books, 1997.

9

CAN BOYS GROW INTO MOTHERS?

MATERNAL THINKING
AND FATHERS' REFLECTIONS

Andrea Doucet

Introduction

In a recent issue of the journal *Feminism and Psychology* devoted to the topic of "Mothering Sons," Robyn Rowland and Alison M. Thomas write that one of the challenges for mothers raising sons is that of finding "ways to create a generation of men who can live in a world where women—feminist or not—will no longer put up with the old version of masculinity" (1996a, 93). This "old version of masculinity" would include R. W. Connell's well-known concept of "hegemonic masculinity," which is the dominant form of masculinity at any given historical juncture, one which involves the domination of women and is constructed in relation to varied marginalized and subordinated masculinities (1987, 1995). In eschewing this old version of masculinity, it is worth asking whether, in this process, feminist mothers would want their sons to grow up to be mothers? The question of boys growing into mothering, or more specifically men and mothering, is the subject of my chapter. I attempt to formulate an answer to this question by constructing a hypothetical conversation between Sara Ruddick's views, as expressed mainly in her most recent version of *Maternal Thinking: Towards a Politics of Peace,* and selected narratives drawn from a qualitative research project with twenty-three fathers and twenty-three mothers interviewed in Britain in the early 1990s (Doucet 1995a).

Two aspects of Ruddick's work are of relevance for the arguments developed in this chapter. The first is her view that men can mother and that men can be mothers. She writes: "To be a 'mother' is to take upon oneself the responsibility of child care, making its work a regular and substantial part of one's working life" (1995, 17). Some twenty pages later she reiterates this definition but then adds an interesting twist: "a mother is a person who takes on responsibility for children's lives and for whom providing child care is a significant part of his or her working life; I mean *his or her*" (40). Ruddick has recently acknowledged that there is a slight discomfiture between men and mothering, both for men, "who insist that they are not mothers" (xiii) and for women, for whom "a genderless mother trivializes both the distinctive costs of mothering to women as well as the effects, for worse or for better, of femininity on maternal practice and thought" (xiii). Nevertheless in rethinking her position six years after the first publication of her acclaimed book, Ruddick maintains that men "really can and often do in engage in mothering *work*" (xiii, emphasis added).

I emphasize the word "work" in the above paragraph because it is Ruddick's view of mothering as work, as maternal *practice*, which is the second aspect of her theory that I draw on in this chapter.[1] Her view is that mothering as practice and as work can be gender-free. She writes: "I remain unconvinced by arguments that there not only are but should be distinct paternal and maternal 'roles' and 'tasks'" (1997, 206). I agree with Ruddick in her conviction that it is possible, indeed desirable, to conceptualize mothering as work[2] and also that work, both domestic and nondomestic, can and should be gender-free. Nevertheless, it is important to note that the work, tasks, and "roles" of motherhood and fatherhood occur in distinct sets of gendered social relations, discourses, and identities. While men certainly mother in terms of their practical daily work, they cannot *be* mothers and they are not regarded as mothers by others.[3]

I make this argument while respectfully acknowledging Ruddick's much larger moral, epistemological, philosophical, and political aims, which inform her eloquent and persuasive writing about mothers and mothering. One of her aims is to articulate that the moral and epistemological perspectives developed through maternal practices could form the basis for a peace politics. For Ruddick, maternal thinking—with its emphasis on care, connection, contextual and holistic thinking—informs a fundamentally different way of viewing the moral landscape from that endorsed by liberal, liberal feminist, and neo-Kantian conceptions of individual rights and justice. Maternal thinking can thus function as a social critique. As Ruddick puts it: "maternal thinking is a 'revolutionary discourse' that has been marginal and peripheral but that, as a central discourse, could transform dominant, so-called normal ways of thinking" (1995, 268). In linking maternal thinking and a feminist maternal peace politics, Ruddick radically "envision(s) a world organised by the values of caring labour" (135).

Her second aim is to challenge and disrupt the binary distinction between mothers and fathers and the taken-for-granted ideological and discursive lapsing between mother/carer/homemaker and father/provider/breadwinner. In her words: "The question I want to address is whether there is anything in the 'nature' of children, women, or men that requires a sexual division of parental labor even in postpatriarchal societies" (1997, 207). These are lofty aims that are well worth exploring. Nevertheless, in response to Ruddick's argument that men can mother and that motherhood is predominantly work, I posit that, while theoretically speaking we may wish to dispense with mothering and fathering as distinct domestic practices and roles, they nevertheless exist at the level of community and interhousehold practices, as identities, and within social relations and discourses.

This chapter centers on the three characteristics of mothering as developed in *Maternal Thinking* and my response to these characteristics based upon my interpretation of the narratives of twenty-three fathers. While the bulk of the chapter focuses on the relationship between men, masculinities, and mothering, in the conclusion I return to the issue of mothers and sons, boys and mothering. I begin with a brief outline of the theoretical and methodological approaches that inform my discussion.

Theoretical and Methodological Approaches

Theoretically my research is located in, and informed by, several debates, including household studies, with an emphasis on highlighting intrahousehold divisions of resources,[4] research documenting the persistence of gender divisions of labor,[5] feminist work on gender equality and gender differences,[6] and, finally, research on caring work which focuses on the relationships that exist between households, kin, and community.[7] While informed by a political-economy theoretical approach, the research is also methodologically and theoretically rooted in symbolic interactionism, which accords significance to the meanings people attach to their actions and how they in turn interpret their actions in light of the observations and judgments of other people.[8]

The qualitative research project that informs this chapter was conducted with a "critical case study" of twenty-three heterosexual British couples with dependent children who identified themselves as "consciously attempting to *share* the work and responsibility for housework and child care."[9] These were not couples who claimed to be involved in "50/50 parenting" (Kimball) or "co-parenting" (Ehrensaft), since I was interested in household *variation* in the *meaning* and *structure* of sharing with regard to household work. The sample was predominately white[10] and mainly middle class.[11] While these factors represent limitations of the sample, the gendered findings on domestic responsibility that emerged from the study do have relevance across class and ethnicity lines due to the well-documented gender divisions of domestic labor that transcend distinctions based on class, nationality, and ethnicity.

At least three interviews were conducted in each household: one joint interview with the man and woman together and at least one individual interview with each man and woman. The joint interview revolved around a creative participatory technique called the "Household Portrait"[12] and the individual interviews explored personal and employment histories through the utilization of the "Life Line"[13] and "Mapping Social Networks"[14] techniques. Data were analyzed using an adapted version of the voice-centered relational method which consists of at least four readings of interview transcripts combined with narrative summaries and case studies[15]; in addition, a computer software program, TextBase Alpha, was employed during the final stage of analysis to assist with thematic analysis. The voice-centered relational method accords particular emphasis to issues of social relationships in narratives as well as to processes of reflexivity in research; it also recognizes the epistemological dimensions of both data collection and data analysis.[16] Furthermore, in taking a position of "strong reflexivity" (Harding) I recognize that my own biography is implicated in this research.[17] Worth noting here is the influence of my own parenting of three daughters with a man who has at times been their primary caregiver; I have thus been a participant observer of men's alleged "mothering" in my own family and in other families for over ten years.[18]

Maternal Practice and Men's Mothering

Ruddick maintains that mothers "are committed to meeting three demands that define maternal work." These are "preservation, growth and social acceptability," and, she continues, "to be a mother is to be committed to meeting these demands by works of preservative love, nurturance and training" (1995, 17). In this section, I examine these three demands through the lens of the men's narratives collected in my research and I consider how fathers meet these demands.

I. Preservation

Ruddick defines preservation as "protective care." In her words: "It simply means to see vulnerability and to respond to it with care, rather than abuse, indifference, or flight" (19). Another way of characterizing preservation or "protective care" is to draw on the work of feminist writers who write about the practice of care. Authors such as Joan Tronto, Bernice Fisher, Selma Sevenhuijsen, Hilary Graham, and Clare Ungerson carefully define, describe, and explore care as involving skills which include, among other things, "knowledge about others' needs," which the carer acquires through "an attentiveness to the needs of others" (Tronto 1989, 176–78).[19] That is, it involves both the ability to recognize where care is needed and the actual physical work of caring.

Ruddick's assertion that men can mother is confirmed by men's successful taking on of the maternal task of "preservation" and "protective care." In order to illustrate men's ability to carry out this task of preservation, I draw on the words of two of the men I interviewed for my research study.[20] Both Richard and Adam speak about how they are very much "in tune with" the "rhythms" of their young sons. They meet this criterion of preservation by providing "protective love" and responding to their children in their most vulnerable moments. These men are actually surprised at how much in tune they are with their sons. Indeed each describes, to his own amazement, how he often runs to his child's bedside *just as* the child is waking up. Richard says: "I'm a light sleeper, you see. It's almost as if I wake up just before he does. I'm actually *awake*. I'm actually awake and halfway in the bedroom before he's woken up, really. And I get there and he's sitting up. It's *odd*. It's really odd!" Adam, a self-described househusband and father of one-year-old Dylan, comments on a similar pattern:

"It's very pleasing to me that I feel so much in tune with him sometimes. Because he's asleep upstairs and *I haven't heard* him, but I go up and he's just *waking* up, just when I go in. And I feel that I'm in tune with his *rhythm*."

My research on highly committed fathers joins a large body of research produced over the last two decades which argues that fathers can be just as nurturing, affectionate, responsive, and active with their children as mothers are.[21] It is well documented that fathers who are actively involved with their children can develop skills which enable them to partake in this task of "preservation." In the words of Adam: "There is no mystical skill involved. It's the *willingness* and the *openness*."

II. Growth

The second characteristic of mothering, according to Ruddick, is "growth." She writes: "The demand to preserve a child's life is quickly supplemented by the second demand, to nurture its emotional and intellectual growth. Children grow in complex ways, undergoing radical qualitative as well as quantitative changes from childhood to adulthood" (1995, 19). She goes on to recognize that others are interested in these growth processes: "In the urban middle class cultures I know best, mothers who believe that children's development is sufficiently complex to require nurturance shoulder a considerable burden. Many people other than mothers are *interested* in children's growth—fathers, lovers, teachers, doctors, therapists, coaches. But typically a mother assumes the primary task of maintaining conditions of growth; it is a mother who considers herself and is considered by others to be primarily responsible for arrested or defective growth" (1995, 20, emphasis added).

Although Ruddick recognizes that others are *interested* in children's growth, I would go further to emphasize that others *partake* in ensuring children's growth and that mothering involves coordinating, balancing, negotiating, and orchestrating these *others* who are involved in children's lives. Mothering involves relationships between households as well as among the social institutions of families/households, schools, the state, and the workplace. Within and between households and other social institutions, mothers share the responsibility for their children with others who take on caring practices—caregivers, other parents, neighbors, kin, child care experts, nurses and doctors, teachers, librarians, music teachers, soccer coaches, and so on. Each stage of child rearing introduces its own sets of issues, according to the particular needs and demands of particular children. For all of these issues and decision-making processes—from a child's preschool to university years—*other people* are often consulted and relationships are built up on the basis of a shared interest in a particular child or children.

Mothering thus involves not only a domestically based set of tasks and responsibilities but also a responsibility that is community-based, interhousehold, and interinstitutional. According to one of my research respondents, Saxon, the taking-on of this wider responsibility means that one: "is very good at saying that we should do this and getting it organised and making it happen and finding people to do this, that or the other." While I have termed this work "interhousehold responsibility" (Doucet in press 2001) as well as "community-based responsibility" (Doucet 2000), this work of *mothers and others* appears in varied guises in a wide body of feminist research. For example, Italian sociologist Laura Balbo calls this work "women's servicing work," while Micaela di Leonardo has coined the well-used term "kin work," and Ursula Sharma's research on Indian households refers to women's "household service work." In her work on black motherhood, Patricia Hill Collins points to how "the institution of black motherhood consists of a series of constantly negotiated relationships that African-American women experience with one another, with black children and with the larger African-American community" (118). At the first International Conference on Mothers and Daughters in 1997, Sara Ruddick also highlighted this work when, in her keynote address, she referred to mothers' gatekeeping roles in linking and orchestrating the multiple relationships around child-rearing activities.

While the work described here—the responsibility for children's "growth" as well as the work traditionally performed by women in order to build bridges and social support between families and households—is enacted and experienced in varied ways across class, ethnicity, sexuality, and cultural lines, many feminist researchers have pointed to how it is women and not men who take on this work. With specific reference to mothering, one of the reasons why men do not take on the work of orchestrating and assisting children's growth is because mothering, especially for preschool children, occurs within social networks where many men are, or feel they are, largely excluded (Bell and Ribbens).

One of the most significant findings to emerge from my research was that, in spite of efforts to share most aspects of household life and labor, all twenty-three women interviewed still took on all, or the overwhelming

bulk of, the interhousehold and community-based responsibility for children. That is, mothers initiated, planned, organized, and managed the
bulk of short, medium, and long-range planning between households as
well as between households and other social institutions. Even in three
households where men were doing most of the daytime caring, women
orchestrated the community-based contexts within which men parented.
One example is the case of Jessie, a social worker, and Sean, full-time caregiver of their two young boys. While he does more of the daily and weekly
care of the children, *she* does the planning and organizing of their lives
and activities, nursery and school. With regard to remembering to buy diapers (nappies) and other baby supplies, she says (to Sean): "I mean you're
the one who's here all the time and I have to say, can you go to the shop
and get some nappies." She also takes Luke to the dentist "because Sean
won't go to the dentist" and she organizes birthday parties because "I think
it's important for the child" and "I thought Luke should have one." As for
the children's sporting activities, she says, "I've rung Tumble Tots and Sean
is going to take them."

Why, then, is it difficult for men take on this maternal task of encouraging and assisting in children's "growth"? Three examples from my research
provide a partial answer to this question. Sean, who has been a full-time
carer for his two young sons for a year and a half, reflects: "I still think that
the whole thing about being a male trying to make networks is difficult."
He sometimes feels like he is standing outside an immense "kind of culture" that is run by women. He says: "There is this huge gulf between me as
a male carer and women . . . who have a sort of ready-made context that
they're attuned to, that I haven't got." The words that Sean uses give the
distinct impression that he is standing outside the rather exclusionary
world of women and children and staring in, wondering when and what to
join into. He says: "I thought for a long time I needed to sort of penetrate
that kind of culture, um, for my own sanity and for Oliver." He uses a variety of other words which confirm this image of standing as an outsider:
"slot into," "starting to step back," "click into," "drawn into," "joining it," or
"not joining it."

Sean's sentiments about standing outside of women's culture are
echoed in varied ways for all the men in the study. They include comments
on joining mothers' coffee circles, volunteering at playgroups and in the
classroom, organizing child care arrangements, organizing birthday parties, and arranging babysitters. Lilly and Joe, for example, discuss
organizing birthday parties for their daughter:

Joe: I think it's more you organising it than me, in the sense of sending out invitations and contacting people. I help on the day more, I think. I don't know the other mums. I think they kind of relate more to you.

Lilly: Well, they're very stereotypical women around here, so I think they might find it odd that Joe was doing it.

Eve organizes babysitting because, in her words: "It's probably this business that it's, you know, maybe I just feel that if I'm asking the neighbour and it's—you tend to ask the *wife*, don't you in [this small village]? I mean they are funny about husbands babysitting, aren't they sometimes?"

The difficulties for men to be center stage in the networks of relationships that surround child rearing are most strongly underlined by research on single fathers. Margaret O'Brien's research in Britain stresses this point: "While being a male single parent does indeed transform relationships with kin and friends," it still remains the case that "the lone father is a unique sort of family man whose position invokes both *support and disdain, admiration and suspicion*" (241).

III. Social Acceptability

Ruddick writes about the third demand of mothering: "The third demand on which maternal practice is based is made not by children's needs but by the social groups of which a mother is a member. Social groups require that mothers shape their children's growth in acceptable ways. . . . (T)he criteria of acceptability consists of the group values that a mother has internalised as well as the values of group members whom she feels she must please" (21). This criterion for mothering brings into play a whole new dimension. Who are these "group members" and how will a mother please them? First and foremost, as I mentioned earlier, the majority of these group members are women. Second, these group members often hold very fixed ideas about appropriate masculinity and femininity, mothering and fathering. More specifically I want to suggest that many men find it difficult to mother because of how they think they will be viewed by other men within their kin networks, their social networks, and their local communities.

One of my findings from my interviews with the twenty-three British men who were attempting to share child care with their female partners was that men, particularly those men who were primary daytime carers of young children, did gauge themselves by, compare themselves to, and feel observed by, other men. Sean, for example, explains how he feels like he is "looked at oddly by other men," thus indicating that, at least in some way, he is concerned about how other men regard him in his role as a primary carer. In this regard he mentions: "I was passing a postman cycling by . . . and I was pushing the push chair [stroller] and holding Luke's hand and I thought he's given me a sort of . . . 'what a big sissy. A big sissy!' "

Although Joe seems to be less "worried" about what other "blokes" think, he nevertheless does "sometimes wonder what they think" when he does the laundry, a task more traditionally associated with women and mothers. In his words: "I'm not particularly worried about being—you know—sometimes I think when I meet another bloke, you know, I wonder what they think. There's a couple of blokes [in the village]. They're always doing building work. And farmers—they're very sort of macho. And there's me hanging out the washing and getting the washing in, and I sometimes wonder what they think. It doesn't really bother me, but it passes through my mind."

The burgeoning literature on masculinity can assist us in making sense of why it is that men do not mother and why boys will not grow up to become mothers. R. W. Connell, for example, argues that hegemonic masculinity tends to be characterized by power, authority, aggression, and technical competence (1987, 183–87). Connell also points out that while few men actually enact hegemonic masculinity, and while it is more useful to talk about masculinities, hegemonic masculinity remains the dominant concept by which many men and boys continue to measure themselves. One of the findings from my study was that men felt that they were observed by other men and against a masculine ideal. Men who attempted to *mother* could not seem to escape the gaze of other men, or of women. Even for men who stated that they felt comfortable with their role as a primary or shared caregiver for young children, there was a sense that they were looking out from the corner of their eye to view how they were being judged by other men and how their newly enacted masculinity measured up to other dominant conceptions. Adam, full-time househusband, poignantly expresses this when he attempts to convince me that he doesn't "care what other men think: "I was watching some workmen in the street, digging up the roads, and I was giving Dylan his food and taking him to the shops, and I felt just as *manly*, whatever that is, if not more so. Because I could dig up the road any day. But if you told one of those men—'Right, you're looking after this baby day after day, here you are'—

he'd be dead scared. . . . I enjoy the fact that being at home with the baby is just so unquestionably necessary as *work*. No one can say that it's not a useful job."

Conclusions

Men can and do increasingly partake in maternal practices. They can care for and nurture children in ways that are indistinguishable from mothering. On any given day in virtually every community around the globe there are fathers cuddling babies, taking toddlers to the park, and calming a child through a schoolyard trauma, and many men carry out these tasks in ways that are largely free from gendered characteristics. But mothering and fathering occur in gendered social worlds where masculinities and femininities, mothering and fathering, remain largely distinct as experiences and as institutions. The argument made here is informed by the work of sociologist Barrie Thorne as articulated in her excellent book, entitled *Gender Play: Girls and Boys in School.* She writes: "I begin not with individuals . . . but with *group life*—with social relations, the organization and meanings of social situations, the collective practices through which children and adults create and recreate gender in their daily interactions. . . . Gender is not only a category of individual identity and the focus of symbolic constructions, but also a dimension of social relations and social organization" (4, 158).

While men can do the tasks and work of mothering, it is the larger "social relations and social organization" of mothering and fathering that preclude men from being socially accepted as, or wanting to be called, "mothers."

What are the implications of these arguments on men and mothering for the central theme of this book, that of mothers and sons? I return to the edited journal mentioned in the introduction of this chapter, that of Rowland and Thomas on "Mothering Sons" in *Feminism and Psychology*; their collection aptly captures the tensions and contradictions involved in allowing boys to wrestle in the worlds of the masculine while also developing new forms of masculinity. In their words: "It seems that as feminists we cannot expect to fulfil the superficially egalitarian ideal of bringing up sons and daughters in the same way, since the social context in which we are rearing them itself creates an asymmetry of power and privilege" (1996b, 148). If we accept the views of these mothers grappling with feminist ideals and the socially located practice of raising sons, as well as those of diverse writers such as William Pollack in his book *Real Boys*, Paul Willis in his research on working-class "lads" in the 1970s, and R. W. Connell, Martin Mac an Ghaill, and Barrie Thorne in their work on boys in schools, then there is a masculine code, or what Pollack calls a "Boy Code," that boys have to live with and navigate. In addition, the last decade has witnessed the emergence of a very large body of literature detailing the construction of masculinities, although some authors note that the *perceptual weight* attached to gender differences may at time supercede practices.[22] Overall this literature investigates the continual social construction of masculinities and gender differences in schools (Connell 1989; Thorne; Mac an Ghaill; Haywood; and Mac an Ghaill), in families (Connell 1987; Heward; Seidler), and at work (Cockburn; Hearn; Morgan). In light of such weighty empirical and theoretical evidence, it seems to me that there will be awkward and conflict-ridden rites of passage for men who have grown up from these masculine playing fields—of boyhood and manhood—and then attempt to join into "complex maternal worlds" (Bell and Ribbens), particularly those of early child rearing.

Of course it is possible to argue that in the conceptual space between social relations, social organization, and self/identity, there is possibility for movement and maneuver (Connell 1987). Barrie Thorne's work is again useful, particularly her concept of "gender crossing": "I have carefully chosen the word 'crossing' to allude to the process through which a girl or a boy may seek access to groups and activities of the other gender. . . . *The process of crossing is complex and often contradictory, affected by matters of definition, activity, and the extent to which an individual has developed a regular place in social networks of the other gender*" (121, emphasis added).

In a similar way the social worlds of mothering and fathering involve some degree of "crossing" borders, and while some aspects of maternal work are easily taken up by men, other activities are not. I have highlighted in this chapter, and elsewhere,[23] that interhousehold responsibility and community-based responsibility are social dimensions of mothering where men may encounter particular difficulties. Part of the explanation for this, building again from Thorne, is that most men have not "developed a regular place in social networks of the other gender" (121). Indeed there is ample evidence to suggest that many men's difficulties in sharing in domestic labor and responsibility are rooted partly in the predominantly female networks that surround child rearing (Radin, Russell, O'Brien, Bell and Ribbens).

To end on an optimistic note, however, there are possibilities for change.

In conducting my new research project on fathers as primary caregivers in Canada at the end of the twentieth century, I have found one issue particularly striking. In stark contrast to the situation I encountered in my research on shared parenting in Britain nearly a decade ago, fathers are no longer fathering in isolation from other parents. Over the past five years there has been a profound proliferation of fathering networks and support groups for young fathers, single fathers, and primary caregiving fathers.[24] These networks represent new possibilities for fathering and the social institution of fatherhood. In a sense these attempts by men to carve out a new space at the center of parenting can be seen as parallel, metaphorically, to the movement of boys crossing into girls' activities in the schoolyard. Again, in the words of Barrie Thorne: "When girls and boys cross into groups and activities of the other gender, especially at the earnest end of the continuum, they challenge the oppositional structure of traditional gender arrangements. Teasing and labelling can be seen as strategies for containing the subversive potential. But incidents of crossing may chip away at traditional ideologies and *hold out new possibilities*" (133, emphasis added).

When men cross into maternal work, they can be viewed as radically challenging the traditional gender order. This chapter has highlighted the "teasing and labelling" particularly by men of other men who recognize the radical and "subversive potential" in men attempting to change fathering and ultimately masculinity. I am more inclined to see men's efforts as primary caregivers as examples of constructing and reconstructing *fathering* and *fatherhood*, rather than as examples of men's mothering.[25] These men are helping to "chip away at traditional ideologies" of mothering and fathering as they "hold out new possibilities" for women's and men's lives. Like the tempered hopes expressed by Rowland and Thomas for feminist mothers raising sons, it is important to view fathering through a lens that can balance contemporary versions of gender relations with radical visions of what a new order could look like. There is some resonance between the call for new ways of mothering sons, *doing boyhood* differently, and *doing fathering and fatherhood* in ways that benefit women, men, girls, and boys.

NOTES

I am indebted to the forty-six mothers and fathers who participated in my doctoral research study, to R. M. Blackburn who supervised the project, to Carol Gilligan who acted as a second supervisor, particularly during data analysis and writing up, and to M. P. M. Richards for his insights on fathering. Funding for the project that informs this chapter was generously provided by the Commonwealth Association of Canada and the Social Science and Humanities Research Council of Canada (SSHRC).

1. I am grateful to Jane Ribbens for drawing my attention to this issue.

2. There is some debate within the feminist literature over whether or not caring, domestic labor, and mothering should be viewed and conceptualized as *work*. For a review of some of this literature see DeVault; Daniels; Mirchandani.

3. See Doucet 2000, in press 2001. An important qualification underlines this discussion. As Ruddick acknowledges, with greater emphasis in the second edition of her book, motherhood varies between women of varied cultures, ethnicities, races, classes, and sexualities. Futhermore, within a particular class, ethnicity, or sexuality, mothering differs dramatically (see McMahon; Ribbens; Epstein; Segura). The experience of mothering also varies for mothers based on their personal biographies and histories, number and ages of children, and the social contexts and relationships within which they mother.

4. See for example, Brannen and Wilson; Morris; Bogler and Pahl; Whitehead.

5. Examples of this literature include Brannen and Moss; Pahl; Morris.

6. See Bacchi; Bock and James; Rhode 1989, 1990; Meehan and Sevenhuijsen; see also Doucet 1995b.

7. See for example Collins; Di Leonardo; Finch and Mason; Hessing; Doucet 2000.

8. Works drawn on include Blumer; Finch; Finch and Mason; Barker. See Doucet in press 2001.

9. The couples were found through a combination of snowball sampling and criterion sampling (Miles and Huberman) through varied community, employment, and parenting organizations in the villages, towns, and small cities of southeastern England. The number of children in each household ranged from one to four and the ages of children were between one year and twenty-five years of age. The ages of the individuals in the sample ranged from twenty-six to fifty-one years of age, with the average age being thirty-eight years of age. I sought couples whose first child was at least one year old as I was aware of difficulties experienced in the early "transition to parenthood" period (Entwistle and Doering).

10. Three persons of color participated.

11. Although the individuals in the sample represented a broad range of occupations, they were largely "middle class," with 87 percent (n=20) of the sample having educational qualifications, technical or academic, beyond secondary school. Average individual earnings were £16,800 ($27,400 US dollars per annum). The social-class composition of the sample should not be surprising given that patterns for sharing housework and child care were relatively rare

in Britain in the late 1980s and early 1990s (e.g., Brannen and Moss; Morris; Gregson and Lowe 1993, 1994).

12. See Doucet 1996; Doucet in press 2001; Dunne.

13. See Doucet 1995a.

14. See Ribbens.

15. See Brown and Gilligan; Mauthner and Doucet 1998a, 1998b; Way.

16. See Doucet 1998; Mauthner and Doucet 1998a; Doucet and Mauthner 1999a, 1999b.

17. See Doucet 1998.

18. I am continuing my work as a participant observer and ethnographic researcher of new models of fathering and fatherhood in my current research, funded by the Social Sciences and Humanities Research Council of Canada, on fathers as primary caregivers. My researcher assistants in this project are Erin Mills and Phil Robinson.

19. See Fisher and Tronto; Tronto 1989, 1993, 1995; Graham; Ungerson, Sevenhuijsen.

20. These and all other names of research participants are pseudonyms.

21. See, for example, Ehrensaft; Lamb; Russell 1983, 1987; Radin; Wheelock.

22. See Thorne; Walker.

23. See Doucet 2000, in press 2001.

24. From a feminist perspective, it is important to distinguish between fathers groups; not all groups have similar objectives, and there are differences in politics, philosophy, and strategy between profeminist and antifeminist fathers groups (see Bertoia and Drakich; Messner).

25. See also Richards; Brandth and Kvande.

WORKS CITED

Bacchi, C. L. *Same Difference: Feminism and Sexual Difference.* London: Allen and Unwin, 1990.

Balbo, L. "Crazy Quilts: Rethinking the Welfare State Debate From a Woman's Point of View." *Women and the state.* Ed. A. S. Sassoon. London: Unwin Hyman, 1987.

Barker, R. W. *Lone Fathers and Masculinities.* Aldershot: Aversbury, 1994.

Bell, L. and Ribbens, J. "Isolated Housewives and Complex Maternal Worlds: The Significance of Social Contacts Between Women with Young Children in Industrial Societies." *The Sociological Review,* Volume 42 (2) (1994): 227-262.

Bertoia, C. E. and Drakich, J. "The Fathers' Rights Movement: Contradictions in Rhetoric and Practice." *Men's Lives.* Eds. Kimmel, M. and Messner, M. Boston: Allyn and Bacon, 1998.

Bock, G. and James, S. eds. *Beyond Equality and Difference: Citizenship, Feminist Politics and Female Subjectivity.* London and New York: Routledge, 1992.

Brandth, B. and Kvande, E. "Masculinity and Child Care: The Reconstruction of Fathering." *The Sociological Review*, 1998.

Brannen, J. and Wilson, G. eds. *Give and Take in Families: Studies in Resource Distribution*. London: Allen and Unwin, 1987.

Brannen, J. and Moss, P. *Managing Mothers: Dual Earner Households after Maternity Leave*. London: Unwin Hyman., 1991.

Brown, L. M. and Gilligan, C. *Meeting at the Crossroads: Women's Psychology and Girls' Development*. Cambridge, MA: Harvard University Press, 1992.

Blumer, H. *Symbolic Interactionism: Perspective and Method*. Berkeley: University of California Press, 1969.

Cockburn, C. *Brothers: Male Dominance and Technological Change*. London: Pluto, 1983.

Collins, P. H. *Black Feminist Thought: Knowledge, Consciousness, and the Politics of Empowerment*. London: Routledge, 1990.

Connell, R. W. *Gender and Power*. Cambridge: Polity Press, 1987.

——. "Cool Guys, Swots and Wimps: The Interplay of Masculinity and Education." *Oxford Review of Education*, 15 (3) (1989): 291-303.

——. *Masculinities*. Sydney: Allen and Unwin, 1995.

Daniels, A. K. "Invisible Work." *Social Problems*, 34: 403-415.

DeVault, M. L. *Feeding the Family: The Social Organisation of Caring as Gendered Work*. Chicago: The University of Chicago Press, 1991.

Di Leonardo, M. "The Female World of Cards and Holidays: Women, Families and the World of Kinship." *Signs,* 12 (3) (1987): 440-453.

Doucet, A. *Gender equality, gender differences and care: towards understanding gendered labour in British dual earner households*. Unpublished doctoral dissertation, University of Cambridge, Cambridge, (1995a).

——. "Gender Equality and Gender Differences in Household Work and Parenting." *Women's Studies International Forum*, 18 (3), 1995b.

——. "Encouraging Voices: Towards More Creative Methods for Collecting Data on Gender and Household Labor." *Gender Relations in the Public and the Private*. Eds. L. Morris and S. Lyon. London: Macmillan, 1996.

——. "Interpreting Mother-Work: Linking Methodology, Ontology, Theory and Personal Biography." *Canadian Woman Studies*, 18, 2&3 (1998): 52-58.

——. "'You see the Need Perhaps More Clearly than I Have': Exploring Gendered Processes of Domestic Responsibility." *Journal of Family issues*. (in press 2001).

——. "'*There's a huge gulf between me as a male carer and women*': Gender, Domestic Responsibility, and the Community as an Institutional Arena" *Community Work and Family*. (2000).

Doucet, A. and Mauthner, N. "Strong Reflexivity, Strong Methods: Linking Data Analysis and Feminist Epistemologies." Paper presented at The First International Conference on Advances in Qualitative Methods, International Institute for Qualitative Methodology, University of Alberta, 1999a.

———. "Subjects and Subjectivities in Feminist Theory and Research." Paper presented at the British Sociological Association Conference. Glasgow, Scotland, 1999b.

Dunne, G. A. "Why Can't a Man Be More Like a Woman? In Search of Balanced Domestic and Employment Lives." LSE Gender Institute Discussion Paper Series, No. 3, 1997.

Epstein, R. "Lesbian Parenting: Grounding Our Theory." *Canadian Women's Studies*, 16(2), 1996.

Entwistle, D.R. and Doering, S.G. *The First Birth*. Baltimore: Johns Hopkins University Press, 1980.

Finch, J. *Family Obligations and Social Change*. Cambridge: Polity, 1989.

Finch, J. and Mason, J. *Negotiating Family Responsibilities*, London: Routledge, 1993.

Fisher, B. and Tronto, J. "Towards a Feminist Theory of Caring." *Circles of Care: Work and Identity in Women's Lives*. Eds. E. K. Abel and M. K. Nelson. State University of New York Press, New York, 1990.

Graham, H. "Caring: A Labour of Love." *A Labour of Love: Women, Work and Caring*. Eds. J. Finch and D. Groves. London: Routledge and Kegan Paul, 1983.

Gregson, N. and Lowe, M. "Renegotiating the Domestic Division of Labour: A Study of Dual Career Households in North East and Southeast England." *The Sociological Review*, 41 (3) (1993): 475-505.

———. *Servicing the Middle Classes: Class, Gender and Wages and Domestic Labour in Contemporary Britain*. London and New York: Routledge, 1994.

Haywood, C. and Mac an Ghaill. "Schooling Masculinities." *Understanding Masculinities*. Ed. Mac an Ghaill, M. Buckingham: Open University Press, 1996.

Harding, S. *Whose Science? Whose Knowledge?* Milton Keynes: Open University Press, 1992.

Hearn, J. *Men in the Public Eye: The Construction and Deconstruction of Public Men and Public Patriarchies*. London: Routledge, 1992.

Hessing, M. "Mothers' Management of Their Combined Workloads: Clerical Work and Household Needs." *Canadian Review of Sociology and Anthropology*, 30 (1) (1993): 37-63.

Heward, C. "Masculinities and Families." *Understanding Masculinities*. Ed. Mac an Ghaill, M. Buckingham: Open University Press, 1996.

Hochschild, A. R. *The second shift*. New York: Avon Books, 1989.

Kimball, G. *50/50 Parenting: Sharing Family Rewards and Responsibilities*. Lexington, MA: Lexington Books, 1988.

Lamb, M. E. "The Development of Father-Infant Relationships." *The Role of the Father in Child Development*. Ed. M. E. Lamb. New York: John Wiley and Sons, 1981.

Mac an Ghaill, M. *The Making of Men: Masculinities, Sexualities and Schooling*. Buckingham: Open University Press, 1994.

Mauthner, N.S. and Doucet A. "Reflections on a Voice Centred Relational Method of Data Analysis: Analysing Maternal and Domestic Voices." *Feminist Dilemmas in*

Qualitative Research: Private Lives and Public Texts. Eds. J. Ribbens and R. Edwards. London: Sage, 1998a.

——. "Reflexive Accounts and Accounts of Reflexivity." Paper presented at the American Sociological Association Conference. San Francisco, August, 1998b.

McMahon, M. *Engendering Motherhood: Identity and Self-Transformation in Women's Lives.* New York: The Guilford Press, 1995.

Mead, G. H. *Mind, Self and Society.* Chicago: University of Chicago Press, 1934.

Meehan, E. and Sevenhuijsen, S. eds. *Equality, Politics and Gender.* London: Sage, 1991.

Miles M. B. and Huberman, A. M. *Qualitative Data analysis: An Expanded Sourcebook.* London: Sage, 1994.

Mirchandani, K. "Protecting the Boundary: Teleworker Insights on the Expansive Concept of 'Work'." *Gender and Society.*

Morgan, D. H. J. *Discovering Men.* London: Routledge, 1992.

Morris, L. *The Workings of the Household: A US-UK Comparison.* Cambridge: Polity Press, 1990.

O'Brien, M. "Patterns of Kinship and Friendship Among Lone Fathers." *Reassessing Fatherhood: New Observations on Fathers and the Modern Family.* Eds. C. Lewis and M. O'Brien. Sage, London, 1987.

Pahl, R. E. *Division of Labour.* Oxford: Basil Blackwell, 1984.

Pollack, W. *Real Boys: Rescuing Our Sons from the Myths of Boyhood.* New York: Owl Books.

Radin, N. "Primary Care Giving Fathers of Long Duration." *Fatherhood Today: Men's Changing Role in the Family.* Eds., P. Bronstein and C. P. Cowen. New York: John Wiley

Rhode, D. L. *Justice and Gender: Sex Discrimination and the Law.* London: Harvard University Press, 1989.

Rhode, D. L. ed. *Theoretical Perspectives on Sexual Difference.* London: Yale University Press, 1990.

Richards, M. P. M. "How Should We Approach the Study of Fathers?" *The Father Figure.* Eds. L. McKee and M. O'Brien. London: Tavistock, 1982.

Ribbens, J. *Mothers and Their Children: A Feminist Sociology of Childrearing.* London: Sage, 1994.

Rowland, R. and Thomas, A. "Mothering Sons: A Crucial Feminist Challenge." *Feminism and Psychology,* 6(1) (1996a): 93-99

——. "Editors' Commentary: Pulling Together the Threads – The Way Forward." *Feminism and Psychology,* 6(1) (1996b): 142-154.

Ruddick, S. *Maternal Thinking: Towards a Politics of Peace.* Boston: Beacon, 1995.

——. "The Idea of Fatherhood." *Feminism and Families.* Eds. H. L. Nelson. New York: Routledge, 1997.

——. "Legacies of the 'Ethic of Care'." Keynote Address presented at the International Conference on Mothers and Daughters: Moving into the Next Millennium. York University, September 1997.

Russell, G. *The Changing Role of Fathers.* London: University of Queensland Press, 1983.

———. "Problems in Role Reversed Families." *Reassessing Fatherhood.* Eds. C. Lewis and M. O'Brien. London: Sage, 1987.

Seidler, V. J. *Man Enough: Embodying Masculinities.* London: Sage, 1997.

Segura, D.A. "Working at Motherhood: Chicana and Mexican Immigrant Mothers and Employment." *Mothering: Ideology, Experience and Agency.* Eds. E. N. Glenn, G. Chang and L. R. Forcey. New York: Routledge, 1994.

Sevenhuijsen, S. "Paradoxes of Gender: Ethical and Epistemological Perspectives in Care in Feminist Political Theory." *Acta Politica,* 2 (1992): 131-149.

———. *Citizenship and the Ethics of Care: Feminist Considerations on Justice, Morality and Politics.* London: Routledge, 1998.

Sharma, U. *Women's Work, Class and the Urban Household: A Study of Shimla, North India.* London: Tavistock Publications, 1986.

Thorne, B. *Gender Play: Girls and Boys in School.* Buckingham: Open University Press, 1993.

Tronto, J. "Care as a Basis for Radical Political Judgements' (Symposium on Care and Justice)." *Hypatia,* 10, 1995.

———. *Moral Boundaries: A Political Argument for an Ethic of Care.* New York and London: Routledge, 1993.

———. "Women and Caring: What Can Feminists Learn About Morality From Caring?" *Gender/Body/Knowledge: Feminist Reconstructions of Being and Knowing.* Ed. A. M. Jaggar and S. R. Bordo. New Brunswick and London: Rutgers University Press, 1989.

Ungerson, C. ed. *Gender and Caring: Work and Welfare in Britain and Scandinavia.* London: Harvester Wheatsheaf, 1990.

Vogler, C. and Pahl, J. (1994) "Money, Power and Inequality Within Marriage." *The Sociological Review,* 42 (1994): 263-288.

Walker, K. "'I'm Not Friends the Way She's Friends': Ideological and Behavioral Constructions of Masculinity in Men's Friendships." *Masculinities,* 2 (2) (1994): 38-55.

Way. N. "Using Feminist Research Methods to Understand the Friendships of Adolescent Boys." *Journal of Social Issues,* 53 (4) (1997): 703-723.

Wheelock, J. *Husbands at Home: The Domestic Economy in a Post-Industrial Society.* London: Routledge, 1990.

Willis, P. *Learning to Labour: How Working Class Kids Get Working Class Jobs.* Aldershot: Saxon House, 1977.

Whitehead, A. "'I'm Hungry Mum': The Politics of Domestic Budgeting." *Of Marriage and the Market: Women's Subordination in International Perspective.* Eds. K. Young, C. Wolkowitz and R. McCullagh. London: S E Books, 1981.

III

MOTHERS AND SONS:

CONNECTIONS

AND

DISCONNECTIONS

10

RAISING RELATIONAL BOYS

Cate Dooley

and Nikki Fedele

Introduction

Achilles, mightiest of the Greeks, hero of the *Iliad*, was nearly immortal. According to myth, his mother, Thetis, dipped him into the river Styx. The sacred waters of this river that led to Hades, the world of the dead, rendered whomever they touched impervious to harm. But Thetis, good mother that she was, worried about the dangers of the river, and so she held onto Achilles by his heel. As the story goes, because of that one holding spot, Achilles remained mortal and vulnerable to harm. Thetis would be blamed forever after for her son's so-called fatal flaw, his Achilles heel.

However, the holding place of vulnerability was not, as the myth would have us believe, a fatal liability to Achilles. It was instead the thing that kept him *human and real*. In fact, we consider it *Thetis' finest gift* to her son. Every mother of a son hopes to prepare him for life's "battles" while also preserving his emotional/relational side. Because mothers value connection, they want to "hold on," to keep open that place of vulnerability. But, faced with cultural pressures that suggest restraint and withdrawal, rather than comfort and nurture, many mothers feel conflicted about their desire to stay connected to their sons. Traditional wisdom cautions that "holding on" will be damaging and create psychological problems for sons. Faced with this dilemma, mothers often give in to cultural pressures and disconnect from their young sons because they think it is the right thing to do.

This chapter describes the application of relational theory to a model of parenting-in-connection. We describe the natural ebb and flow of parent-child relationships through a cycle of connection, disconnection, and new connection, while detailing issues and conflicts specific to boys' development at four distinct stages. The mother-son relationship is, we argue, the most important context within which boys can learn how to move from disconnection to even better connection. Highlighting the dominant cultural model for boys' development—which we believe affects all mother-son relationships despite variations based on race, class, and other factors—we use specific examples drawn from our workshops and clinical work to demonstrate the potential of the alternative parenting-in-connection approach.

Our work with mothers of sons is based on relational/cultural theory, a view of development for women and men, which grew out of Jean Baker Miller's 1976 book, *Toward a New Psychology of Women*. In her book, Miller introduces a new view of women and their development. After many years of listening to and studying women, she concludes that relationship and affiliation are essential to their healthy development. She notes the attitudes about women and their roles embedded in the fabric of Western culture. She further states that this cultural view diminishes women's self-worth.

We highlight the mother-son relationship because we feel that this same devalued view of women affects mother-son interaction. The culture tells mothers to disconnect from their sons. Closeness with mom has often been misunderstood and pathologized. The mother-son connection is ridiculed ("go run to mama"; "crybaby"), cautioned against ("you better let him go"; "push him out to the world"), prohibited ("don't coddle him"; "no more hugs and kisses"), and maligned ("she's turned him into a mama's boy"; "he's tied to her apron strings"). We feel that this disparaging attitude and the early call for separation from their mother isolates boys "from relationship"—first with their mother and consequently with others.

In this chapter we are referring to the dominant cultural model for boys in the United States. We recognize that there are many variations of this model dependent upon race, ethnicity, religion, sexual orientation, family structure, socioeconomic class, as well as other factors. We focus on the mainstream model supported by media images and messages, because of the strong negative influence it has on boys' development. We feel that all mothers, regardless of diverse circumstances, are impacted in their relationship with sons by this culturally prescribed paradigm of disconnection.

Infant studies show that physical and psychological development is dependent upon a good mother-infant connection. Without such a connection we see a developmental "failure to thrive" in babies. Ed Tronick of the Brazelton Touchpoint Project (1998), notes that infant development occurs only within relationship. This is also Miller's belief about our life-long experience. In *Toward a New Psychology of Women* she states that "all growth and learning takes place within the *context* of relationship." While the relational presence of mother is essential for babies to thrive early on, it continues to be essential for boys' emotional and relational growth.

Jean Baker Miller and Irene Stiver speak of the need for relationship and connection as a *human need* in *The Healing Connection* (1997). They see this as a universal need, best met through the development of mutually empathic and mutually empowering relationships. But young boys, if deprived of sufficient opportunities to learn how to make real connections, try to meet these needs in superficial and manipulative ways. They are taught in "boy culture" to fulfil their desires and get ahead, even at the expense of others. In acting this way, boys and men are simply following established rules of the culture for males. A false bravado model not only deprives boys early on of parental empathy, but also infuses them with a sense of esteem and power devoid of internal resonance. As a result, mutu-ally satisfying connection with others becomes impossible. In our clinical practice, men tell stories of "working the room" in executive meetings, assured that they will, ultimately, sway others and (right or wrong) get what they want. These men complain, however, that they feel no internal gratifi-cation in these interactions. All this attention and power fail to gratify and, in fact, leave them feeling empty and even more alone. We see in their expe-rience how learned behaviors make it impossible for many men to connect authentically, leaving them with a debilitating sense of internal isolation.

This problematic developmental course may account for what appears to be a predominance of men who are self-absorbed and cut off from relation-ships. Perhaps if we understand more deeply the impact of culture on boys' and men's development, we can bring a compassionate and understanding perspective to our male children, partners, friends, and clients as they sort through these difficult, deeply embedded relational patterns. Perhaps if we create more empathic possibilities, these new experiences can prevent in boys, and heal in men, the wounds of this early disconnection.

A Mother's Prospective View

We have found in our work with more than three thousand mothers of sons that in spite of the cultural message, many mothers follow their inclination and stay in relationship with their sons. Tentatively questioning established norms, these mothers keep a place of emotionality open in their sons through continued connection. Yet at the same time, they worry that they will affect their son's development in negative ways. Mothers who resist the cultural call to disconnection are in need of validation and support. These courageous mothers are potentially the real experts in boys' development. Keeping a strong connection is the way to teach sons how to navigate the many and complex nuances of relationship. We believe it is within the mother-son context that relational learning occurs and that the groundwork is established for future relationships. Olga Silverstein and Beth Rashbaum, in their book *The Courage to Raise Good Men* (1994), demonstrated that the root of sons' difficulties as adults is linked to distance and disconnection in the mother-son relationship. Our workshops with mothers and adult sons, as well as our clinical work with men and couples, tell us that boys with a secure maternal connection develop stronger interpersonal skills and enjoy healthier relationships as adults.

Although relational theory originally developed as a way to understand women's psychology, the capacity to create and sustain growth-fostering relationships is equally crucial for boys and men. Traditional views of boys' and men's development are embedded in men's experiences and men's fears. Men who have grown up in this culture often feel that the old model is best for their sons. Even men who want to change things may worry about these new directions for boys. Fathers can be pulled unwittingly into a retrospective analysis of present-day issues because of old fears based on their own experience. Because becoming a man is closely linked with traditional ideas about being one's own man (individuation), being dominant, and not being a "girl," evolving their thinking into the realm of emotional and relational development about boys can create worry for some men. They can have much fear about turning boys into girls. Women, on the other hand, not having grown up in boy culture, may have a clearer lens in viewing the currently evolving possibilities for boys and men. Most mothers today *do* keep connection with sons, and sons *are* more aware of the benefits and possibilities open to them in relationship. These newly evolved attitudes and behaviors are actually already much more a part of everyday life for boys than is reflected in the media. Just as Jean Baker Miller (1976) insisted, we must listen to women in order to hear about their experiences; we must listen to mothers of sons to formulate a *prospective view* of the possibility of relationship for boys. It is our opinion that listening to mothers of sons will inform us about current realities and possibilities for boys.

At a recent lecture about middle-school children, a mother asked the speaker how to talk to her twelve-year-old son. The psychologist answered: "There's bad news and there's good news. The bad news is that you won't be able to get him to talk. The good news is that it won't last long, just a few years." Most of the mothers gathered at the back of the lecture hall disagreed with this notion. Even though it was difficult, they had managed to stay connected with their sons. As the "keepers of the connections" in our culture, women know about relationship. Mothers hold the hope for change in their son's relational growth.

New developmental attitudes and directions for boys can change development in many positive ways. Changing cultural expectations to include relational development for boys can change outcomes for both boys *and girls*. Valuing relational skills and emotional awareness in boys will increase respect for girls in our culture. In creating a new vision for boys, we modify the course of development for both genders. Both girls and boys are born with the capacity to have responsible and collaborative relationships. It is the work of parents to provide a safe context for boys, as well as girls, through the development of family, community, and social values that support relationship.

Boy Culture: What Is It? How Does It Affect Boys?

Invisible forces in our culture take hold in the form of implicitly communicated expectations of boy behavior we call "boy culture" (fig. 1). Images of male dominance are projected by the media and modeled daily by older peers in countless ways. These expectations are not consciously taught or supported in most of our homes, schools, or communities. Rather, they are the insidious behavioral messages boys in our culture receive regarding boy behavior. These occur in the form of put-downs and intimidating threats in everyday interactions on the playground and in the halls of our schools. When we do nothing to intervene, thinking "boys will be boys," we implicitly give our approval to and help normalize behaviors that are disconnecting and domineering and that can later lead to what has become a pervasive societal problem of violence.

When we name and question the impact of boy culture, we are not critical of boys and men but rather of the gender straightjacket imposed on

```
┌─────────────────────────────────────────┐
│              BOY CULTURE                 │
│       IMPLICIT EXPECTATIONS FOR BOYS     │
│                                          │
│   • CLOSENESS WITH MOM IS FOR            │
│     SISSIES/BABIES                       │
│   • FEELINGS ARE FOR WIMPS /             │
│     GIRLS (EXCEPT ANGER)                 │
│   • BE FIRST, BE IN  LIMELIGHT           │
│   • DON'T BACK DOWN                       │
│   • POWER-OVER MODEL OF                  │
│     COMPETITION                          │
│     –WIN–LOSE                            │
│   • PRIDE IN NON-COMPLIANCE/             │
│     DISRESPECT                           │
│   • DESENSITIZATION TO                   │
│     VIOLENCE                             │
│   • CODE OF SILENCE                      │
└─────────────────────────────────────────┘
```

Figure 1

boys by the culture. Boy culture focuses on who is in the limelight. It says "be first"; "win." It is built on a competitive, power-over model, in which there are winners and there are losers. Boy culture encourages young men and boys to take pride in expressions of noncompliance and disrespect, to act out, and to pretend not to care about their failings.

Teachers rate boys as problems in the classroom 90 percent over girls.[1] Research shows that as the number of *boy* siblings in a family increase, so does the incidence of acting out, school truancy, and social delinquency.[2] The fact that this is not the case with an increase in the number of girl siblings may speak to the powerful influence of boy culture within families. Behaviors such as bullying, teasing, stealing, noncompliance, swearing, teacher disrespect, and the like have become serious problems, even at the elementary-school level. Children, largely boys aged five to ten years, are imitating offensive, interpersonal behaviors portrayed by the media and observed in older peers.

Boy culture also says that if you retreat, if you shrink from competing, you risk being labelled "wimp," "chicken," "sissy," "scaredy cat," "baby," or even "girl."

> A group of first-grade boys respond to a simple question posed by their teacher by rising up out of their seats and onto their toes, hands waving high, whispering "me first, pick me." They are so eager to be first, all their energy goes into this quest. When called on, they have forgotten the question and have nothing to say.

A third-grade boy creeps along a high wall, egged on by his peers. He is terrified but continues on for fear of being called a "wimp" or "scaredy cat."

A fifth-grade boy proudly boasts to his friends that he chased another boy down, took his prized art project, and made him cry.

A seventh-grader jokingly brags about not studying and takes pride in his prediction of a poor grade on a math test scheduled for that day.

One eight-year-old explained, "If my friends ever found out that I come home from school and go through my backpack with my mom and show her everything I did in school that day, they'd really make fun of me and call me a baby."[3]

Our culture's established standard of individuation and independence moves both girls and boys away from relationship. But for boys this push is especially difficult because it happens at a very young age and within the most intimate of relationships, their relationship with their mother. This move toward independence and away from mom occurs at a time in development for boys when they are still thinking in concrete ways (Piaget and Inhelder). Boys' concrete view of the loss of mom at age five is that they have lost a relationship and are on their own emotionally. Carol Gilligan (1996) and others link the increase in Attention Deficit Disorder (ADD) to this early separation from mother. Diagnostic ADD rates are higher than ever and occur predominantly in boys. Boys' loss creates sadness and anxiety, which may manifest as hyperactivity and inattention. Maybe the first diagnostic criteria to look for in these hyperactive boys should be symptoms of what we call CDD, or Connection Deficit Disorder!

The development of learning and behavioral problems in young boys has become alarmingly common. Boys learn that it is "cool" to be distant, inauthentic, and disconnected. They lose their *relational* voice, the voice that reflects authentic feelings and affiliative needs. What replaces real interaction is banter and bravado. Caught up in the expectations of boy culture, imitating behaviors seen in older peers and siblings, boys often become alienated from their own inner world. When boys disconnect from their mother, they lose access to the relational way of being with others that she represents. They lose the ability to be responsive and receptive (Miller 1986).

Steve Bergman (1991) coins the phrase "relational dread" as a phenomenon in boys and men that grows out of early emotional disconnection from mothers. Boys lose their place within the relational context. Eventually, in the face of emotion and relationship, they freeze. They become immobilized. Isolated in the disconnection from mother, they do not know what to do or how to be in relationship with others. Bergman and Surrey aptly describe this experience of dread and the resulting avoidance of connection that has become an intrinsic part of traditional developmental models for boys. Girls and women do not always see this dread because men cover it up with avoidance, denial, and bravado (Stiver 1998). Its impact, however, is great. This is what makes mutually empathic interactions with and between boys and men so difficult.

When mothers move away from young sons and push them toward independence, boys are denied empathic resonance with their emotions (Stiver 1986). Without the safe relational context provided by his mother, a boy feels alone. He is too young to protest. He knows no alternative. He thinks that disconnection is what is supposed to happen. He still longs for connection, and quite rightly. But now he feels shame and confusion about his inner longings. To deal with his pain and confusion, he shuts down emotionally. He has not yet learned to differentiate and name feelings. Confused, he suffers alone, in silence. The cost of this break in relationship from mother is significant for boys' evolving relationships with others. They deal with this inner confusion and pain by shutting down access to their emotional world and by avoiding relationship. When this happens, relational and emotional development slows down.

From this point on, there are fewer empathic possibilities for boys than for girls. This early loss of parental empathy creates a void in the area of responsiveness to and identification of emerging feelings. Judy Jordan (1989) notes that a lack of empathic response will result in a feeling of personal shame. Boys learn early that emotional needs, longings, feelings, or dependencies are shameful, and subsequently they have a more difficult time developing a healthy sense of self-empathy. Their emotional needs and longings often become covered up by angry expressions and aggressive behaviors. Eventually, through continued exposure to boy culture put-downs and power-over behavior, boys seem to lose much of their capacity for empathy toward others.

There is a further twist. We all yearn for a sense of connection. Yet the inevitable disconnections that happen in relationships can be painful and threatening. Everyone experiences this flow of connection and disconnection in life, but often because of these repeated interpersonal disconnections, we pull back from relationship while we at the same time yearn for connection. Miller and Stiver (1997) write about this as the "paradox of relationship." Boys feel this paradox at a young age; they learn early not to represent themselves fully in relational encounters. Shamed by expressions of emotion, they begin to keep important parts of themselves hidden from others. They do this by developing a repertoire of behaviors for staying out of relationship. Miller and Stiver call these "strategies of disconnection." These strategies keep boys from experiencing the shaming and put-downs of boy culture, but at the cost of keeping them out of real connection with others. Some examples include silence, smart remarks that discourage conversation, elaborate demonstrations of disinterest, sarcastic humor, and the exchange of glances between boys that convey disrespect for the speaker. Yet beneath the bravado and banter, boys are hungry for connection and emotional expression. This is the paradox of relationship for them. Carol Gilligan (1996) describes adolescent girls as sacrificing relationship for the sake of relationships. Boys sacrifice authentic emotional connection with others for the sake of inclusion within boy culture. This accommodation helps them avoid being teased and shamed, gains them the approval of peers, and creates surface connection, but at the expense of real relationship.

Bullying, competitive banter, and bravado; these are the hurtful, power-over interactions that pervade boy culture. At the same time, boys learn about the code of silence built into these interactions. You cannot "tell" on another, even if you know his behavior is damaging and wrong. Boys learn early in life that to survive with peers they have to put up with harsh, mean, even hurtful verbal and physical behavior. Our culture expects boys to be tough, and shames them when they are not. They cannot let on when they have been hurt or humiliated. If they break the code of silence, they risk humiliation, peer isolation, and further harassment. Boys plead with their mothers not to intervene. They would rather submit to the bullying than be shamed by turning to someone for help.

> Walking home from school, a group of nine-year-old boys stop at the ballpark to hit a few fly balls. Waiting his turn, Max stands behind the backstop, his fingers curled around the metal links. Whack! One of the boys smashes the bat against the backstop and hits Max's finger. Max screams and crumples to the ground in tears, clutching his hand. The group of boys stares at him, then one says,
>
> "Oh c'mon. I don't see anything wrong. It's not bleeding. You're faking."
>
> "What a wimp!" yells another.
>
> "Poor baby hurt his finger?" chimes in Andrew, Max's best friend.

Bewildered, Max gets up, trying without much success to hold back the tears. His finger throbs.

"Maybe you should go over and play with those girls" taunts Andrew, shaking his head in disgust, as he and the others walk off together, leaving Max behind.

Max arrives home upset. His mother sees his tears and the finger swollen and black and blue now. She offers ice, but it's not the finger that hurts most. She tries to comfort Max, and asks what happened. "Nothing Mom, it's okay," insists Max as he retreats to his room in shame.

Mothering can be seen as a political act. It is a form of the political resistance that Carol Gilligan so eloquently describes for women—their need to speak their truth. In this case it is the truth about boys' "code of silence."

The experience of being shamed by the culture, by peers, or by parents because of vulnerable feelings can have a significant impact. Because of the recent episodes of violence in young adolescent boys (Jonesboro, Arkansas; Littleton, Colorado; Paducah, Kentucky; Pearl, Mississippi), we, as a nation, are examining the roots of this behavior. James Gilligan (1996) in his recent work on violence in men, cites the experience of intense shame as an important dynamic in the histories of violent men. The act of shaming around vulnerable feelings is a major contributor to acts of violence in these men. Shame becomes a precursor to the expression of the only feelings acceptable for boys and men, anger and aggression.

A liability built into boy culture is the expectation of repeated exposure to violent play, movies, and video games. Boys eventually become desensitized to violence. To avoid being teased or shamed, they stifle their natural emotional reactions of fear and vulnerability. Gradually, with daily exposure and practice, boys lose access to their real feelings and normal reactions to violence. Before long they can sit and watch violence, abuse, and horror on the screen, in video games, even in peer interactions without flinching!

The Ebb and Flow of Relationship

Connection occurs when we experience a sense of mutual engagement, empathy, authenticity, and empowerment within the context of relationship. We have the mutual feeling of knowing and being with the other, immersed in their experience along with our own. Such connections provide a continual source of growth for the individual and the relationship.

This form of connection has startlingly positive effects, which Miller (1986) calls *the five good things*: zest (vitality); a more accurate picture of oneself and others; increased sense of self-worth; increased desire and ability to act; and desire for more connection. When we are in a disconnection, the opposite happens. We feel cut off from the person, experience the pain of not being understood and not understanding the other, and feel confusion about what is happening. The five outcomes of disconnection are; decreased energy; confusion and lack of clarity; decreased self-worth; inability to act; and turning away from relationship.

Relationships are not static. Figure 2 illustrates the natural movement of all relationships. The cycle of connection-disconnection-new connection demonstrates how working through disconnections can enhance relationships. Understanding this is the key to mutually satisfying relationships. The inevitable disconnects become the signal that work needs to be done in the relationship. When we do not acknowledge this and when we do not try to find a solution together, distance replaces closeness. The relationship suffers. The connection becomes derailed in the confusion and ambiguity of the disregarded issue. On the other hand, when addressed, disconnections can become opportunities to work together toward mutual understanding and solution (Bergman and Surrey 1992).

Reconnection can be quick and easy, or take time, effort, and creativity. This is the strengthening work of relationship. When we find the way back, it is not just a reconnection, but a strengthened, enhanced, growthful leap for the relationship. Even when sons seem to be disinterested and uninvolved in this process, a mother's efforts are extremely important. This is how we continue to build relationship with sons.

The creative work looks different depending upon the unique characteristics of each family: family structure, values, importance of the issue at hand, temperament, culture, ethnicity, religion, and race. This work provides opportunities to widen the lens for sons. For example, in dealing with a power issue, white mothers can talk with their sons about how many different power differentials create disconnection. By raising their son's awareness of the dominant culture's racist views and how they affect relationships, we can help boys begin to see and deal with issues of privilege and power early in life. Discussions about social esteem[4] can help boys understand how their view of themselves and others is affected by (often negative) stereotypes and attitudes deeply embedded in our culture.

The mother-son relationship is a safe place for boys to learn how to work through disconnection. In this relationship they can use disconnections as

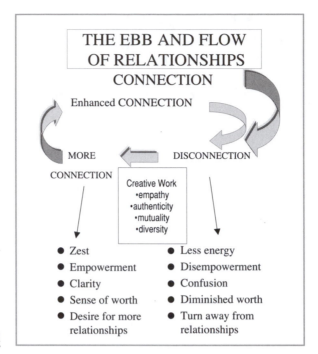

THE EBB AND FLOW
OF RELATIONSHIPS
CONNECTION

Enhanced CONNECTION

MORE
CONNECTION

DISCONNECTION

Creative Work
•empathy
•authenticity
•mutuality
•diversity

● Zest
● Empowerment
● Clarity
● Sense of worth
● Desire for more
   relationships

● Less energy
● Disempowerment
● Confusion
● Diminished worth
● Turn away from
   relationships

Figure 2

cues, not to let go, but rather to find creative ways to reconnect. Mothers can then support, guide, and reassure their sons through small and large conflicts in relationship. These happen first with mom, then with other family members, and eventually, in peer and adult relationships outside the home. The following example illustrates how a mother's emotional connectedness to her son enhanced his relational and emotional development:

> When thirteen-year-old Andy got home from school he learned that his best friend Sam's dog had been killed by a car. His own dog had died the same way just a year ago. Andy, in hearing the news, froze. His body stiffened, his face registered fear. What could he possibly say or do to help his friend at this point? He had no words. He was confused, overwhelmed, and inundated with feeling about his own dog's death. He knew the horrible loss he experienced a year ago was what Sam was feeling now but felt immobilized by his own grief and discomfort. How could he possibly approach Sam in this vulnerable state? And what about Sam? Wouldn't he be embarrassed by his own sadness?
>
> His mom put her arm around him and said, "You know how sad Sam must be. Remember how sad we all were when Trumpet died? Sam could really use a friend right now, especially one who knows exactly how he must be feeling."

Andy panicked, "No, Mom, I can't. I don't know what to say. I'd sound really stupid."

"You know it's a really important part of a friendship to go to your friend's side when something bad happens. He needs you now," said his mother.

Andy couldn't move. He couldn't go to Sam's. He couldn't call. He was angry with his mother for her suggestion. He started walking out of the room, but his mother said, "Wait, let's do this together. We can write it out and then call him."

Andy stiffened further insisting he couldn't even think, saying, "I'm stupid. I don't know what to say."

His mother wrote it out for him, encouraging him all the way, "Look Andy, all you have to say is 'Sam, I'm sorry. I just heard about your dog. I'm so sorry. I know how you must feel. You know Trumpet died last year the same way and it crushed me. I'm really sorry.'"

Andy backed away from the phone, but his mother dialed and handed it to him. As the phone rang he mouthed "No" to his mother, dangling the receiver her way. Finally, the answering machine picked up. With a sigh of relief Andy read the message.

Later his mom was worried about how these two teenagers could make a face-to-face connection. So she offered to let Andy have a Beanie Baby she had just bought for his younger brother. "You could give this to Sam in memory of Rumpus because it looks just like him," she said. Andy was insulted.

"Wow! Step back, Mom! A *Beanie Baby*? Give me a break!" At this point his mom dropped the idea.

The next day, Sam came over to find Andy, who wasn't home yet. He repeated over and over to Andy's mom, "Tell Andy that it was so cool he called me. No one else did. Tell him I said thanks. Tell him I came over. Tell him to come over to my house when he gets home. Tell him that was really great to call."

When Andy returned, his mother told him Sam had been there. Andy stiffened in fear. But when his mother related how appreciative Sam was for the call, Andy's whole body relaxed. His eyes brightened, he had a burst of energy, and was out the door to Sam's. His mom was relieved, and then a few minutes later heard him come back into the house. As he ran up the stairs he smiled and sheepishly asked if he could give the Beanie Baby to Sam.

On his way out the door his mom gave him a quick hug and told him what a great job he'd done. He smiled as he pulled away, saying, "That's because I've got a *buena madre!*"

Andy moved from alienation to emotional involvement. He moved from disconnection not only to reconnection, but even better connection with his mom and his friend. When he first heard the news, Andy disconnected and became immobilized. He exhibited all five outcomes of disconnection: lack of clarity or confusion ("I don't know what to say"), decreased desire and ability to act ("I can't"), decreased self-worth ("I'll sound stupid"), turning away from relationship (walking away), and decreased energy. With empathy, support, and mutual involvement from his mom, he was able to make the move back into relationship with his friend and with his mom. By the end of the story we see how the individuals and both relationships benefit from the move back into connection.

Andy exhibited all of the five good outcomes. He was motivated to act and did (went to his friend, came back for the Beanie Baby), he felt better about himself (smiling, joking), he had a more accurate picture of himself and others (*buena madre*), he had a desire for more connection (with his mom and Sam), and he had more energy (went to his friend, energized in his interaction with his mom). Andy learned something important about relationship and loss. His relationship with Sam will deepen because the two shared a new awareness of themselves in relation to each other's grief. And his relationship with his mother is enhanced as he more fully appreciates her efforts to help him with the difficult work of relationship.

Parenting-in-Connection

Embracing the natural ebb and flow of relationship is the basis for a model of child raising we refer to as "parenting-in-connection." The goal is to enhance connection and to circumvent distance and separation. As noted above, disconnections are *opportunities* to deepen and strengthen the relationship. Thus the inevitable disconnections of parenthood become a signal that work is needed in the relationship. Mothers can teach sons by example to move toward reconnection rather than becoming derailed by disconnection. A mother's knowledge and ability can enable this learning process for boys and enrich the connection with her son. This model offers a way for mothers to stay tuned in.

In a recent two-year longitudinal study of twelve thousand teenagers from across the country, researchers found that a close relationship with a parent is the best predictor of a teenager's health and the strongest deterrent to high-risk behaviors. The study, published in 1997 by the *Journal of the American Medical Association,* was part of a $24 million project funded by the National Institute of Child Health and Human Development and other agencies. A strong emotional connection with at least one parent or significant adult figure reduces the odds that an adolescent will suffer from emotional stress, have suicidal thoughts or behavior, engage in violence, or use substances (tobacco, alcohol, or marijuana). Feeling that at least one adult knew them and treated them fairly buffered the teens against every health risk except pregnancy. This finding held up regardless of family income, race, education, specific amount of time spent with a child, whether a child lives with one or two parents or in an alternative family structure, and whether one or both parents work. The evidence is overwhelming. Good relationships help create resilience against dangerous acting-out behaviors in our children.

As parents and educators, we share the painful dilemma of having important family and community values that conflict with the realities of peer culture for boys. Together, mothers and sons can develop new ways of approaching these dilemmas. We help mothers introduce the notion of repair and reparation when dealing with interpersonal violations and injuries. There is a growing need to set limits on emotionally, socially, and physically hurtful behavior toward others. But setting limits for the sake of limits does not work. Punishment without a relational context only further alienates boys. They take pride in getting busted. Acting out and noncompliance earns them points with peers. Naming the behavior that we want changed, providing alternatives to the old way, and adding interpersonal reparation making (see below), are all essential parts of limit setting with boys. They often love structure and tend to go along with a clearly outlined and defined model that they *and their friends* are expected to follow—"If you build it, they will come!" Boys need adults to point out that the behavior is hurtful, offer better alternatives, and provide concrete consequences for relational injuries.

We are suggesting a simple yet powerful change in boys' development: move the emphasis of the mother-son relationship away from separation and isolation, toward connection. When we do that, we have a chance to help sons with healthy emotional development daily in dozens of small but significant ways. We just might change the course of their lives by teaching them, through these everyday interactions, how to develop mutually empathic, mutually empowering relationships.

In reviewing boys' relational growth, we identified four stages in the development of mother-son relationships. Each developmental period has cultural expectations that influence the mother-son relationship, creating conflicts and dilemmas. We have set relational goals for each stage and defined ways mothers can counter these cultural influences and keep sons on the path of relational development. Each stage is outlined in terms of age, imposed cultural pressures, problems created, and specific methods for meeting relational goals (fig. 3).

I. The Early Years, 3–7 years. The cultural message is the invincibility of the superhero. Little boys are besieged by superhero figures that imply that becoming a man depends on independence, strength, stoicism, total invulnerability, and the defeat of all others. The relational goal is laying the groundwork for relationship by naming, demonstrating, and validating relational abilities.

II. The Middle Years, 8–13 years. The cultural message involves banter, bullies, and bravado. Middle-school boys are indoctrinated with the competitive ethic of winning at all costs and exploiting power over others. The relational goal is setting limits and offering alternatives by guiding sons toward interactive, fun-filled, authentic relationships.

III. The Teenage Years, 14–18 years. The cultural message is shutting down to real feelings and interactions and engaging in the "locker room" culture of social, physical, and sexual dominance. The focus is on dominance, not real relationship. The relational goal is maintaining relationships as multidimensional and encouraging mutual dialogue. It also involves viewing conflict and difference as opportunities to stay in connection and learn more about each other.

IV. The Adult Years. The cultural message is disconnection and separation from mother. Adult sons worry about being too "attached." The expectation to disconnect can feel like disinterest and distance to their mothers. The relational goal is to encourage a mutually responsive, mutually empowering mother-son relationship.

Parenting-in-connection provides a new way of understanding and responding to disconnections. It can be teaching a two-year-old to share, helping a nine-year-old to deal with the hurt and unfairness of being bullied, empathizing with a teenager's pain in being rejected romantically, or sorting through the many decisions of adulthood together.

The Early Years

One mom recalls how her son, Aaron, went from being the "best boy" in preschool to becoming the "wild boy" in kindergarten. "The kids he sat

---

PARENTING IN CONNECTION

- STAGE I. YOUNG BOYS
  AGE: 3–7 YRS.
  CULTURAL MESSAGE: The Superhero Years
  RELATIONAL GOAL: Laying the Groundwork

- STAGE II. MIDDLE YEARS
  AGE: 8–13 YRS.
  CULTURAL MESSAGE: Bullies, Banter & Bravado
  RELATIONAL GOAL: Interactive, Fun-Filled, Authentic
  Relationships

- STAGE III. TEENAGE YEARS
  AGE: 14–18 YRS.
  CULTURAL MESSAGE:
  The Locker Room Culture
  Physical & Sexual Dominance and Submission
  RELATIONAL GOAL: Maintaining Relationships as
  Multidimensional

- STAGE IV. COLLEGE/ADULT
  CULTURAL MESSAGE: Disconnection and Distance
  from Mother
  RELATIONAL GOAL: Reconnection as Adult

Figure 3

---

with on the first day of kindergarten were rambunctious, wild boys," she recalls. He sat at the same table day after day and very soon "he became a wild boy."

Before entering a traditional school setting, Aaron was an empathic little boy who asked his preschool teacher, "Are your feelings hurt?" after another child snapped at her. He was always the first to step forward and offer a welcome when a new child entered the class. With the move to kindergarten, Aaron entered a larger, traditional setting that reflected more mainstream boy culture expectations. His new teacher seemed to assume that all boys were rowdy, and did not really know Aaron. Feeling isolated and disconnected, he sought to establish connection by mimicking the boys at his table. He became loud and boisterous, winning acceptance by succumbing to pressures to join in with "wild boy" behavior.

In the parenting-in-connection model, the early years (figs. 4 and 5) are the time to lay the groundwork for relational mothering. Noting how essential mutual respect, honesty, empathy, and listening are to every interaction can do this. Mothers can show sons how to put these skills into action, verbally and nonverbally. Mothers often direct boys outside or into

Early Childhood
Cultural Issues:
Disconnect from Mom; Superhero
Influence

PROBLEMS	SOLUTIONS
• LOSE ACCESS TO RELATIONSHIP AND EMOTIONS	• SHOW & TELL
	• CHAT TIME
• LOSS/SADNESS	• FAMILY RITUALS
• CONFUSION	• TEACH RESPONSIVENESS
• BEGIN EXPOSURE TO MEDIA & SUPERHEROES	• MODEL & PRACTICE EMPATHY
• LOSE ACCESS TO VULNERABILITY	• PRAISE RELATIONSHIP & EXPRESSION
• LOSE EMPATHIC RESPONSE	• REFRAME
• AGGRESSION	– STRENGTH
	– COURAGE
	– BRAVERY
	• TIME OUT/IN REPAIR

Figure 4

the basement to watch a video when company arrives because their aggressive energy feels too incongruent to the occasion. Why not, instead, teach boys to stop, look at, shake hands with, respond to, and initiate conversation with guests that we welcome into our homes. Keeping boys in the picture offers an opportunity for practicing interpersonal skills. Over time, these relational skills will become second nature to boys and possibly replace the high-activity behaviors they seem to use to cover their anxiety.

Boys need to be told and shown how to interact in situations that extend beyond family and friends. Mothers can be clear about expecting receptivity and responsiveness to others in the home and community. Early childhood is the time to inculcate values like these. It is also the time to note the importance of being honest in communications with others and of respecting others' feelings, even though we might feel differently. These are the show-and-tell years, a time when children are open to learning and guidance that the culture does not offer and even opposes.

Our culture convinces boys early on that invincibility and imperviousness are hallmarks of strength. Little boys are fascinated by stories about Superman and they love to play superheroes. They learn that they have to be able to fix everything and protect everyone from evil forces. There is little room for expression of their vulnerable, dependent side. This inner part of boys can be quickly buried beneath shame if parents let the message of the culture take hold at this age.

Superman is powerful and invincible. But, as the story goes, his survival and strength depend upon his being apart from any trace of his "mother" planet, Krypton. Like Achilles, the underlying mythology presents the allure of invincibility and the dangers of the mother connection for sons. And the price for these illusions of strength for boys is the loss of access to feelings and authenticity in relationship.

In these early years, children are beginning to practice skills of empathy. Being responsive to family members' feelings and expressive of his own can give a little boy the opportunity to learn about mutually empathic relationships. Highlighting and validating the relational part of an activity, not just the activity itself, form another lesson for the early years.

> Maria takes her seven-year-old son cross-country skiing for the first
> time. When they come to a hill, John has a rough time. His mom

Figure 5

braces him from behind, to keep him from backsliding. Resting against her, he looks up and says, "You must really hate skiing with me. I'm terrible and you're awesome."

"Oh no," says Maria, "I love this. I love being with you and helping you. That's what important to me."

"Really?" says John, smiling broadly.

Another simple way to create a space for relationship at this early age is to make a daily chat a part of a boy's routine. Mothers can designate a time for a private chat. This can be done in the car on the way to an activity. It can be done at bedtime as a way of wrapping up the day. It can be combined with a game or other joint activity. Mothers need not pressure their son to speak, but rather let him know that he has the opportunity. As the chat becomes ritualized, this will be a special time together. This sets a relational frame within which he can learn that it's safe to talk about *anything*.

Parenting-in-connection in the early years is a matter of teamwork. Instead of sending a little boy out to master a two-wheeler without any preparation, mother and son start by peddling a bicycle built for two. Mom is there to help her young son navigate life's inevitable bumps and twists. Working through difficult feelings and problems with Mom not only teaches the boy relational skills, but also nourishes and enriches his self-worth and their relationship. These lessons and experiences with his mother give him the confidence to remain in touch with his inner world as he ventures into the greater world beyond family.

The Middle Years

At this age we see the "playground" influence of teasing and bullying (figs. 6 and 7). This behavior can be both emotionally and physically hurtful. Boy culture behavior says: "I'm tough"; "It doesn't bother me"; "You can't hurt me"; "I don't care." As noted above, when we stop responding to boys from an empathic, compassionate perspective, we give them the message that they should be tough and independent both emotionally and behaviorally.

In the earlier story about Max at the ballpark, his mother went to her son's room and sat with him. Her acknowledgment of and compassion for his pain offered both validation and comfort to Max. Left on his own to deal with this experience, Max would learn to avoid the shame he felt by denying his feelings of physical and emotional pain. Mothers sometimes worry about embarrassing sons further by acknowledging and responding

MIDDLE CHILDHOOD
BOY CULTURE:
DISCONNECT FROM FEELINGS
TEASING, BULLYING

PROBLEMS	SOLUTIONS
• BOY CULTURE BRAVADO	• HUMOR
• LOSS OF <u>RELATIONAL VOICE</u>	• REFRAME STRENGTH AND COURAGE
• DENIAL OF FEELINGS	• EXPAND RELATIONAL EXPECTATIONS
• FEAR OF HONEST EXPRESSION AND CONNECTION	• ENCOURAGE FEELING TALK
• DISCONNECTION FROM MOTHER/FAMILY VALUES	• LEARN TO SIT WITH FEELINGS, ESP. ANGER
	• ENHANCE RELATIONAL CHATS
• DESENSITIZATION TO VIOLENCE	• RELATIONAL VIOLATION & REPARATION
– VIDEO GAMES	• SHARE DILEMMA BETWEEN HOME VALUES AND CULTURE
– MOVIES, TV	
– INTERNET	
• "BAD BOY" BEHAVIOR	• FAMILY ACTIVITIES TOGETHER
• DISRESPECT	• INCLUDE FATHER'S STORY
• POOR JUDGMENT	
• DAREDEVIL TACTICS	• TALK ABOUT ALTERNATIVES
• HIGH-RISK BEHAVIOR	• ENCOURAGE BOY-GIRL <u>FRIENDSHIPS</u>
• POOR PERFORMANCE	

Figure 6

to their vulnerable emotions. Yet it is this very naming of and feeling compassion for hurt feelings that offers empathic response where they otherwise feel shame. This interaction teaches boys alternatives to avoiding shame by denying feelings.

We encourage mothers to jump into their son's world and react authentically to what they see and feel. Naming their emotional reaction and eliciting their son's view of the situation creates a dialogue. Mothers and sons can then further the process of sharing differences and exchanging values. While this process does not always give immediate answers, being together in a real way can create the connection necessary for them to work toward possible solutions.

A couple of years ago, a year-long, weekly values class became the setting for teaching relational skills to ten nine-year-old boys. Previous teachers warned about the impossible task of working with this group of boys, stating: "Every one of these boys meets criteria for ADHD [Attention Deficit Hyperactivity Disorder]"; "They are impossible to work with in a classroom

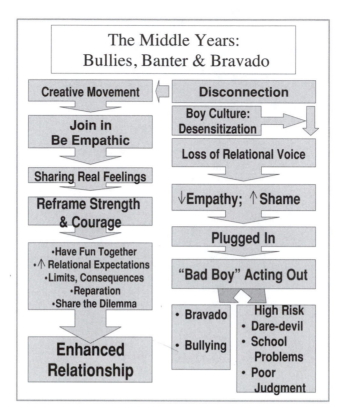

The Middle Years:
Bullies, Banter & Bravado

Creative Movement ⇐ Disconnection

Join in
Be Empathic

Boy Culture:
Desensitization

Sharing Real Feelings

Loss of Relational Voice

Reframe Strength
& Courage

↓Empathy; ↑Shame

•Have Fun Together
•↑ Relational Expectations
•Limits, Consequences
•Reparation
•Share the Dilemma

Plugged In

"Bad Boy" Acting Out

Enhanced
Relationship

• Bravado

• Bullying

High Risk
• Dare-devil
• School
  Problems
• Poor
  Judgment

Figure 7

setting"; "Let them outside to run off their energy"; and "This group desperately needs girls to tone it down." Similarly, the boys greeted the new teacher with: "We are powerful"; "No one can control us"; "We rule"; and "You have to let us go outside and run around." The teacher of the special values class spent the first month reinforcing good relational behavior with pennies and letting the boys trade these for candy at the end of the period. She walked around the classroom dropping pennies into paper cups whenever someone was *not* participating in disruptive behavior. She was eventually able to reinforce the new relational behavior as it appeared. Slowly the boys, through the introduction of a new model of interacting, started to engage with one another in a real way. The class brainstormed ideas about old and new models of relationship for boys. As they shared their experience in the old model, they were able to share feelings of isolation and an awareness of how unfair the old model is to boys. One child likened the expectations of boy culture to racism: "It's like racism, you can't even have a friend who's a girl without being called her boyfriend or a wimp for hanging around with her!"

The group created its own new culture and value system for boys. Instead of running wild, they talked about relationship. They interacted honestly and respectfully with one another. They even learned to meditate to the resonance of a meditation bell!

In the same classroom Nan Stein's and Lisa Sjostrom's "Bullyproof" curriculum (1996) introduced language and concepts for participation with peers outside the group. The boys brought in examples of boy culture from their school life and talked about the dilemma of doing the right thing in the face of peer pressure to do the opposite. Stein's "web of courage" exercise renamed being honest and supportive with friends as bravery and strength. There are countless ways we can praise and build confidence in boys for going against the cultural model. One boy's brave act was calling his friend on the phone. He expressed his hurt feelings to this friend who had joined with other boys mocking him on the way home from school. The boys seemed relieved to tell their real stories and talk about feelings in a place that was relationally safe. When we create new models with new values, boys can grow in new ways.

Middle-childhood-age boys respond well to structure. Mothers can name the relational violation they see, stop the hurtful interactive behaviors, and provide meaningful concrete consequences. We teach the notion of relational repair to boys. When a behavior is hurtful to the person and the relationship, we call it a relational violation and expect that reparation be made in some concrete form of giving to the relationship to get back into connection. Boys are responsive to structured ways of coming back into connection. Making reparation to a younger brother who has been hurt can mean engaging him in his favorite game and having fun together. This can be a quick fifteen-minute interaction between siblings during which all other freedoms are on hold. The reparation piece fits with a boy's desire to fix things. The shift is important—move the focus from fixing concrete things to repairing relationship.

Mothers can draw on established family relational rituals to open and process feelings and interactions with sons. Trade the stories of your lives. Welcome all their stories and tell them yours. Children are particularly interested in their parent's stories of childhood. How did you struggle at their age? Encourage a son's daily stories. Show interest in a son's day-to-day struggles with peers and praise his creative attempts to deal with these. When mothers do this they can enhance skills that are otherwise ignored or even put down by peers and the culture at large. By joining her son in his dilemma, a mother can widen his view of new possibilities and change.

The Teen Years

As boys enter the teen years the cultural message is to get as far as possible from their vulnerable emotions (figs. 8 and 9). The power-over model of boyhood is transformed into a model of dominance in adolescence. Social, physical, and sexual dominance replaces authentic interactions. Because they shut down to awareness of feelings and are disconnected from parents, adolescent boys tend to act out rather than talk out their problems and conflicts. This leaves them at risk for forming insecure or abusive relationships. They may experiment with drugs, alcohol, and other risk-taking behaviors. Peer competition and pressure often motivate premature sexual intimacies. Because this type of quick intimacy is devoid of relational depth, it can often lead to a pattern of frequently shifting sexual partners.

Confusion about who they are and what they feel extends to their future and their goals. Often this translates into a state of underachievement in school and a feeling of general discontent with their lives. This path for boys leads to further disconnection and alienation from relationship. They learn to resist influence and become relationally silent.

ADOLESCENCE
LOCKER ROOM BRAVADO
PHYSICAL & SEXUAL DOMINANCE

PROBLEMS	SOLUTIONS
• FOCUS ON PHYSICAL STRENGTH/DOMINANCE	• VALUE MUTUAL RESPONSIBILITY AND MUTUAL EMPATHY
• UNAWARE OF FEELINGS, EXCEPT ANGER	• EMPHASIZE POWER WITH OTHERS
• ACT OUT PROBLEMS AND CONFLICTS	• PARTICIPATE IN SON'S WORLD
• COMMUNICATION SHUT DOWN	– ASK QUESTIONS
• DESENSITIZED TO VIOLENCE	• CONTINUE TO DEFINE A MOTHER-SON RELATIONSHIP
– MOVIES, GAMES	• VIEW CONFLICT AS AN OPPORTUNITY FOR CONNECTION
– SPORTS	
– RELATIONSHIPS	
• CONFUSION ABOUT SELF & FUTURE	• NAVIGATE THROUGH TRANSITIONS; PREDICT FEELINGS
• UNDERACHIEVEMENT	
• DISCIPLINE PROBLEM	• NAME AND PROCESS FEELINGS; SIT WITH CONFUSION
• PRESSURE TO DRINK, TO BE SEXUALLY ACTIVE	
• USE DRUGS/ ALCOHOL TO DEAL WITH ANXIETY	• TALK OUT RATHER THAN ACT OUT
• SHIFTING SEXUAL INTIMACIES	• KNOW LIMITS
• VULNERABILITY TO	• EXPECT REPARATION
– DATE RAPE	• LEARN ABOUT MALE SEXUAL DEV.
– TEEN PREGNANCY	
– AIDS	• FRIENDSHIP PREREQUISITE TO SEX & INTIMACY

Figure 8

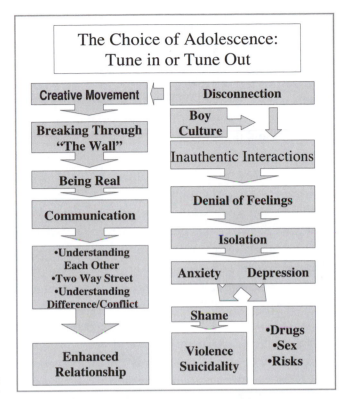

Figure 9

Mothers of teenagers often interpret their son's silence as rejection or as a desire for independence. They retreat from their son's distance. They are fearful that if they pursue connection they will be ignored or will increase the animosity they already feel from him. They are also afraid of being intrusive. They think they should respect their son's need for distance.

> A group of fifteen-year-old boys responded to the question: "What are the important mother-son issues for you?" One boy went on and on saying, "She should stay out of my room, leave me alone, stop telling me to do my homework and to clean up my room." This same boy, when questioned further about whether his mother ever tried to talk with him about important things, responded, "Yeah, but she gives up too easily."

In our work we encourage mothers to work hard at keeping the connection with sons. Adolescence is a time developmentally when sons need their mothers to hold onto the relationship. Even when it seems to mothers that they are "talking to a wall," these efforts mean something to boys and can become the early threads of connection. Mothers can raise issues and questions and let their son know what they think and feel. As boys mature, mothers can expect increased mutual responsibility for the work of their relationship. Mothers need to remain authentic in dealings with sons. For example, voicing frustration because she is doing all the work of the relationship and wanting more effort on his part can be the spark that wakes a son up and makes connection start to happen. Even if interactions seem to be conflicts and disagreements, the dialogue itself moves the relationship out of silence and distance into connection. Mothers need to make explicit the work of relationship so that boys learn what to do. Boys need guidance and real-life examples.

At the same time as a son's relationship with his mother becomes more balanced relationally, it can also become more balanced regarding the concrete work of family life. Mothers sometimes hold onto the role of provider and caretaker in a concrete way because that is all they have with their sons. As roles and responsibilities evolve, boys feel better about themselves and the growing mutuality with mom. They are learning how to be in relationship in a real way. Mothers can share their feelings and perspective while remaining receptive to a son's effort to communicate his viewpoint. Receptivity to a son's initiative is essential, whatever form this may take. Sometimes just being together in silence can create enough connection for sons to share a little bit more of who they are. As the relationship evolves, boys will begin to include mothers in discussions regarding dilemmas they face in the world and with peers. Learning to communicate with parental support gives boys the skills they need to deal with complex and difficult situations in life. As mentioned earlier, when there is a strong connection with at least one parent, teens do not need to turn to drugs, alcohol, or other forms of distraction and acting out.

As boys start to deal with bodily changes and emerging sexuality, mothers can provide a safe place to learn about both physical and interpersonal changes in relation to romantic and sexual partners. Mothers can keep the dialogue open, being responsive to questions, initiating concerns, and even sharing their own story. When it comes to teaching and guiding sons through the emotional, developmental topography of intimacy, mothers (as well as fathers) can be quite a good resource! Today's teens have no guidelines or structures in place to set the pace of intimacy for them. There are no rules. Teens "hook up" at parties. Dating does not exist. "Going out" and "hooking up" are loosely defined descriptions of partnering which can mean anything from talking on the phone regularly to having some form of sex together. This "no rules" situation creates problems, especially for boys. Our culture shames boys for not knowing facts or for reluctance in moving into sexual intimacy. Boys feel they should know what is going on, be in charge, and take the lead sexually. Even when sons appear to not want to talk about sexuality, it is usually out of the shame of not knowing. If mothers can voice their own feelings about these constraints, it may allow sons to come out of shame and feel safe enough to talk. Mothers need to hold this connection with their sons, creating possibilities for dialogue about relationship, intimacy, sexuality, and issues of power.

The Adult Years

At one of our first workshops, forty of the one hundred participants were mothers of adult sons. There was uniform concern about remaining in connection with sons in college, in marriages, and in adult life. We began the section by saying the refrain: "A daughter is a daughter for the rest of your life; a son is a son . . . " and everyone in unison joined in spontaneously " . . . 'til he takes a wife." The cultural message of disconnection at this stage is the culmination of years of distance between mothers and sons (figs. 10 and 11). The cultural stereotypes are always of the intrusive or meddling mother or mother-in-law. There are numerous negative images in the media of close mother-son relationships. The cultural mandate of disconnection we have talked about is fiercely reinforced through exaggerated stereotypes that mockingly refer to adult men who are close to their mothers as "mama's boys."

> At age thirty-seven a young man was reflecting on the anger and distance he had felt toward his mother since adolescence. At this stage in his life he wanted to establish a better relationship with her. In answer to the question, "What was your early relationship like?" he suddenly recalled: "I remember the wonderful feeling of her sitting on my bed talking with me before I fell asleep every night. Then one night she didn't come in. I called to her, but she said she couldn't come in anymore. She never told me why and she never came in again."

A mixture of pain and shame was evident in the telling of his story. Sharing his past experience seemed to bring him greater understanding of his feelings. The clarity motivated him to discuss this incident from the past with his mother in the present. One way of connecting with adult sons is to revisit past interactions and talk about how cultural pressures affected your mother-son relationship. Mothers who disconnected did so because the

ADULT SONS
Single, Married, Married with Children

PROBLEMS	SOLUTIONS
• ISOLATION & ALIENATION	• VALUE ATTEMPTS AT RECONNECTION
• NEGATIVE IMAGE OF STRONG MOTHER-SON RELATIONSHIP	• EXPECT MUTUAL RESPECT & RESPONSIBILITY
• MEDIA DISEMPOWERS MOTHERS	• BE AUTHENTIC & RESPONSIBLE
• SONS DISCONNECT AND DISTANCE	• HEAR HIS VOICE USE YOURS
• RIVALRY WITH DAUGHTER-IN-LAW	• ACKNOWLEDGE HIS NEEDS
• LOSS OF RELATIONSHIP	• CONNECT WITH THE PEOPLE IN HIS LIFE
• OPPOSING NEEDS IN LIFE STAGES OF MOTHERS AND SONS	• RESPECT DIFFERENCES
	• ACKNOWLEDGE DILEMMA
	• SUPPORT NETWORK

Figure 10

culture told them to, not because they wanted distance from their sons. In opening this dialogue, both mother and son can share their perspective and their feelings about these experiences. Processing old interactions in an effort to understand each other's point of view creates connection. This can be the beginning of the mutual effort and understanding that is needed in order to heal past hurts and misunderstandings.

It is our hope to reframe the relational goal of men's adulthood as discovering renewed connection with their mothers as they enter into more mutually supportive adult-to-adult-child interactions. One mother of an adult son told us that she had been having concerns about the distance in her relationship with her grown son. When she told him that she was attending a mothers-and-sons conference, he suggested that they have lunch afterward to talk about it. It seemed that letting him know about her interest in the conference opened a door for them and had an immediate effect on their relationship.

Mothers of adult sons are represented by many different situations: mothers of single sons, married sons, sons with children, gay sons, separated or divorced sons. The variations are endless. Yet many mothers of

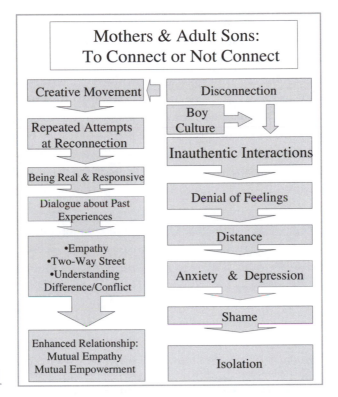

Figure 11

these sons feel isolated and alienated. They feel disempowered in their efforts to maintain some connection with their son or his partner and/or family. His lack of initiative-taking and unavailability in their relationship feels like a statement from him to leave him alone.

Adulthood is composed of many developmental stages for men. The mother-son relationship faces challenges as sons move through these. Some sons live a single lifestyle; others develop intimate relationships and live with partners or marry. The introduction of a new person adds a new level of complexity to the mother-son relationship. At this point, a son's energy may be directed toward developing this intimate relationship. Others may need to invest time and energy into demanding work schedules. Some choose to have children. All of these features influence the mother-son relationship. The son is developing more interpersonal commitments and career opportunities at a time when his mother may be doing the opposite. He is less available and she is often more available. This juxtaposition can create misunderstandings and hurt feelings if not addressed by mother and son. It is important for both to talk about the impact of the situation on their relationship and about how this feels. Talking openly and clarifying feelings created by these differences can help reestablish the connection and decrease the misinterpretation that silence can cause.

The challenge for mothers is to understand their son's expanding relationships and demands while at the same time to voice an interest in being included in some way. Both mothers and sons need to respect and embrace the other's relational efforts across these differences. Mothers can value attempts at connection by sons even when they feel as if they need more. Being authentic about one's own feelings but responsive to the other's needs and circumstances is the challenge of the adult years. At this point the relationship is the mutual responsibility of both mother and son.

Being aware of these conflicting needs and discussing the natural dilemmas they create can result in an atmosphere of acceptance. Most importantly, mothers need a strong support network of other mothers and other family members to help them deal with their evolving relational needs. Many mothers of adult sons have voiced the need to talk together about these issues. Joining with other mothers in similar life circumstances can be a healing experience for mothers of adult sons. These groups can help create the kind of connection that is often lacking in their relationships with their sons. This network of connection can empower mothers to find positive solutions to dilemmas with sons.

Conclusion

In the Greek myth, Thetis worried about what was best for her son, Achilles. In order to be a good mother, she chose to protect him from harm. In so doing, she affirmed his vulnerability. The decisions mothers face in raising boys are no less challenging today. Faced with cultural pressures that impose emotional straitjackets on boys, mothers feel unsure about how to handle their relationships with their sons. Over two thousand mothers who attended mothers-of-sons workshops intuitively knew that boys needed their emotional help but felt enormous pressure to disengage from them. In this supportive environment, they related stories of true connection and working through disconnections with sons throughout the life span. Time and time again they demonstrated that a mother's emotional connectedness to her son enhances his relational and emotional development. Good relationships are the cornerstones of psychological health and help create resilience in our sons to cultural pressures.

NOTES

1. See Lewis, Lovely, Yeager et al., Boston Public Schools, 1997.

2. See, for example, Jones, Offord, and Abrams.

3. From an interview the authors conducted with a teacher discussing her experience with boys.

4. See Jenkins.

WORKS CITED

Bergman, S. J., and J. L. Surrey. "Couples Therapy: A Relational Approach." In *Work in Progress, No. 66.* Wellesley, MA: Stone Center Working Paper Series, 1992.

———. "Men's Psychological Development: A Relational Perspective." In *Work in Progress, No. 48.* Wellesley, MA: Stone Center Working Paper Series, 1991.

Boston Public Schools. Survey of classroom behavioral problems by gender. Unpublished raw data, 1997.

Brown, L. M., and C. Gilligan. *Meeting at the Crossroads.* New York: Ballantine, 1992.

Federal Bureau of Investigation. *Uniform Crime Reports for the US.* Washington, DC: US Department of Justice, 1987.

Gilligan, C. "The Centrality of Relationships in Human Development: A Puzzle, Some Evidence, and a Theory." In *Development and Vulnerability in Close Relationships,* edited by G. G. Noam and K. W. Fischer. Mahwah, NJ: Lawrence Erlbaum, 1996.

Gilligan, J. *Violence.* New York: Vintage Books, 1996.

Jenkins, Y. M. "Diversity and Social Esteem." In *Diversity in Psychotherapy: The Politics of Race, Ethnicity, and Gender,* edited by J. L. Chin, V. De La Cancela, and Y. Jenkins. Westport, CT: Praeger, 1993.

Jones, M. B., D. R. Offord, and N. Abrams. "Brothers, Sisters and Antisocial Behavior." *British Journal of Psychiatry* 136 (1980): 139.

Jordan, J. V. "Relational Development: Therapeutic Implications of Empathy and Shame." In *Work in Progress, No. 39.* Wellesley, MA: Stone Center Working Paper Series, 1989.

———., ed. *Women's Growth in Diversity.* New York: Guilford, 1997.

Lewis, D.O., R. Lovely, C. Yeager, et al. "Toward a Theory of the Genesis of Violence: A Follow Up Study of Delinquents." *J Am Acad Child Adolesc Psychiatry* 28 (1989): 431–436.

Miller, J. B. *Toward a New Psychology of Women.* Boston: Beacon Press, 1976.

———. "What Do We Mean by Relationships?" In *Work in Progress, No. 22.* Wellesley, MA: Stone Center Working Paper Series, 1986.

healthy sense of their maleness. Ten years later the feminist sociologist, now psychoanalyst, Nancy Chodorow put Greenson's thesis in feminist terms. She pointed out that as long as the current unequal allocation of child care persists, then the child's primary caregiver will, more often than not, be a woman—usually the mother—from whom sons will indeed have to lose their attachment and identification to achieve a separate male identity.

Recalling their early childhood, men often recall the pressure put on them to detach themselves from their mothers and from the feelings involved in losing them. The psychoanalyst Wilfred Bion, who was taken to boarding school in England when he was eight by his mother, who then returned to their family home in India, remembers the following conversation on his first evening in the dorm:

> "What's the matter?" asked one of the three boys. . . .
> "I don't know," I wailed. . . .
> "Are you homesick?"
> "Yes." At once I realized what an awful thing I had done. "No, B," I hurriedly said.

Bion adds, "As my powers of deception grew I learned to weep silently" (1982, 34).

Men interviewed for a recent television program recalled similar misery at being detached from their mothers upon attending boarding school. A seventy-year-old man, Tony Kildwick, recalls:

> When I got to the school, the excitement of getting there, and the misery of being separated from my parents was very great. I was absolutely miserable when I arrived. But once I was in the dormitory with other boys of the same age, though I do remember very much crying of homesickness, I did it under the bedclothes so that they wouldn't discover. I think probably we were all crying under the bedclothes if the truth were told. But one simply did not, and one should not, show emotion. And even at that age—at eight—I wasn't going to let on to even the other little boys, who were probably feeling exactly the same as I was, er, that I was homesick, that I was blubbing, as we used to call it. (*A Man's World: The Boy*, 1)

Men who went to day school remember much the same pressure to stem the tears evoked by attachment to their mothers and homes, so as to prove themselves boys, not "weepish" girls, as Geordie, another contributor to this program, put it. He poignantly went on to recall how, having been taught since infancy not to express his feelings, he found himself at age eleven unable to shed a single tear when his mother died suddenly of a heart attack:

> When she died it was three parts of my life went. I wanted to cry but I couldn't. I just had the big lump in my throat, no tears. I don't think I knew how to do it. And, of course, on the other hand, there were quite a few neighbours at the funeral. And I didn't want to be classed as a softie and cry. None of me brothers cried. And you felt a sort of tautness around your chest. But you just couldn't get anything out. I think that was the feeling. It was an awful feeling happening, and you remember it to this day. (*A Man's World: The Boy*, 1)

Many men describe a similar feel a "tautness" about expressing their feelings. Some literally gag on their feelings. They stammer in keeping their emotions down.

Stammering

Stammering occurs almost three times more often in boys than girls (Yairi and Ambrose 1992). It often begins in boys, not girls, at the age when they first detach from their mothers to go to nursery school. This cost to men of detaching prematurely from their mothers and suppressing their feelings has recently been movingly described by the novelist Pat Barker in her World War I trilogy, *Regeneration*. She draws attention to the frequency with which, having learned early to "keep a stiff upper lip," shell-shocked officers stammered in preventing their feelings from showing. She recounts the origin of the stammer of W. H. R. Rivers, famous for using Freud's "talking cure" method to treat these officers. Rivers's stammer began when he was four and cried at the barber. Rivers learned from the example of his father, who said nothing to his mother about the incident, that he too must say nothing.

It was the same with his patients—they too stammered rather than express their feelings, so much had they been taught to repress them at school. Or, as Rivers explains, fear and its expression are especially abhorrent to the moral standards of the public schools at which the majority of officers have been educated. The games and contests that make up so large a part of the school curriculum are all directed to enabling the boys to meet without manifestation of fear any occasion likely to call forth this emotion (Rivers, quoted in Young, 65). But repression does not do away with fear, and it returned to haunt Rivers's patients in recurring nightmares of the traumas they had suffered in the trenches. The solution was to undo the repression, or, as Barker puts it, to tell them, "Go on . . . cry. It's all right to grieve" (Barker, 96).

Recurring Nightmares

The pediatrician and psychoanalyst Donald Winnicott once described a seven-year-old who was dealing with detachment and separation from his mother by repeatedly reattaching to her, as it were, with string. Asked to write down their best remembered recurring childhood dream, high-school boys today sometimes recall similarly wishful reattachment. A fourteen-year-old, living with his father and siblings but without his mother, writes:

> My most repeated [childhood] dream was that I was hanging from a building trying to paint a statue of a lady gold. I only had 3 pots of paint and I had 24 hours before the sun came up. I then painted it completely apart from the legs, but I could not paint them as the rope was too short. The 24 hours was up and the rope holding me up snapped. I fell and as I reached the floor I woke up. (Sayers, 23)

Others recall recurring nightmares of maternal separation. A seventeen-year-old writes:

> I used to have a dream about being separated from my mother as she was taking me to school. There was always a very strong sense of loss in this dream—it was particularly vivid, and at the same time quite frightening. It was a dream that reoccurred very frequently for some time. (Sayers, 24)

Another seventeen-year-old remembers the following recurring nightmare of separation from those to whom he would otherwise be attached:

> I could see waves, not necessarily sea waves, but they were often like that. They created a horrible, distressing distance between myself and the object of the dream I was having. (Sayers, 24)

Others recall nightmares of being threatened and attacked while being separated, isolated, and unattached. A fourteen-year-old describes his best-remembered recurring dream:

> All that happened . . . was me looking up towards the sun and every-thing went white. I then found myself walking in a place that was totally white. I couldn't distinguish between anything, and then a

black spot appeared in front of me. The spot grew and grew until I was engulfed by it. I then found myself falling into nothingness with everything being black. (Sayers, 24)

Another fourteen-year-old wrote:

I often had a strange dream in which there was a piercing noise. There was an infinitely small "thing"—maybe me—and it was "over-taken," crushed, by a much larger "thing." I had this dream maybe three times. (Sayers, 25)

In the words of another teen of the same age:

My most repeated childhood dream was that I was being chased through some woods by a monster, and he kept gaining on me. (Sayers, 25)

Nor are these nightmares any surprise given the theory that, for children to experience their fears not as monstrous and as attacking them, they need to experience their fears as contained and understood by their mothers, so they can in turn regard them as containable within themselves (Bion 1962). But premature separation and distance between mothers and sons threatens this process. As the poet William Morris, who was sent away to boarding school after his father died, wrote in versifying a mother's words to her infant son:

> twixt thee and me
> Shall rise that wall of distance, that round
> each one doth grow,
> And maketh it hard and bitter each other's
> thought to know.
> (McCarthy, ii)

Too distant from the mother to experience their feelings as contained and containable by her, boys often arrive at adolescence experiencing their feelings as uncontained, monstrous, and out of control.

Self-Division

Young men have to live with a division between the uncontained feelings they experience and the external control they know they're supposed to demonstrate. Some deal with this self-division through remaining silent about what they feel, lest expressing their feelings expose them as uncontained and out of control. Thus, for example, a group of working-class fourteen- to sixteen-year-old boys attending a Glasgow secondary school recently told a researcher:

> If you ask any boy if he's a virgin every one will say "No," "I done it on holiday," and all that. That's the pure one: "I done it on holiday at Ayr." . . . You would not go and have a big conversation amongst all your mates. . . . You may come out with a joke and that. You never have a pure conversation at all. . . . You don't go and pour your heart out and all that. You keep your feelings to yourself. (Wight, 722)

Talking about feelings—about love, at least—is too "soppy," as a nineteen-year-old in another Glasgow-based study put it.

New York teenagers tell a similar story. An African-American boy tells a researcher how he too has to keep his feelings to himself:

> I had a couple [of close friends] once when I was real young, around ten. . . . But right now, nobody really 'cause it seems that as I've grown, you know, everybody just talks behind your back and stuff. . . . With my girlfriend, I could relax . . . with a girl you can express certain feelings and stuff, you know . . . you can talk about certain things and with boys it's just harder to like . . . some of the things you may want make you seem you're gay or something. (Way)

Others likewise divide themselves off from expressing their feelings. Dreading their feelings will expose them as homosexual, they attribute them to others. A nineteen-year-old recalls a nightmare:

> I dreamt I saw group male sex in a college toilet. Then I was raped from behind by another male whilst urinating. After leaving the toilet (the rapist had run off) in tears, someone I knew in the dream . . . comforted me and sat me down and told me not to worry and then chased off after my attacker. This dream seemed so real I woke up thinking I had been really raped in my bed and covered in sweat. (Sayers, 36–37)

Others divide themselves from incestuous feelings. A fifteen-year-old's description indicates that his self-image fluctuates between guilty and innocent, incestuous and virginal:

> My most recent dream was last night—I dreamt I was with my sister. . . . She said she wanted to lose her vaginity [sic] but not to be a bastard. She asked me to have sex with her. . . . So I agreed, but I actually wanted to have sex with her! . . . She pointed to my trousers, and she took them off and pulled me down on top of her . . . I then got my

penis and put it into her vagina and we started having sex . . . she reached her orgasm as I ejaculated. Then she got dressed and went to her bedroom. I am still a virgin! (Sayers, 37)

Writers at the turn of the century told similar tales of being divided from themselves by sex. They also told tales of their feelings and experience of sex not being contained for lack of being put into words through speaking or writing to others about it. A teenager in Wedekind's play *Spring Awakening*, first performed in 1906, says of his sexual fantasy:

There were these legs in sky-blue tights climbing over the teacher's desk . . . I'd never felt anything like it before—such a craving—for such unbearable excitements. Unbearable! Why wasn't I left to sleep through it—and wake up when it was all over? . . . I can hardly speak to a girl without my brains going into a kind of spin down a drain—I think the most horrible things . . . I've been through the encyclopedia from A to Z. Huge, ponderous volumes, solid with words. Masses and masses and masses of words. But not one plain description of what actually goes on. (Wedekind)

Others note ways in which sexual fantasy fills the gap left by loss of attachment. In his 1906 novel, *Young Törless*, Robert Musil describes a teenager who is separated from his mother upon going to boarding school. While she weeps at the station waiting for the train to take her home, Törless walks back to the school and finds his mind filled with a confusing riot and "mesh" of "obscure" sexual images and longings:

[He] looked through the little windows and the crooked, narrow doorways into the interior of the cottages with a gaze burning so hotly that there was all the time something like a delicate mesh dancing before his eyes. Almost naked children tumbled about in the mud of the yards; here and there as some woman bent over her work her skirt swung high, revealing the hollows at the back of her knees, or the bulge of a heavy breast showed as the linen tightened over it. . . . He was waiting for something . . . some monstrous sight of which he could not form the slightest notion; something of a terrifying, beast-like sensuality; something that would seize him in its claws and rend him, starting with his eyes; an experience that in some still utterly obscure way seemed to be associated with these women's soiled petticoats. (Musil, 23–24)

Arriving at the school, and through the next few days, Törless feels horribly alone. He associates his loneliness with being abandoned by his nursemaid as a child. Ungovernable sexual ideas fill the void—fantasies of the "lure of woman" and of "perverted lust in the secrecy of it." He finds himself "disturbed by the thought that his lustful imaginings might overwhelm and gain more and more ascendancy over him" (Musil, 34).

James Joyce wrote similarly of the threat of sex dividing him from himself, overwhelming him while filling the void of being unattached, separate, and alone. Pressed as an eight-year-old not to say anything of his attachment to his mother when he leaves for boarding school, he subsequently depicts himself in his autobiographical novel, *A Portrait of the Artist as a Young Man*, as a teenager detached and self-divided between sexual fact and fantasy:

> On the desk he read the word *Foetus* cut several times in the dark stained wood. The sudden legend startled his blood. . . . His monstrous reveries came thronging into his memory. They too had sprung up before him, suddenly and furiously, out of mere words. He had soon given in to them and allowed them to sweep across and abase his intellect, wondering always where they came from, from what den of monstrous images. . . . The letters cut in the stained wood of the desk stared upon him, mocking his bodily weakness and futile enthusiasms and making him loathe himself for his own mad and filthy orgies. (Joyce, 90, 91)

Given these self-divisions resulting, at least in part, from young men's early suppression of and division from their feelings, in the first place on losing their attachment to their mothers, it is no surprise that young men are more likely than others to suffer the extreme self-divisions and self-destruction of schizophrenia and suicide.

Schizophrenia and Suicide

A recent worldwide survey found that, among those younger than thirty-five, men outnumbered women by nearly three to two in being diagnosed as schizophrenic, with men aged fifteen to fifty-four in the United Kingdom sample outnumbering women by nearly two to one (Jablensky et al.). A 1995 study found that the first rank symptoms of schizophrenic self-division increased in men, but not in women, through adolescence (Galdos and van-Os). Sex differences in suicide are even more marked: in 1988, for instance, the suicide rate for England and Wales was 11 per 100,000 in men compared to 3 per 100,000 in women (Diekstra et al.).

The link between suicide and loss of attachment to others is indicated by evidence that many are driven to commit suicide when they feel cut off from others by what they experience as shameful, unmentionable, homosexual longings and desires (Raymond). One commentator attributes men's high suicide rate to the pressure on men both to prove their success and not to talk about their failures. He concludes that "men have remained the silent sex and increasingly become the suicide sex" (Farrell, 13). Suicide, it seems, remains linked to loss or lack of community with and attachment to others (Offer et al.), just as the sociologist Emile Durkheim famously reported in 1888.

Examples abound of young men whose schizophrenic and suicidal breakdowns are linked to early loss of attachment to their mothers and to their subsequent attempts to fill the gap with fantasies of sex, which has the effect of dividing them from others (Laing; Laufer). Examples from my own work as a psychotherapist include Simon, a nineteen-year-old modern languages student, referred to me following a very serious suicide attempt in which he nearly died.

Simon

Simon began therapy by describing his mother's indifference to him and her almost total physical and emotional absence from his life. His mother's indifference, Simon complained, included her disbelief when he told her a man in the train had grabbed him, pulled his head back, and spat into his mouth, leaving his intrusive stink inside him.

He also complained of his father's hostility toward him. He recalled his father calling him an "alien" and "the black sheep of the family." He recalled his father ganging up with his older brother to deride him as "schizophrenic." To defend himself he took refuge in self-division. Or, as he later put it, "I wanted to hide the real me behind something else."

On the one hand he felt he was indeed the hated, alien figure his brother and father accused him of being. He remembered himself, aged twelve or thirteen, going home from school with his younger sister and encouraging her to go to a sweetshop with a stranger who had been courting them, later feeling he was the same as this stranger who used the lure of the sweetshop to abduct his sister and abuse her. Simon felt he too was an abuser, a pedophile, and a rapist, not least because he had several times gone along with his older brother's invitation to have sex with him.

On the other hand, Simon cultivated a contrary image of himself as a young woman—akin perhaps to the dead baby girl his mother had borne early in his parents' relationship, whom his father still very much grieved. Simon imagined himself being made love to as a young woman by another young woman. That was why he stole women's underclothes, he told me. Wearing them gave him sexual satisfaction. But he also hated himself for his cross-dressing. That was why he tried to kill himself.

He hated his sexual, bodily self. But he loved his intellectual, rational self. He regaled me with his near-perfect achievements at school. But he had also begun worrying that he could not keep his body and mind divided. He worried that his bodily impulse to wear women's clothes had damaged his mind. He was convinced that a lump on his head was an effect of the bones of his skull being fed by his sexual drive—by excess sex hormone.

He had been to see his doctor about it. But his doctor was no more understanding than his father. Simon could no more talk about his feelings with his doctor than he could with his father or with anyone else. His doctor would not tell him honestly what was wrong with him. He regarded him as a "pest" and evidently felt uncomfortable being with Simon, just as Simon's father did. Simon complained that he also could not communicate with his fellow students. Nor could he share his feelings with his college tutors. He had tried. But, like his mother, they did not believe what he said. They laughed at him behind his back. They treated him as a pariah.

If only he could establish the closeness he wanted with me, free of the division between being a hated man and a loved girl—a division that it became apparent was the legacy of his parents' destructive indifference to and hatred of him, in contrast to the love his father felt for Simon's dead baby sister. Simon signaled his longing for closeness with me, for me to recognize his worth, by bringing a school photo of himself, aged eight, handing his work—a beautifully detailed poem, quirkily about a poisonous snake—to a visiting woman dignatory, famed for her motherliness.

He wanted to be close to me. But he was also inhibited from emotional closeness and talking about his feelings with me, just as he was with others. Instead he often wrote long letters to me about what he felt. He wrote about his hated, sexual self; about his suicidal self-loathing at giving in to his urge to wear women's clothes; and about his rapacious, murderous thoughts about women and children. He wrote about his attempt, at age eleven or twelve, to kill and punish himself for stealing his father's typewriter and outdoing him as a poet in composing verses that had earlier won him the motherly woman dignatory's approval and attention at school.

He felt diffident about being with me and about confiding in me. He left sessions early. Later he wrote to me about his anger at my not taking in the fact of his initial "crush" on me. Long since alienated and separated from his mother, he wrote, "I wanted to be close with you." His longing had evidently been a major source of his nervous laughter when he was with me. I had not noticed. He told me he had concluded that I did not take him seriously, that I had distanced myself from him out of fear lest he become too intimate and emotionally involved. He was angry that I seemed not to understand. But he was also more confident than with his parents that I might understand and withstand "the mess" of his trying to convey what he felt. He became hopeful that I might withstand his longing and hatred without rebuffing him. He wrote between sessions, saying: "I know that if I tell you what bothers me you will try to help."

Perhaps it was his confidence of both of us being able to retain something of the closeness that—despite its conflicts—he had shared with me that enabled him to leave therapy to pursue his university studies, first in England and then in Germany. Many months later, before going abroad, he wrote, saying: "You probably remember me. . . . You are one of the few professional people who has known me."

He wanted to see me—the manifest reason being that he wanted me to endorse his identity card photo. When we met it transpired that he also wanted to renew his previous attachment to me—just as he renewed the closeness he experienced with the motherly figure at school by repeatedly returning to the photo of the two of them together. Simon's cultivation of the divided man-woman story was his answer to the disruption of emotional togetherness with his parents and his resulting "keeping secrets and bottling things up," as he put it.

His divided-self story was on a continuum with many men's experience of being or becoming unattached and divided, first from their mothers, then from others and themselves through adolescence. Many more young men resolve this division not through suicidal self-hatred but through manic self-glorification.

Manic Self-Glorification

Given that boys are pressured to distance themselves from their mothers to forge a separate and superior male identity, it is not surprising that this identity often becomes grandiose and manic as they reach adulthood. Feminist theorist Carol Gilligan describes this phenomenon as men being compensated for "attenuating their connection with their mothers" by being "stuffed with grandiosity and privilege" (Gilligan, 25).

When asked to record their dreams anonymously in school, several pre-teen and teenage boys told recurring nightmares of maternal loss followed by dreams of heroic grandiosity. After writing about a recurring dream of losing his mother, a fourteen-year-old writes that recently he dreamt of scoring the winning goal in the Wembley Football Association Cup Final. Another fourteen-year-old, after recounting a recurrent childhood dream of isolation from family and friends in a desert, goes on to write that in his best-remembered recent dream:

> There was crowds and crowds of people. I was playing tennis against Andre Agassi and Pete Sampras at the same time. They didn't win a point. And I won. The grass tennis court was bright green and the crowd cheered me. (Sayers, 119)

A third fourteen-year-old begins with a recurring dream that he tells in the following detached, third-person terms:

> A nightmare where you are in darkness alone, in the middle of nowhere, with a massive army all around you—that approach you . . . but just when they reach you and are about to kill you, the dream starts all over again.

He then arguably compensates for this "alone," "nowhere," third-person world of darkness and attack with an image of himself as a man who, far from losing attachment to those around him, is surrounded by girls all longing to have sex with him. He wrote:

> My most recent memorable dream which occurs over and over again is where I start at a party, with lots of really nice girls, and they all really fancy me and aren't afraid to show it. I know all of the girls in my dream. Then two of them follow me home, and I shag them both, lick them out and they give me a blow job. (Sayers, 119–120)

But compensating for loss—first for lost attachment to their mothers—through self-glorification comes at a cost. It may lead to delinquently attacking others. One example comes from an eleven-year-old who tells a recurring nightmare of isolated walkers on a windswept beach being sucked into the sand and threatened by "a crimesquad" hidden below. He then gets away from the "crimesquad" terrors of being alone. He makes himself big by evoking these terrors in others. He tells a recent dream in which, he writes:

we had been playing football all day and then we went to Pete's. We raided the fridge and freezer and got legless. Then we all went up to John's house but on the way we met the unfriendly dog. We started to annoy it. So it chased us. We all turned around and kicked it until it was unconscious and didn't move. (Sayers, 139)

Others dread that their grandiosity might excite others' envious attack. A twelve-year-old dreams he won Wimbledon and collected the trophy but was then rewarded by a man machine-gunning him and the admiring spectators. A fourteen-year-old dreams he was in a rock group, adored by girls who then beat him up. Another fourteen-year-old dreams of glory transmuted into disaster. He writes:

I dreamt I had become a member of a really big rock/grunge band and that I was really rich and all our records had gone platinum. I was in the middle of singing the song called the "4th of July" by Soundgarden which is about the end of the world when everything in the song came true. The floor opened and engulfed everything and everyone except me and I was left alone on a completely deserted Earth.

Still others tell nightmares of self-aggrandizing victory turning into humiliating defeat. A seventeen-year-old tells a dream of "missing an open goal in Holland against Germany when playing for England in the European Cup." They tell nightmares of disillusion: a thirteen-year-old dreams he was playing for Liverpool at Wembley for the Football Association Cup Final only to discover that the applause of the crowd came from tape recorders, not people, in the stands.

Len

The ills of manic self-glorification can persist well into adulthood. An example was Len, a man I saw in private therapy some years ago. He was an architect and began therapy in his mid-thirties. An architect colleague had suggested he might find therapy helpful in enabling him to get out of the rut in which he felt he was stagnating both at work and at home. At least, that was what he initially told me.

Like many men, Len went on to tell a story of himself that began with early loss of his mother. In his case the loss had been total. His mother died when he was thirteen. Her loss reminded him of other losses: the death of his older sister in childbirth when Len was nine; and the loss of his father when his father remarried a year after Len's mother died.

At some level Len worried that he might have contributed to the loss of his mother and sister. He worried that, like the damage he felt his architecture clients inflicted on him by intruding into his personal life, he might damage his wife by having sex with her when she was pregnant. He remembered dreading that he might cause her, like his sister, to die in childbirth. He was horrified at the sight of his wife giving birth—her flesh putrid and disgusting like that of his dying mother.

More often, however, feelings of depression and guilt at the thought of damaging and contributing to the loss of those he both loved and was horrified and disgusted by were obscured by another story he told himself. He described how, following his mother's death, he became the supremo in his family. Just as he told me he allayed vulnerability to attack by his peers by patronizing them as "disadvantaged" and giving them cigarettes, he allayed vulnerability to his mother's loss by patronizing his father as more bereaved than him by her death.

Meanwhile, at school he triumphed over any upset he might have felt about the loss of his mother by becoming a "big deal" artist. He also became a Don Juan. Seducing women into crediting him with being the perfect lover kept at bay the discreditable hatred, as well as love, of his mother and others, which might otherwise have accompanied his sense of loss at their death. Sex, he told me, is a "fuck off" to death.

It was the same with his politics. He recalled a dream of his car being boxed in when he was visiting a friend, and of his saving the day by giving the lads a loudspeaker. It was his solution to being "boxed in" by attachment to, dependence on, and fear of losing those he loved. Rise above it all. Speechify. That was the motto impelling him to become a demogogue student activist. It had similarly impelled him to become a "wild cannon" and "maverick" at work. He kept the firm together. Without him, he said, the business would collapse.

It was the same with his wife. Just as he had grandly taken his father under his wing when he was a teenager, he had grandly taken his wife under his wing in marrying her. Just as he derided his father's dependence on him and his mother's nervous debility following the death of her daughter and father, he derided the dependence of his wife that led her to marry him, saving her from the misery and abjection of growing up an unwanted foster child.

It was the same with me. He derided me. He had no respect for my trade. He bad-mouthed psychoanalysis as endless talk of "murderousness and death." He dismissed therapy with a finger gesture of contempt. He called it "furtive." He likened me to the fool who, going to the theater, hangs up what little intellect he has along with his hat in the cloakroom outside. He short-changed me; he told me it was my fault, that I must have made a mistake in calculating his bill. He resented paying. Anyway why should he pay? He was "a special case," too important to be bothered with such financial trivialities. He had no need of me. Rather I needed him. He spoke of my being lost without him when his work prevented him from attending one of his appointments.

Slowly, however, his attitude changed. Cracks began to become apparent in his self-glorifying façade. Long-suppressed and -negated feelings of attachment and loss began to surface. Faced with the prospect of losing me over the Christmas break, he recalled a dream:

> Mr Bouverie [a senior partner in his architecture firm] and I were having Christmas lunch. But there was only very measly turkey legs. We asked for some more and got some wine. But I lost the turkey leg. I woke up looking for it.

The loss of his "measly turkey leg" was a striking contrast to his previous self-glorifying image of himself as having the phallus, as the Freudian analyst Jacques Lacan might have put it. His dream reminded him of his car. It was a crock but he could not bear to lose it. He assumed he could magically fix it, just as he imagined he could fix everything and everyone when his mother died. Thinking of her loss reminded him of one of his customers who, when Len's job for him ended, could not bear to say "Goodbye." He talked of those who, rather than face loss of those they love, escape into suicide. Along with his dawning recognition of his and others' difficulties in facing separation and loss came increasing recognition of the divided feelings involved. Now, as well as remembering his mother as someone he hated and was horrified by, he also remembered loving her. He remembered her goodness. He wished she had lived to see his achievements so he could stop driving himself to ever more superlative feats.

He began to acknowledge his initial fear of depending on and of losing his identity were he to become attached to, dependent on, and involved in therapy with me. Having begun therapy by idealizing himself, he now idealized me as "an omniscient therapist" whom he also hated and wanted enviously to spoil and depose. Anxious about our work together, he recalled a recurring dream of being chased by a clown and of tearing off the clown's mask not so much to expose him as a fraud but out of "livid" hatred of the clown, now equated with me, for making him feel so beholden to others helping him.

Following the next vacation break, he told me he had realized he valued and missed therapy when it was not there. He confessed to having begun therapy in a "grandiose" fashion and to now feeling quite the reverse—that he was not very "adept" at it. He despaired of taking in anything good. All he took in, he said, was bad—cigarettes and beer. He was preoccupied with bad people, with a news story, for instance, about boys killing a two-year-old. He became depressed lest, contrary to his former grand image of himself as ensuring his teenage daughter's success at school where her teachers had failed, he could not get her through her exams.

He was laid low with the flu. He worried lest his debility lose him his wife. He worried that she might heartlessly "dethrone" and "dispense" with him, as he had dispensed with his mother and others rather than countenance their loss. Having previously characterized his wife as useless compared to him, he now acknowledged that she also helped him. It was because she had suggested he might find therapy helpful, he now told me, that he had first asked me to take him on as a patient.

He began to value not only his wife's help but also his father's ability to use help, so unlike his own inability to rely on others when his mother died. A memory came back to him of himself, aged eight, miserable at losing his father one day in a crowded supermarket. Facing his unhappiness at these and other losses, he acknowledged wanting therapy. He wanted its "containment," he said. He wanted me to keep an eye on him, as he kept an eye on his teenage daughter, so as to work to resolve, rather than flee into self-glorification from, his divided feelings about being with others and fearing their loss. He asked me to help him with his job. He also increasingly faced the fact of his poverty, which he had previously indicated and brushed aside, leaving me, not him, to worry about it. Beyond therapy, he set about remedying his lack of money. He set about furthering the skills he needed to become the good son, husband, father, worker, and friend he had previously imagined he already was in the self-glorifying story with which he had begun.

Conclusion

Therapy—in Len's, Simon's, and many other similar cases—can centrally involve seeking to heal the ills done to sons by division from and loss of early attachment to their mothers and others. These ills, as I have sought to indicate, include such reactions as stammering, recurring nightmares, teenage self-division, schizophrenia, suicide, and manic self-glorification. Their treatment accordingly entails addressing men's early loss of attachment to their mothers. Hence the recent enthusiasm of feminists for Bowlby's attachment theory, with which I began and which is, as I have sought to demonstrate, highly germane to redressing the losses and wrongs done by sexism—in this case to mothers and sons.

WORKS CITED

Barker, P. *The Ghost Road*. London: Viking, 1995.

Bion, W. R. "A Theory of Thinking." In *Second Thoughts*. London: Heinemann, 1962.

————. *The Long Week-End*. London: Free Association Books, 1982.

Bowlby, J. *Maternal Care and Mental Health*. Geneva: World Health Organisation, 1951.

Chodorow, N. *The Reproduction of Mothering*. Berkeley: University of California Press, 1978.

Diekstra, R., et al. "Suicide and Suicidal Behaviour among Adolescents." In *Psychological Disorders in Young People*, edited by M. Rutter and D. Smith. Chichester: Wiley, 1995.

Durkheim, E. *Suicide: A Study in Sociology*. London: Routledge and Kegan Paul, 1952 (1888).

Farrell, W. *The Myth of Male Power*. London: Fourth Estate, 1994.

Freud, S. "Beyond the Pleasure Principle," In *Standard Edition of the Complete Collected Works*, vol. 18, 1920.

Galdos, P., and J. van-Os. "Gender, Psychopathology, and Development." *Schizophrenia Research*, vol. 14, no. 2 (1993): 105-112.

Gilligan, C. "I Don't Want to Talk about It." *New York Times Book Review* (Feb. 16, 1997): 25.

Greenson, R. "Dis-identifying from Mothers." *International Journal of Psycho-Analysis*, vol. 49 (1968): 370–374.

Jablensky, A., et al. "Schizophrenia." In *Psychological Medicine: Monograph Supplement 20*. Cambridge: Cambridge University Press, 1992.

Joyce, J. *A Portrait of the Artist as a Young Man*. London: Penguin Books, 1916.

Laing, R. *The Divided Self*. London: Penguin, 1965.

Laufer, M. "The Central Masturbation Fantasy." *Psychoanalytic Study of the Child*, vol. 31 (1976): 297–316.

MacCarthy, F. *William Morris*. London: Faber, 1994.

Musil, R. *Young Törless*. London: Panther Books, 1906.

Offer, D., et al. "A Study of Quietly Disturbed and Normal Adolescents in Ten Countries." In *International Annals of Adolescent Psychiatry*, edited by A. Z. Schwarberg. Chicago: University of Chicago Press, 1992.

Orbach, S. "Why Is Attachment in the Air?" *Psychoanalytic Dialogues*, vol. 9, no. 1 (1999): 73–83.

Raymond, D. "Homophobia, Identity, and the Meaning of Desire." In *Sexual Cultures and the Construction of Adolescent Identities*, edited by J. Irvine. Philadelphia: Temple University Press, 1994.

Sayers, J. *Boy Crazy: Remembering Adolescence*. London: Routledge, 1998.

Testimony Films. *A Man's World: The Boy*. BBC2, March 6, 1996.

Vallely, P. "When Jon Snow Told His Family Secrets." *The Independent*, 2 (November 1996): 21.

Way, N. *Experiences of Desire, Betrayal, and Intimacy*. New Psychologies Conference, Tarbert, Scotland. June 28–July 1, 1996.

Wedekind, F. *Spring Awakening*. London: Faber, 1995 (1891).

Wight, D. "Boys' Thoughts and Talk about Sex in a Working Class Locality in Glasgow." *Sociological Review*, vol. 42, no. 4 (1994): 703–737.

Yairi, E., and N. Ambrose. "Onset of Stuttering in Preschool Children." *Journal of Speech and Hearing Research*, vol. 35, no. 4 (1992): 782–788.

Young, A. *The Harmony of Illusions*. New Jersey: Princeton University Press, 1995.

12

MOTHER-SON RELATIONSHIPS

IN THE SHADOW OF WAR

Amia Lieblich

This chapter, based on the Israeli-Jewish[1] experience, aims to explicate how the mother-son relationship in modern Israel is deeply linked to the sociopolitical circumstances in which private life is embedded, and in particular to the ongoing state of war and hostility in the Middle East. Thus it demonstrates how in Israel, as probably elsewhere, the private domain of a mother-son relationship interacts with, and is constructed by, the cultural-political sphere. As changes occur in the political arena, they infiltrate the private domain and produce time variations in mother-son relationships. Thus while in some of the phenomena to be described almost no changes have occurred in the last fifty years of Israel's history, others have undergone important transitions. It can be hypothesized that as progress occurs toward achieving peace in the Middle East, we may observe further changes in mother-son relationships in Israel as well as in the Arab states.

The chapter is divided into three parts: 1) The mother-son relationship in the context of obligatory military service—normal life course development; 2) motherhood of soldiers as a political position; and 3) the voice of mothers as mourners. Each of these sections reflects on the topic from a different perspective. The first part deals mainly with the private domain, the second, with the public or cultural domain, and the third represents an interaction of the private and the collective discourse.

1. The mother-son relationship in the context of obligatory military service—normal life course development

In Israel, military service in the Israeli Defense Force (IDF) is compulsory for all eighteen-year-old Jews and lasts three years for men and about two years for women. Although this is the legal requirement, there are several exceptions to this rule. The largest group being released from military duty are Jewish ultra-orthodox males who provide evidence that they are full-time students in religious academies (yeshivas), and orthodox females who declare that service in the military is against their beliefs. Among the nonreligious too, there is a growing number of individuals who manage to get exemption from military duties due to psychological maladjustment or health problems. Nevertheless, the norm that young men and women serve in the army prevails, and this phase of life is a normal part of the Israeli life course developmental pattern, both for the conscripted soldiers and for their parents.[2]

Military service in Israel is considerably more dangerous for men than for women, since combat duties are restricted exclusively to male soldiers. Men also have a longer compulsory service and an almost life-long reserve duty. Therefore, for the majority of Israelis, manhood is highly related to being a soldier, and the relationship of mothers to their sons, from childhood to adulthood, is deeply colored and affected by this fact, as will be demonstrated by four different relevant issues. It should be emphasized, however, that fathers' attitudes and feelings are often similar to those of mothers, and, at any rate, the terms "mother" and "father" should not be taken "essentialistically," but rather as possible modes of experience and relationships which may emerge in the lives of both females and males.[3]

When a boy is born—and on

The birth of a boy in Israel always evokes slightly ambivalent reactions on the mother's part: with all the happiness of having a boy, the birth of every son is anxiety-provoking—because of the imminence of his military service. On the same grounds, many mothers accept daughters with great relief. This anxiety may be conscious or unconscious at different periods and stages of development. Many parents declare immediately after the birth of a boy something like: "If this son will have to serve in the army, we are getting out of here"—a threat that is rarely materialized later on. The most apparent expression of this anxiety is in the saying: "When you grow up, we will have peace, and you will not have to serve in the army"—a saying that has been contradicted so far by three generations of parents and sons serving in the army. A popular song of recent years starts with the words:

> We are the children of the winter of '73.
>> [talking to their parents, and referring to the October 1973 War]
> We were conceived at the end of the war,
> And you promised there will be no more wars when we grow up.
> We know you are honest, and you taught us that promises have to be
>> kept. . . .

As the situation in the Middle East is still far from a peace settlement, the promise of "no more war, no more bloodshed," or "no more army," is frustrated again and again, a frustration that deeply influences the feelings of Israeli mothers toward their sons.

Such feelings find their ways into individual or group therapy sessions in which women share their feelings. The following is a quotation from Sara, a member of a Gestalt-therapy group.[4] (Sara is speaking in the present tense, as usually required in Gestalt therapy. Unspoken reactions of the therapist appear in italics):

> It is a clear summer morning when the idea that my son, Yuval, will become an Israeli soldier materializes in full color for me. He is ten years old. It is the last day of school, before the summer vacation. My son has volunteered to bring a cake to school to celebrate the end of fourth grade, to make this last day a special one. I bake a big cake, put frosting on top to please the children, and walk to school to hand it to the teacher. I arrive in the deserted schoolyard, which seems so vast when all the children are in their classrooms. In the center of this yard a new metal sculpture has been erected. It is a large, brown structure on which the children can climb and play. It has an inscription—a sentence from the Bible about children playing in the streets of Jerusalem. I like the sculpture, yet it makes me sad. I don't know why.

> *Some unconscious fears start to emerge at this point, because the woman "knows" what she will see next.*

> I enter the building slowly, waiting for the bell to ring for the break, and automatically my eyes fall on a stone plate. Engraved on it are the names of all the school graduates who were killed in the wars.

> *This feature is naturally out of place in an elementary school, with students of grades one to six only!*

Brightly colored drawings of students are hanging all over the wall around the plate. From one room I hear children's voices singing: "Jerusalem, City of Peace." Suddenly I know I am going to cry, and I rush outside, back to the sculpture. This time, through the tears, I know why it makes me sad. Now it looks like a monument. I am asking myself: For whom?

And the mother concludes:

Life is rough here on mothers of soldiers and future soldiers. I am frightened by it all. At the same time, there is a sense of value and significance to my life here rather than somewhere else. (Lieblich 1978, 97–98)

Thus the sense of future risk is never far from mothers' awareness as their boys grow up.

On pampering boys

Israeli children are considered to be very free and often undisciplined—boys much more so than girls. Can this be related to the pattern of anxiety and guilt on the part of parents? Clinical material and general observations indicate that boys' upbringing by mothers is often permissive, guided by an unconscious wish to compensate them for future hardships.

Many clinical examples demonstrate this phenomenon. In one of my Gestalt groups, a father of three boys, a new immigrant from Argentina, spoke to his seven-year old son—represented by an empty chair—after bringing up his problems in getting this boy to obey him. At the end of the therapy session he reached an understanding that in making his choice to move to Israel, he had actually determined the future of his sons to go to the army. He said:

I hope it will be more peaceful here when you grow up and your turn to serve in the army comes around. Sometimes I feel guilty for making the choice for you, for the fact is I am afraid it will still be wartime when you're eighteen, or when your brothers are. I pray to God you'll all survive.

This work helped the father in understanding the origin of his feelings toward his sons and in making clear his demands from them.

A similar example is of a mother of a thirteen-year-old, who asked to work in the group on her relationship with her son. After starting to speak about her difficulty in disciplining him, for example in keeping his room in order, she recalls an episode that happened recently when they went shopping together for gym training clothes:

> Dan is never fancy in his clothing. . . . But in the store, he suddenly picks out the most expensive outfit, some imported goods of very high quality. . . . He insists on having just this one, and I feel very displeased. No, even worse, I feel angry. . . . Although I am not usually tight-fisted, not at all.

As she reflected on her reactions she had what she called a "terrible thought," and she heard an "inner voice" telling her:

> How dare you? He is becoming a young man, and pretty soon he will be a soldier, and then what? If the worst happens. . . . You have to compensate him now. There is no time, you have to make him happy, give him the best possible childhood, since as a young man in Israel, who knows? (Lieblich 1978, 110)

These short excerpts demonstrate how parents' lenient relationships with their sons are influenced by their feelings of guilt regarding the future risk involved in their sons' service in the army.

Growing apart

Since women do not experience the same military service as men, a distance or even a gap often materializes between mothers and sons as the time approaches for their military service. In preparation for their future in the military, boys turn to other men—fathers, brothers, or male teachers. Women are rejected as not understanding the real world of men. Within the family, boys—especially those who see themselves as combat soldiers or members of elite units in the future—often draw closer to their fathers, who are more likely to support their choices, to show pride in them, and to provide expertise and contacts. Women's fears and worries are scorned, and the mother's voice is silenced and repressed in an attempt not to discourage her son from "acting like a man." The world of men, fathers, and boys grows gradually apart from the world of mothers, sisters, and girlfriends, and a "macho" culture, where masculinity and militarism intermingle, is greatly reinforced.[5]

Being protected

At eighteen, the age when one may begin to establish an egalitarian relationship between parents and children, boys are conscripted and given uniforms and guns, symbolizing their social, functional legitimization for feeling/acting superior to all women, including their mothers.[6] The major role of the soldier, even at this young age, is "to protect women and children." On the surface, a complete reversal in roles and power positions takes effect in the family. At the same time, research demonstrates that young soldiers are highly dependent on parental help and solicitude during military service (Lieblich 1989), and the participation of the entire family in the various ordeals of their sons is a well-known feature of Israeli society. Thus, even though "a child remains always a child of his mother," the shift in social roles and responsibilities cannot go unnoticed in the interpersonal and intrapersonal space connecting mothers and sons.

A single mother of a recently drafted young man told the author in an interview an anecdote which clearly demonstrates how mothers experience the shift from protecting to being protected:

> On Thursday morning I saw him off at the bus depot, one of about a hundred young boys, all in shorts and sandals, as if they go together to a summer camp, not to the army. . . . But the feelings among the parents, as I clearly noticed, were so heavy! And yet, I was not prepared for the encounter the next day, on Friday, when Amir was sent home for Shabbat, already a soldier. As he came home with his new uniform, his boots, and a gun, he looked so much taller and more serious. The first thing he did as he came home was to look for a safe place to put his rifle away, till he returns to camp on Sunday. He was going around the apartment with his gun, searching for the most secure location, while I followed him, behind him. I didn't make any suggestions to him, it was his responsibility, not mine. And suddenly I realized—now Amir is the stronger and more adult between us. He is beyond my protection. My safety will be in his young hands. All I can do is just watch him from afar and pray for him.

Thus the so-called traditional feminine passivity and dependence become all the more salient in comparison to the social-military power given to the son, the young male, the soldier. Family life of mothers and their sons, the soldiers, have other specific manifestations which are beyond the scope of the present discussion.

2. Motherhood of soldiers as a political position

A different perspective on the relations of mothers and sons in the shadow of war concerns the public domain and mothers' role in the political sphere. Many important questions can be raised in this area: What is the place of women in peace movements and political protest? Does being a woman—and a mother on top of it—impose a certain view in the political world? Does the fact that women relatively lack resources, and are more distant from the institutionalized power positions like the army and government, make them more sensitive to changes in society and more aware of dangers which may threaten it? Do these factors lead to special feminine practices of activism and protest? Are mothers closer and do they show more empathy to pain, suffering, and the subordination of others? Does the mere fact of being a mother dictate an immanent tendency to protect her children and therefore be more adamant in pursuing peace?

Sara Ruddick (1989) strongly supported the position underlying the last question (apparently essentialist), claiming that there is a direct link between the practice of care, as in mothering, and a pacifist political stand. According to Ruddick, motherhood has a social-political significance, since from its practice peace-aspiring patterns of thinking and awareness have to emerge. This neo-Marxist position has been severely criticized by other feminist scholars, who see womanhood and motherhood as socially constructed, having no predetermined values, attitudes, or habits.

This debate can hardly be solved, however, using Israeli data. A vast majority of Israeli adult females are mothers,[7] and therefore it is impossible to compare fairly mothers to nonmothers. Like men, Israeli mothers are distributed among all parties and political camps. In Women in Black, a prominent protest movement against occupation of the West Bank, whose sole activism for six years was regular Friday noon gatherings on picket-lines in several urban intersections, 75 percent of the women were mothers (Helman and Rapoport)—a high rate considering the fact that many of the protesting women were young, unmarried students. When interviewed, one of the Women in Black first said: "I don't care what others think and feel here, whether they are feminist or gather here to prove something to men. I'm here only because of my sons, so that they will not have to serve as soldiers in the occupied territories" (quoted by Helman and Rapoport, 180).

Mothers are at least as prominent among the right-wing. In one of the settlements in the occupied territories, religiously orthodox mothers (each having seven to thirteen children) participated with their children in a sit-in against banning new settlements. When interviewed, they also declared that the whole point of their demonstration is a struggle for peace and security for their children (Elor). However, their definition of peace is different and may look "messianic" and "colonial" to some of the more moderate Israeli citizens.

Motherhood of soldiers as a separate status legitimizing political activism in Israel came to public attention recently with the emergence of the new protest movement named Four Mothers. The term "four mothers" relates to the four women who started the movement, all mothers of combat soldiers in active service. But it has a biblical connotation, too, referring to *the* four matriarchs of the Jewish nation—Sara, Rivka, Rachel, and Lea. The Four Mothers protest movement was born on a tragic night in 1997, in which two IDF helicopters transporting soldiers to their duty in South Lebanon, collided and crashed, leading to the loss of seventy-three Israeli soldiers and officers. Four female kibbutz members from the north of Israel, whose sons—all graduates of the same regional high school—were serving in elite combat units at the time, decided to initiate political activities toward immediate, unilateral withdrawal from Lebanon, where most casualties among Israeli soldiers have occurred in the last few years. The movement's public activities started in August 1997. Since then, it has been able to mobilize a lot of action, interest, and identification—as well as vehement opposition. Although the core of activists consists of no more than ten women, more than ten thousand individuals signed petitions expressing their identification with the Four Mothers.[8] Among their activities were demonstrations in public locations, such as the front of the Security Ministry building in Tel Aviv or along the border with Lebanon, picket-lines in traffic intersections, as well as meetings with the prime minister and members of the cabinet, the Knesset, and the diplomatic corps. Their actions were highly creative—for example, in a demonstration on the border, flying white balloons with the picture of a dove to Lebanon. Among their famous posters, raised in demonstrations and also displayed as a bumper sticker are those saying: "Out in peace from Lebanon" and "Stop war. We want our sons back home."

In their discourse through the mass media, spokeswomen for the movement said that as mothers of soldiers who might pay the highest price for the Israeli position in Lebanon, they have the moral right to evoke a public debate on, and support for, the withdrawal. They said that while their sons keep fighting, they do all they can for their sons. In several interviews they said: "Enough with feminine helplessness and avoidance of political action" and "We gave birth to these sons, we raised them, and handed them to the army on a silver tray. It is now our duty to act for their survival." They said that they advocate one supreme value, the holiness of life. They refuse to accept the "masculine distorted thought pattern that war is the solution for conflicts, or that it is a heroic challenge." Furthermore, they refuse to accept the claim that Israelis are on the defense, that we are the victims, and that the ongoing loss of lives of Israeli soldiers in South Lebanon is the minimal price required for maintaining security of the north of Israel.

Not surprisingly, public opponents to the movement on various levels claimed that these are "hysterical women" (although the movement included men!), who have no experience in the army and absolutely no understanding of the complicated political situation in the Middle East. One can assume that the status of mothers-of-soldiers actually protects them from even more severe attempts to silence their voice. During the summer of 1997, a new movement—Three Fathers, also referring to the three biblical patriarchs—was announced by fathers of soldiers in Kiryat Shmone, the northern town that suffers most from hostilities from Lebanon. This group argued that the Israeli Defense Force should remain in Lebanon and protect the north, and that "women who sit in coffee bars in Tel Aviv have no right to experiment on the safety of our babies in Kiryat Shmone." This movement ceased to exist immediately after its only public appearance, however, while the Four Mothers persists in its protest activities.

The following quote from Irit Letzter, an activist of Four Mothers, succinctly expresses their credo, using the old myth of the binding of Itzchak:

> I am a mother of four. When my eldest son went to the army, and volunteered to the paratroopers, I had such a panic reaction, that right away I got pregnant with another child—a girl this time, thank God. She is now a year and a half old. I know the association is terrible, it terrifies me, too, but that's a mother's instinct, there's nothing you can do. . . . When God told Abraham: "Go get your son, your only one, the one you love, Itzchak"—Abraham obeyed right away, he didn't argue with God. Had God asked Sara for the same, she would have certainly said: "Go away, forget it. I will not sacrifice this child." (*Ha-Aretz*, Jan. 2, 1998)

The idea that fathers, more than mothers, would be willing to sacrifice their sons is highly provocative and, so far, beyond empirical support. It implies, however, the existence of a notion that Ruddick (1989) termed "maternal thinking" which one hopes might have the power to reduce violence in the world.

3. The voice of mothers as mourners

The third and last perspective to be explored in this paper, as a manifesta-tion of mother-son relationships in the shadow of war, focuses on loss and mourning, and represents the interaction of the private and collective dis-course on this subject. There is no doubt that bereaved mothers (and other family members) are—like their sons—victims of a tragedy. Is their loss any different because their sons were killed in a war or a political strug-gle, rather than by a disease or a car accident? In what way is this tragedy a social role as well as a personal experience?

During the fifty years since the establishment of the state of Israel, more than twenty-two thousand Israeli soldiers have been killed in military ser-vice. A vast proportion of these casualties is, of course, male, since women have rarely been exposed on the front line in combat functions. Bereaved families are very common in Israeli society; everybody knows some. As psy-chologists usually comment, for parents, the death of their grown-up son or daughter is the hardest loss from which to recover.

In the past, the mother who lost her son in a "just war," defending the homeland, has been one of the most powerful images of the hegemonic Zionist culture. Like Mary and Jesus in the dyadic position of the "pieta," so has the sorrow of bereaved Israeli mothers been depicted in pictures and poetry. A mother who had given life to her son was then presented as the tragic heroine facing his death. In the discourse of loss of this kind, the primordial, biological, mother-son relationship, which is aimed at giving life and protection from harm, is confronted with the national relationship between citizen and state, which—in two steps—has first taken the child from his mother, and then taken his life from him. In public discourse, the mother frequently represents the nation as its symbol. Indeed, many languages use the term "motherland." In Hebrew as well, "moledet"—homeland, and "yoledet"—mother, the one who bears children, have the same root.

The individual loss of each son is also a collective, national loss, as in the famous quotation from Jeremiah the prophet: "A voice is heard in Ramah, lamentation and bitter weeping, Rachel is weeping for her children, she refuses to be comforted for her children, because they are not" (Jer. 31: 15). This point has been made universally for other nations as well, as in the following quote: "The nation . . . as a mother who lost her sons in bat-tle, is a frequent part of the particular nationalistic discourse in national liberation struggles or other forms of national conflicts, when men are called to fight 'for the sake of our women and children' or to 'defend their honor'" (Hutchinson and Smith, 311).

In Israeli culture, a very famous male poet, Uri Zvi Grinberg, known as the poet of the nationalist camp, presents most of these ideas in a five-part poem. It was written during the War of Independence in November, 1948. The poem is titled "By Virtue of a Mother, Her Son, and Jerusalem."[9] It describes a mother whose son was killed in battle (in Hebrew "fell," a term used much less in English) trying to open up the blocked road to Jerusalem. The poem presents the narrative of a single mother whose whole world darkens and shatters as her son dies. At first she loses the will to live. But she copes with her tragedy and finds a way to accept her bereavement, and integrates her private experience with the collective Jewish history of loss and redemption. This integration, says the poet, is the true victory, the spiritual-moral war triumph of the mother—even though the battle came to nothing. Dan Miron (1992), in his analysis of this poem, points to the curious fact that the father is totally absent from this poem, so that a complete love story unfolds between mother and son. The death of the son is conceived as the mother's defeat in a duel with her rival—another female lover, namely Jerusalem. But the woman loves Jerusalem, too, and, at the end of the poem, she invokes the people and the soldiers never to forsake it, for any price at all.

The following lines clearly demonstrate the spirit of taking the private loss into the public domain:

> A mother laments her son.
> My son, my son, nine months of labor
> nights before pregnancy, nights of longing.
> How were you lost, my own flesh and blood. . . .
> My son fell among the heroes, my son was a hero
> on the way to Jerusalem, thirsty for blood.
> She, too, is our mother, and my son—her son
> and he's all hers now.

And, at the very end of the poem:

> By virtue of a mother who donated her son as a torch for your night
> your dawn will break and your army will soon march high.

This is a representative example of the cultural discourse in Israel until the beginning of the 1980s, when the atmosphere started to change. Until then, Israeli mothers of soldiers killed in action were presented—both in the mass media and in art—as state symbols, as heroines, and as victims. At present, following a general cultural trend, individualistic modes of discourse and experience have taken over this area as well, as will be soon demonstrated.

While held up as public symbols, however, bereaved mothers of the past were silenced by society, their voices not to be heard. For both mothers and fathers, the highest level of valor was in carrying their pain in silence, in other words—according to the Western culture—in a masculine manner. In his recent book about the Sabra, the first generation of native-born Israelis Oz Almog (1997) describes funerals and mourning practices in the first thirty years of the state's existence. He characterizes the entire Israeli culture of that period as suppressing emotions, especially pain and sadness. In military funerals, no crying was heard in public from either men or women. Open emotional manifestation was considered to be weakness as well as "primitive" behavior (Ben-Ari; Lieblich 1978, 1989). Moreover, crying was interpreted as protest against the need for and justness of fighting—something totally taboo at the time. This norm seems to be highly masculine and probably harder to practice for mothers than fathers. Men, as fathers, were at least given the voice of the rituals of Jewish religious mourning, such as in saying Kadish in public after their sons. The voice of mothers (and other females) was totally silenced, their needs for emotional expression completely denied. Their self-control was considered as signifying patriotism. It also conveyed the message that "I can take care of myself, I will not fall as a burden on others, who have more important, national duties to carry out."

Recently, with the decline of nationalistic ideologies, the rise of the peace movements, the crumbling of consensus about the need for war, and the greater influence of Sephardic subculture, there has been a change in this trend in Israel. Today, the private sphere and normal individual needs are not dominated to the same extent by the public sphere and the needs of the collective (Samocha). Recently, mothers' voices, women's voices, have been heard more in mourning. Men, too, cry more—even young soldiers often cry in public at funerals. The practices of mourning and the discourse about the dead have been returned to the private, feminine realm.[10]

There are many expressions of this trend. Women speak in public, in emotional and personal terms, about theirs sons. Many families resent the ready-made clichés of national language concerning the tragedy of their sons. This was manifested, for example, in opposing the standard inscriptions on soldiers' tombstones, which used to be determined by the state and was identical for all soldiers, and requesting the right of free expression in this context, which is not only individualized but frequently subversive (Bilu). In other words, women as mothers are taking their rightful place as mourners for their sons and in doing so, they change the entire discourse around death in military action.

A recent interview with Manuella Deviri, a bereaved mother, stirred much interest as well as protest in Israeli press and media. Many letters were received by the newspapers following her interview, several of them claiming that Deviri's interview signifies the end of the "cult of bereavement" in Israeli culture.[11] It is certainly not a lonely voice in Israeli society today. Deviri, an Israeli-Italian woman, talked to a female journalist Neri Livna, who published the interview in *Ha-Aretz* on July 31, 1998. Deviri's youngest son, Yoni, had been killed in Lebanon on February 26, 1998. Two generations down from Grinberg's heroic mother (although there are still sectors of Israeli society that would see Grinberg's depiction as completely relevant), Deviri is not crying in public, yet refuses to be politically silenced. She is speaking out loudly against the "holy cows of bereavement"[12] and especially the image of the bereaved mother. She says:

> To be a bereaved mother is such a big and meaningful title that from this terrible moment of the night of the 26th of February, when I was informed that I earned this title, for many people I ceased to be Manuella Deviri the woman, the human being. . . . Even if for a moment I felt that, okay, something terrible has happened to me, but I am still alive—nobody would let me.
>
> What people actually tell me all the time since then is that "you are a broken person, all you do or say just proves it. You are not a whole person anymore, don't pretend to talk or to act like one. You are a bereaved mother, don't smile, don't laugh—and, God forbid, don't dance at weddings. If you don't cry and lament all day long, it means you are not a bereaved mother as you ought to be. . . . If you don't look like your life is totally ruined, it means you didn't love your child enough."
>
> One of the problems of bereavement is that its description is so banal. Everyone is sick and tired of watching TV pictures of mothers crying on their sons' graves. If until now more than 22,000 people lost their lives here, it means that their parents all adjust to their suffering, bend down and take life for what it is. But this show cannot go on!

Her reaction to what she calls a "show" is both personal and political:

> I personally do not think that since I feel so much pain, it is impossible for me to feel glad and happy at the same time. . . . One of the first

things I said after Yoni was killed—that it's enough that he died, there is no need to ruin our lives, too. Anyway, you cannot kill Yoni twice—first when he was killed, and second, when I, also, die with him.

I think that it is harder for fathers. Because women's business is to bear a child and to grow it, and it's men's business to send boys out of the shelter to do war. Therefore fathers feel more guilty. Women are more flexible, more creative. In the funeral, I was the only person who did not cry, for I knew I had to support all the others, my husband as well as Yoni's brother and sister.

The real danger [of this situation is that] you can fall easily into this narcissistic trap and adopt this stance of the bereaved mother. For me, the significance of Yoni's death is that I have discovered how meaningless I am, and that the only thing I can do is to be truthful, to say only the truth from now on. I feel that Yoni's death has given me a great clarity of vision. Suddenly I have no more patience for non-sense.

There are many lies (bluffs) involved in this title of a bereaved mother, and I would like to expose them. The first one is in this saying that "we all hurt with you," "we are a big family in this." I think that if it were true that we all suffer with you, then we would have stopped it a long time ago.

By "it" she means simply the state of war between Israel and the Arabs.

My first duty towards Yoni, the child who keeps living inside me, is to say the truth all the time, never to be silenced again. Not to let people forget for a moment that Israel must withdraw from Lebanon, must make peace with the Palestinians. Perhaps, if I had done something for these goals before, Yoni would not have been killed. I am so angry with myself for not being active before, for not doing something which might have prevented his death and my disaster. The most important thing is to be politically active. If instead of Four Mothers we had ten thousand mothers, mothers whose sons are not with us anymore, if these mothers were not crying on graves but loudly protesting, our situation would have been different.

When the journalist, impressed with her intensity, asked her why her words carry more weight or validity than anyone else's, Deviri's simple answer is "because I had already paid the price."

Deviri's voice represents a new composition of private and public languages, of the feminine and masculine voices and modes of being, in today's Israeli discourse. The time has perhaps come for mothers, "new" kinds of mothers, individualist, feminist, and daring, to enter the public arena in Israel for their sons' sake, for their own sake, and for the sake of the future.

NOTES

1. Israeli citizens are Jewish (the majority) or Arab (the minority). The topic of Arab mothers and sons in Israel deserves a separate presentation.

2. See, for example, Lieblich 1989.

3. This part of the chapter is based on several studies using the life interview method from 1975 onward, on records of Gestalt group therapy sessions with Israelis (Lieblich 1978), on a variety of cultural materials, and also on the author's personal experience as a mother of two adult sons who have served in combat units in the IDF.

4. The Gestalt groups mentioned in this paper were led by me, as part of my professional work, from 1970 onward. For further details see Lieblich 1978.

5. On this point see also Ben-Ari; Ben-Ari and Lomsky-Feder.

6. This is, according to Israeli feminists, one of the main reasons for the weakness of the feminist movement in Israel. Women do not feel they deserve full equality as long as they do not share the risks and perils of military combat service.

7. According to the last census conducted in Israel, in 1995, 76.8% of Jewish females over eighteen have had at least one child. This figure is, however, considered by experts (e.g., David Newman, the Central Statistical Bureau, personal communication) as a greatly underestimated rate, since the ultra-Orthodox did not participate in the census, and their fertility rates are very high.

8. Most of the facts and quotes on the Four Mothers movement are based on a thorough review of all items in which the movement's actions were reported or mentioned in the daily paper *Ha-Aretz*, the most serious—yet left-oriented—newspaper in Israel.

9. For a complete analysis of this work, see Miron, 141–152. All translations into English are mine.

10. See Gur; Hendle; and Naveh. The works of Hendle and Gur are novels on bereaved families, and present, in particular, the individual anti-collective voices of bereaved mothers. Both of the authors are female Israeli writers. Gur's novel is based on a real story.

11. See *Ha-Aretz*, Letters, Aug. 7, 1998 and Aug. 14, 1998.

12. Translated from Hebrew by the author.

WORKS CITED

Almog, O., *The Sabra—A Portrait.* Tel Aviv: Am Oved 1997 (Hebrew).

Ben-Ari, E. *Mastering Soldiers: Conflicts, Emotions and the Enemy in an Israeli Military Unit.* Oxford: Berghahn Books, 1998.

Ben-Ari, E., and E. Lomsky-Feder. "Military, Identity and War in Israel: Cultural Constructions." In *The Military and Militarism in Israeli Society,* edited by E. Lonsky-Feder and E. Ben Ari. Albany: State University of New York Press, in press.

Bilu, Y. *Transformations in the Construction of War-Related Loss and Suffering in Israeli Society.* in press.

Elor, T. "The Rachelim Event." In *Alpayim, A Multidisciplinary Publication for Contemporary Thought and Literature,* 7 (1993): 59–81. (Hebrew).

Gur, B. *A Stone for a Stone.* Jerusalem: Keter, 1998.

Helman, S., and T. Rapoport. "Women in Black." *Theoria u-bikoret,* 10 (1997): 175–192. (Hebrew).

Hendle, J. *The Mountain of the Erring.* Tel Aviv: Kibbutz Ha-Meuchad, 1991. (Hebrew)

Hutchinson, J., and A. D. Smith, eds. *Nationalism.* Oxford and New York: Oxford University Press, 1994.

Lieblich, A. *Tin Soldiers on Jerusalem Beach.* New York: Pantheon, 1978.

———. *Transitions to Adulthood during Military Service.* New York: State University of New York Press, 1989.

———. Private records of a Gestalt group.

Miron, D. *Facing the Silent Brother: Studies in the Poetry of the War of Independence.* Jerusalem: Keter, 1992. (Hebrew).

Naveh, C. "On Loss, Bereavement and Mourning in Israeli Experience." *Alpayim,* 16 (1998): 85–120. (Hebrew).

Ruddick, S. *Maternal Thinking.* New York: Ballantine Books, 1989.

Samocha, S. "Transition in Israeli Society—Fifty Years. *Alpayim: A Multidisciplinary Publication for Contemporary Thought and Literature,* 17 (1999): 239–261.(Hebrew).

13

THIS IS LEAVE-TAKING

MOTHERS, SIGNATURES,

AND COUNTERMEMORY

Douglas Sadao Aoki

Calligraphy by June Yuriko Aoki

> *. . . a use of history that severs its connection to*
> *memory, its metaphysical and anthropological model,*
> *and constructs a counter-memory—a trans-formation*
> *of history into a totally different form of time.*
> *—Michel Foucault*

This is the story of the conference that my mother wouldn't attend. Her name is June Yuriko Aoki. She was supposed to be there—or at least I supposed that she would be there. When I learned about the York University conference on mothers and sons, I called her long-distance to ask if she would like to go and speak with me about our relationship as *nisei* (second-generation Japanese-Canadian) mother and *sansei* (third-generation) son. I hoped that she would say yes, mostly because this would have been a rare chance for us to share my professional world. I also thought, with some self-satisfaction, that we might embody a celebration of mother and son. She did indeed agree; she said she was happy to do so. She could visit with my younger brother and his family, who live not far from the conference site. My father, still very much the academic despite retiring years ago, gave his enthusiastic support. Everything was set.

Except shortly thereafter, my brother called me and, barely concealing his incredulity and contempt, told me that it was a very bad idea. After speaking with me, my mother had called him in a panic, saying that she didn't think she could do it, but she did not want to disappoint me. She also pleaded with my brother not to tell me what she had said. He assured her that he would not, and promptly did. I was forced to admit my foolishness and inferiority to my brother, who once again demonstrated that he remembered much better than I what it means to be the son of a *nisei* woman. After a judicious day's wait, I dialed my parents' number again and let her off the hook.

Thus my mother never went to the conference. Instead, she stayed home and waited for me to call and let her know how my presentation fared in her absence. I was left to speak of mothers and sons without her. This was immediately problematic. As my brother would surely ask—as he undoubtedly will ask—on what possible dubious authority could I speak of my mother? Because to speak *of* her was inevitably to speak *for* her, and regardless of how far I regularly fell short of being the feminist that I regularly professed to be, I retained enough of feminism's convictions to remain wary of any man who would once more appropriate and displace a woman's voice. When I stood before the audience at my session, I could not escape the feeling that I was, in a pernicious but ineluctable way, attempting to stand in for my mother, to take her place.

I might have insisted that she was there nonetheless, in me. There is the precedent of another son, who wrote, "Whatever I imagine I know is taken from my mother's body"[1] (a curiously provocative turn of phrase, where imagination claims the necessity of its mediation of a body of knowledge). The banality of genetic inheritance, mirrored in the common desire to find oneself in one's children, gives both biological and psychoanalytic credence to such imagining. Just like many other sons and many other parents, I can look at photographs of my mother when she was young and discover myself in drag, or I look in my son's face and find my mother's mouth.[2] Yet to claim the undeniability of the embodiment of filiation is still to prevaricate. My mother has given me so much of herself, but that does not mean she has given me herself. Blood is never that thick. If I am to reiterate that she was there *in herself* with me at the conference and still here with me now, in however partial a way, I am obligated to offer something which profoundly eludes my possession. The necessity, then, is to give something I do not have.

My Mother and Her Mother: This Is Leave-Taking

Here is what I offer (see fig. 1).

This is my mother's writing, which she sent to me and, through me, to you. Not writing reduced to the text or to meaning, as we in the West are wont to do, this writing is more meaningful than meaning. Lacan argues that the signifier is the "material of language," while meaning is merely imaginary (Lacan, 1993, 32, 54). In that sense, this writing is the materiality of my mother's hand, in all of its equivocality of flesh and ink. This is what she sent of herself.

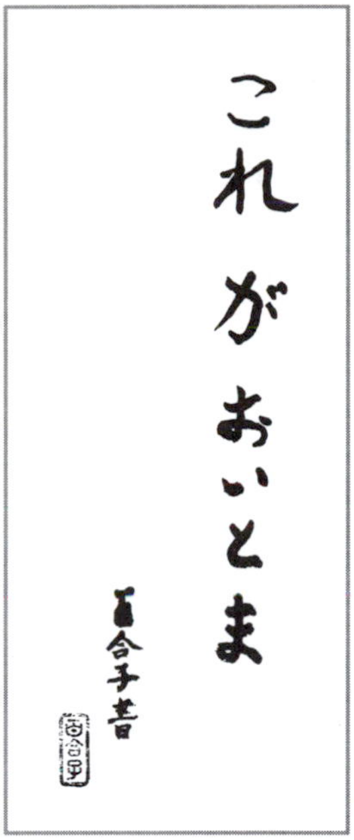

これがおいとま

百合子書

Figure 1

I think it is beautiful, although I hardly have an expert's eye. For the Japanese, calligraphy has an aesthetic status that is of a different magnitude from even the finest drafting of letters in the West. In fact, its aesthetics exceeds itself, for it is a *jutsu*, an art, which has been raised to the status of a *dō*, a way of the national spirit. Japanese calligraphy thus short-circuits the world to materialize Lacan's raising of the signifier above the signified, in an inversion of the Saussurean sign (1977, 147).[3] That is, the form of the character/signifier in calligraphy gains a crucial ascendance over its "literal" meaning/signifier because of the philosophical esteem that Japanese tradition has for its aesthetics. There is another parallel between Parisian psychoanalysis and Japanese letters, one that has a peculiar personal force. Lacan's other notable revision of the Saussurean sign is to eliminate the oval surround that contains and unites the sign, thereby foregrounding the bar that separates the signifier from the signified. In other words, Lacan's sign is constituted through a barring of the signified from the signifier, which is the barring of the passage of meaning itself. I am barred from the "meaning" of Mom's calligraphy in several important ways, not the least being that I am too much a son and a *sansei*, and too little a Japanese, to be a fair judge of how well Mom's brushwork fares against the elevated standard of *dō*. That doesn't really matter to me. I think her calligraphy is beautiful, although I know it has become a little shaky.

But I can't read it.

I know what it says, but only because Mom told me. I can pronounce the characters, *kore ga oitoma*, after a fashion and with a bad accent, but only because she coached me. Today I cannot read Japanese at all, except for a pitifully few characters. I can barely recognize my own name in Japanese, and I write it much worse than I say it. My name's language is vastly and irrefutably different from my own. It is strange to be alienated by one's own name, but stranger still to realize that such alienation is the gift of a more common divided heritage: my surname, *Aoki*, is my father's name and remains so, even though it is now also my mother's. Each and every time I say our name, especially on those occasions when I enunciate it with care for the non-Japanese ear, my insistence on a "proper" pronunciation asserts an authenticity to which I have no legitimate claim. A "real" Japanese might well laugh at the way I say *Aoki*, except she would likely be too polite to do so openly. She might well say, at least to herself, that I cannot even say who I am.

This wasn't always the case. When I was young—when I was just my mother's boy—I spent each Saturday morning in Japanese school, in the warm, bright kitchen of my paternal grandparents. They were school-teachers who immigrated early in the century so that Japanese-Canadian children might learn their Japanese letters, and they dutifully continued that tradition around their kitchen table in the 1960s for young *sansei* like me, growing up on the prairies. But then they moved to Vancouver and we moved to Edmonton, and my rudimentary grasp faded away. Now, like many *sansei*, all I remember is a handful of words. Ironically, among them are the names of the Japanese systems of letters that I have forgotten. In my mother's calligraphy, elements of *hiragana*, the simpler syllabary, rise above the more elaborate *kanji* beneath them. She says that together the characters mean, "This is leave-taking." I can only believe her. So here is that crucial piece of June Yuriko Aoki herself, something that always resists my appropriation. My mother's voice metonymizes through her hand—and now, of course, through mine.

This citation of my mother, like any strategy of disavowing appropriation, must fail even if it succeeds.[4] Questions are immediately begged: "Why this calligraphy? Why these words? Why this leave-taking?" The answer that must be admitted is: "Because I asked for them." They are my mother's words, but they remain my choices. I asked Mom to write this particular calligraphy for two reasons. First, because its weight in our mutual worlds far exceeds its meaning, its articulation, or its translation—this is why it is more meaningful than meaning. Second, because something special happens when my mother writes out words that are at once her own and not her own. And third, because these words are passed to me from not just my mother, but also her mother, and her mother's mother. To be accurate, these words were not spoken by Mom but transcribed by her. This is what her mother said to her, in a transgenerational iteration.

I remember my grandmother vividly. Her name was Tomo Yoshida or, in the Japanese order of things, Yoshida Tomo, but she was always just Grandma to me. My parents and my little sister and I would go and visit her and Grandpa in their dark, cramped farmhouse (such a mysteriously different place from the bright kitchen of my schoolteaching paternal grandparents), where she would stroke my head and croon Japanese that was no less comforting for being incomprehensible. I was only seven years old when she died, but that was old enough to remember. Many years later, Mom told me about *kore ga oitoma*, which is a story of Grandma's passing. Mom was at the hospital attending to Grandma, who was almost completely consumed by the cancer within her. As my mother knelt to lace up her shoes, Grandma leaned over and gently grasped my mother's face, and said: "*Kore ga oitoma.*" Those were the last words that she ever spoke.

The striking thing was that Mom at the time did not know what those words meant. While she was fluent in Japanese—at least as fluent as any girl growing up in an isolated Vancouver Island village could be (she was later accused of speaking like a lumberjack by a professor of Japanese)—the expression was strange and impenetrable to her. At the time, Mom assumed that they were well-intentioned but essentially meaningless, bubbled up from looming death and its mollifying drugs. Still, she did remember the shape and sound of the words, the tremulous materiality of signifiers upon the air. More than a decade later, when she was refining her Japanese at the University of British Columbia, she pored through her expensive dictionaries and discovered, to her astonishment, that *kore ga oitoma* is the most formal way possible of saying farewell. Years before, it had been the extremity of that formality that had confounded her, because of its deliberate estrangement from familiar discourse, but now that same extremity both moved and comforted her. I can think of no better emblem of the Japanese-Canadian ethos, at least as Mom lived and lives it, than that embodiment of the ultimate in intimacy via the strictest of impersonal form.

Kore ga oitoma therefore effortlessly wings across all the generations of Mom's life. She wrote it for me so you could see it, but even here and now it reaches back to her beloved mother. And back again and even further, for it cannot be separated from another generational story. Grandma was *issei*, or first-generation—a linguistic nicety that immediately implodes, for no one could ever have been the *first* generation. Such is the generative definition of motherhood: everyone has always had a mother, so there was always a generation before. Every mother, even though she is the archetypal embodiment of birth, repudiates the solemnities of the origin (Foucault 1977, 143). Motherhood constitutes and defines the perpetuation of passage figured in the delivery of childbirth. It passes from body to body, from mother to son and mother to daughter.

So instead let us say that in 1918 Grandma was of that Japanese generation that was conventionally the first to leave for Canada. When she set sail, she promised her mother that she would return in a year. But, through the common vagaries of emigration, war, relocation, and sometimes poverty, Grandma never saw her mother again. Mom, as a young girl, would watch Grandma gaze past the horizon of Vancouver Island toward Japan and the mother she had lost. Grandma never had the chance to say *kore ga oitoma* to her own mother, never had the chance to hear it from her. But then, through the decades of longing for her mother, Grandma remained so devout that she never doubted that she would see her again, in the glorious company of Buddha.

Or perhaps I have it wrong. Perhaps *kore ga oitoma* was exactly what Grandma's mother said to her when Grandma set sail; perhaps her mother somehow knew exactly what Grandma could not possibly believe, that Grandma's passage to Canada was indeed the final leave-taking, and that it was necessary and merciful for any farewell to be veiled in a way that would not be understood until much later.[5] Perhaps, then, Grandma's loving farewell to my mother was a final gift, a passage of her own mother's farewell. This fragment phrase is the only thing I know of my great-grandmother, besides that of Okumura, the family name Grandma took from her and left behind. And even this knowledge turns out to be ambivalent. In my profound ignorance and loss, I cannot know which of these histories of *kore ga oitoma* might be "true," if either. Yet it does not really matter. Grandma and Mom have at least given me a haunting possibility, one of an endlessly repeated passage of *kore ga oitoma* stretching back into the shrouded ancient history of Japan, pronounced and echoed by a line of women who have lost even their patronyms, the names that were never theirs, but who will nonetheless be forever connected by leave-taking. Nameless, these women cannot constitute a history; unremembered, they can persist in no recollection. Yet they still abide, though severed from history and memory, through my mother and in her countermemory.

My Mother and My Son: Obligated to Philosophy

Mom has told me the story of *kore ga oitoma* often. She has always liked to repeat her stories, and I have always teased her about it, only half-feigning my exasperation as I flash my fingers in front of me, indicating that I have heard that particular story five or ten times before. But I never tire of hearing the story of *kore ga oitoma*. In fact, I never really tire of hearing any stories about Grandma. The homely magic of them, conjuring that smiling wrinkled face, never falters. These days, Mom repeats her stories more often. About two years ago, she had a series of small strokes, so small that they were not diagnosed until some indefinite time afterward. Because of those little catastrophes of blood and mind, Mom's short-term memory is not very good anymore. She is still funny and outgoing, and if you spend just a couple of minutes with her, she seems very together, especially for a seventy-year-old. But if you linger a couple more, she will start brightly saying the same things she just said and asking the same questions she just asked, and it will become very apparent that something is not right, that something has been lost.

Mom herself knows her memory is unreliable, and despite the doctors' reassurances that her condition has not materially deteriorated, it does appear to be slowly getting worse. She constantly apologizes and berates herself for her failures of memory. When she came to visit us last summer, I peeked in her bedroom while she was supposed to be napping, and I caught the confusion on her face as she struggled with all her might to remember and did not succeed. It is partially because I saw forgetting made flesh in her face then that I wanted her with me at the mothers- and sons-conference. But of course, the fact of her forgetting is also exactly why she did not want to come. The strokes are also why her calligraphy has become a little shaky.

Yet short- and long-term memory are separate parts of us, and Mom's recollection of her childhood and mine appears undimmed, regardless of the treachery of her remembrance of things not long past. As a result, our conversations now turn through uncanny cycles, where the remembering of the past interleaves with the forgetting of the present, again and again. Mom's history of herself has transfigured her relations to time, which reflects back upon the ongoing narrations of that history. She is no Foucaultian genealogist, but the failure of memory has necessitated her reconfiguration through a kind of countermemory nonetheless, living through what Foucault enumerates as moments of intensity, lapses, extended periods of feverish agitation, fainting spells (1977, 145). She asks the same questions about Alex, her beloved grandson and my son, over and over again, the form of repetition now the very measure of her devotion. She retells the stories of long ago. She re-remembers her mother telling her "*kore ga oitoma*," and retells me that it would be a good thing to write about. And she has given me her calligraphy, which will enter into no historian's narrative of the world. According to Michael Mahon's definition, her current life's work are exactly the methods and manners of countermemory: the dredging up of "forgotten documents, minor statements, apparently insignificant details, in order to recreate the forgotten historical and practical conditions of our present existence" (9). My mother is constructing a countermemory of mothering, and more, for grandmothering is another, if different, form of mothering. She pulls me aside and confides, "I want Alex to remember me."

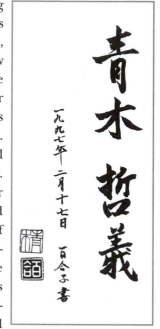

Figure 2

Above Alex's toddler bed hangs another piece of her calligraphy: *Aoki Tetsuyoshi*, his name in Japanese (see fig. 2).[6] This chapter is written between Mom's two calligraphies, and between my mother and my son. Mom wrote *Aoki Tetsuyoshi* to celebrate Alex's birth, and thereby gave him something neither his father nor mother ever could. Yet his name writes out another and different alienation. Alex was a genuine surprise, for he was not supposed to be Alex at all. At a prenatal examination few months before, my wife, Lucy DeFabrizio, had pressed the ultrasonographer for a prediction, and she told us that Lucy was going to have a girl. As a testament to our misplaced faith in medical science, the given names that awaited Alex were *Micheline Helena*, after my late sister and Lucy's mother. The situation forced us to admit we were not truly gender radicals, for we could not keep those names for our son, and we were therefore immediately faced with the problem of renaming. *Alex* emerged from our joint musings. Then, in a spasm of ethnic longing, I suggested that we ask my parents for a Japanese name, and Lucy agreed.

My pleased mother and father went home in the afternoon and

returned with their selection in the evening. Dad produced a paper limned in his elegant hand which diagrammed, in both English and Japanese, how *Tetsuyoshi* united the first part of his name, *Tetsuo*, with the final part of his father's, *Sadayoshi*. He told us that *Tetsuyoshi* meant "obligated to philosophy." Too late, Lucy and I realized, to our chagrin, that we had unwittingly fallen prey to the implacable Japanese reproduction of the father's name and its correlative effacement of the mother's. There was no possibility of refusing the name, although I'm still not sure if that impossibility was instated by our unwillingness to be unkind or my own inability to free myself enough from filial piety. Still, although my mother "officially" assented, she made her characteristic gesture of defiance, there in the hospital: "You can't give him that name; kids will call him 'Tits'!"—which earned her a glare from my always dignified father. But the naming was *fait accompli*, and shortly thereafter my mother brushed *Tetsuyoshi* with love and pride onto rice paper nonetheless.

Lucy and I sometimes rue our decision, although now we cannot think of Alex as anything but Alex. Lucy retroactively but rightfully indicts the severity and sweep of the patronym: all the mothers have been effaced, including and especially hers and herself. The inequity is compounded by the fact that Alex's surname is mine and not hers. That surnaming was a joint and prior agreement, stemming from the profusion of De Fabrizio grandchildren and the absence of any other *yonsei* (fourth-generation) Aokis. Still, the unfairness rankled even then and continues to this day, although we could think of no fairer alternative. After all, Lucy's surname is her father's, just as any tracing back of the passage of a name—a literal genealogy—too quickly arrives at the place where the father eclipses the mother, at least in almost all Canadian and Japanese families. It is a rare person in this country who knows her/his maternal grandmother's maiden name, and much rarer still who knows her/his great-grandmother's. Still, Lucy and I could have and should have done better. Nothing of her Italianness is articulated by *Tetsuyoshi Alexander Aoki*, and we regularly debate the virtues of spending money we do not have to make a name change that would, in whatever limited degree, return Alex to his mother and to his mother's mother.

Yet when I watch over our son as he sleeps, and find my eyes rising to the calm letters above his head, I realize that my mother has found through them another, more indirect and therefore more Japanese, way to return Alex to her and her to him. The issues of sexism and justice that legitimately pertain to the patronym do so only because we habitually reduce a name to what it says. The signifier, Saussure says, is bound to its signified like two sides of a sheet of paper. The presumed function of the name is both to signify and to subjectify: "Alex," I say, and he turns around, in the model performance of interpolation (Althusser, 127–186; Butler). Of course, he has to be awake to turn, yet even when he is asleep, I still come to his room and murmur his name, very softly, "Alex . . . " as if the more quietly I say it, the more precious it will become, and the truer it will be to the silent but ferocious love beneath the beating of my heart. Yet I can never say it as quietly as Mom has written it. There, *Alex* has been silently transmuted into *Tetsuyoshi.* She has brushed his name once so that it can endlessly say and not say its unmistakable and irrevocable love. See what Mom has done: she has taken the patronym, and, by writing it, inscribed herself in its very articulation. Up there: Alex/Tetsuyoshi in my father's name but my mother's hand. Mom's brushwork is a defining passage of his name, just as calligraphy marks, beyond any meaning whatsoever of the words it constitutes, the materiality of a like passage. In its giving forth of the name of the father, motherhood makes itself tangible upon the paper as love.

Signatures

Mom is in her calligraphy in a more explicit way, for, as you can plainly see in her *kore ga oitoma,* there is more to Mom's calligraphy than those words. To the lower left, there is a smaller line of characters, and to the left of that, a yet smaller line that in the original is in red, framed in a rectangle. The latter, which the Japanese call *in,* was not brushed but applied with a carved stamp. Together, these characters are my mother too, in the most conventional form of representation, for they are her signature or autograph, doubled in the traditional Japanese manner. "The effects of signature are the most ordinary thing in the world"—Derrida, 328): authentication, presence, substitution, identity. This specific signature, however, is a peculiar kind of synecdoche in which the middle stands in for the whole. Instead of *June Yuriko Aoki,* it says only *Yuriko,* which means "lily." This is my mother: a lily in black, and another in red, the lily that her own mother gave her to become. If you look closely, you can see that while these lettered lilies are different, they are also the same. Different styles and different scripts, but the same *kanji.*

Or almost the same, for the black outnumber the red. The "extra" black one is not part of my mother's name, although it is part of her signature. It is the character *sho*, which simply means, "written by." This difference once more discriminates Japanese letters from those in the West. Here, in this culture and in this nation, when we say that something was "written by" someone, we speak of the author. But here, upon this paper, "written by" distinguishes the writer *from* the author.[7] Calligraphy announces the literality of its writing: particular characters declare that particular others were written by Mom, that they were brushed onto the page by her hand, not that they were spoken by her mouth. Such a nonauthorial signature is neither disingenuous nor self-aggrandizing, for, to a large extent, the writing is what counts here, not authorship. Who could claim authorship of *kore ga oitoma*, anyway? Grandma said these words, but they were hardly hers to "give," at least in any originary sense. In fact, their consequence derives directly from their dispossession, for it was their general formality that mattered when Grandma spoke them, and, years later, it was that same formality that mattered when Mom finally heard them. Insofar as formality manifests in a cultural symbolic system rather than in any individual heart or mind, the significance of those words thus turns, in a pedestrian Derridean way, on their iteration and not on any singularity. Their origin has been forgotten and remains unmourned and of little consequence to the moment. The point is not one of origin but rather that of the passage from mother to mother.[8] When Grandma spoke those words to Mom, she was already respeaking them, just as I respeak them to you.

But it was Mom who wrote them.

"By definition," Derrida says, in one of his most famous and familiar texts, "a written signature implies the actual or empirical nonpresence of the signer. But, it will be said, it also marks and retains [her] having-been present in a past now, which will remain a future now, and therefore in a now in general, in the transcendental form of nowness (*maintenance*)" (328). The signature signs the part-presence of my mother: she is there and there and there, repeating across space what each reading of *Aoki Tetsuyoshi* does across time. Mom's signature, as Derrida suggests, also marks and re-marks a specific temporality. When she signs her calligraphy of *Aoki Tetsuyoshi*, when she puts her name alongside his and thereby binds him to her through the very proximity of the signifier, she signs even more than she does in her *kore ga oitoma*. Mom's signature and its declaration of being written, *sho*, appear in both pieces. But alongside *Aoki Tetsuyoshi* there is not one stamped signature, but two: *Yuriko*, in an abbreviated form, and *Aoki*, in another discursive echo. There is also a date: February 17, 1997. One might suspect that this would be the date of Alex's birth, which is, at least in the

West, that most vital of statistics, but this is not the case. Instead, February 17, 1997, is when Mom wrote the calligraphy, at which point Alex was already more than three months old. This date, which is, as far as I know, in no way special to history, maps the difference between the signified and the signifier to the axis of time, between the birth of her grandson and the inscription of that birth. Yet the difference in time, which always invokes that between then and now, is, as Derrida remarks, both affirmed and negated in the signature, in which the present slips from the past to the future, just like the words of a mother taking leave. Here is where Derrida converges to Foucault, for countermemory is exactly a transformation into another form of time.

Such a transformation of the signature is recapitulated in the relation between its writing and its reading. Geoffrey Bennington comments: "The text's signature calls up the reader's countersignature, as in the case with all signatures: we can now see more clearly that the countersignature it calls up is essentially the countersignature of the other, be that other myself" (Bennington, 163). Or be that other my mother's mother, or my mother's mother's mother. Or even you. It is therefore Mom's autograph that countersigns her writing into countermemory. Something is given and recovered in her hand: not a substitute for memory nor even a record of imperiled personal history, but rather a counterpoint to both, in a different register.

Perhaps all this is too much of a stretch, too much of a professorial son doing some suspect reconfiguration of his own to bring this writing into his comfortably professional world. The University of Alberta, where I write this, is palpably distant from both Paris and Japan. It's then doubly unfortunate that Mom could not attend the conference on mothers and sons that spawned this chapter. After all those years as a professor's wife, she has developed a talent for casually puncturing academic pomposity and an immunity to its pretensions. Foucault, Saussure, Lacan, and Derrida mean much less to her than Alex. Still, what is often missed, in and out of the academy, is how French theory is so often engaged with much more than academic lives. As Karlis Racevskis notes, "What people *know* constitutes what Foucault calls . . . 'fragmentary' knowledges" (126). Mom still does know, even if she's forgotten. "Tell them about your brilliant mother," Mom laughed, just before I left for the conference.

I will, Mom. I just did.

NOTES

I wish to thank my father, Tetsuo Aoki, and my friend and colleague, Satoshi Ikeda, for their invaluable assistance and advice. I benefited greatly from the careful and gracious reading by Serra Tinic. Finally, it need not be said, but must be acknowledged, that this chapter could not have come to be without my mother, June Yuriko Aoki.

1. Edward Dahlberg, 130.
2. These different but parallel "citations" of my mother's face prefigure motherhood as passage, discussed below.
3. Saussure's structuralist diagram places the concept (signified) over the sound-image (signifier). de Saussure, 66–67.
4. Appropriation is immanent to language in at least two ways that devolve from the fact that we are born into a language that precedes us. First, we must appropriate language and its histories in order to use it—hence the popularity of using *masterful* and kindred terms to praise excellent speakers and writers. Second, from a French theoretical or poststructuralist point of view, language appropriates us. That is, language is constitutive of subjectivity.
5. I owe this insight to Carole Robitaille.
6. My mother did this calligraphy before the *kore ga oitoma*, and before she had her strokes.
7. The status of *sho*/ "written by" incarnates the status of Japanese calligraphy as simultaneously art and text. In the West, artists, not authors, conventionally sign their works, and authors, not artists, have "by," as an abbreviation for "written by," inscribed in the front of their books and attached to their names (although not their signatures). Japanese calligraphers do both.
8. In shifting from authorship to writing, what becomes pertinent are exactly the questions that Foucault raises at the end of "What Is an Author?": "What are the modes of existence of this discourse?"; "How is it circulated?"; and "What placements are determined for possible subjects?" (Foucault, 138).

WORKS CITED

Althusser, L. "Ideology and Ideological State Apparatuses." In *Lenin and Philosophy and Other Essays*, Translated by B. Brewster. New York: Monthly Review Press, 1971.

Bennington, G. "Derridabase." In *Jacques Derrida*, edited by G. Bennington and Jacques Derrida. Chicago: University of Chicago Press, 1993.

Butler, J. *The Psychic Life of Power*. Stanford: Stanford University Press, 1997.

Dahlberg, E. *Because I Was Flesh: The Autobiography of Edward Dahlberg*. New York: New Directions. Cited in S. Neuman "Your Past . . . Your Future: Autobiography and Mothers' Bodies." In *Genre, Trope, Gender*, edited by B. Rutland. Ottawa: Carleton University Press, 1992, 130.

de Saussure, Ferdinand. *Course in General Linguistics*, edited by Charles Bally and Albert Sechehaye in collaboration with Albert Riedlinger, translated by Wade Baskin. New York: McGraw-Hill, 1966. 66–67.

Derrida, J. "Signature Event Context." In *Margins of Philosophy*, translated by A. Bass. Chicago: University of Chicago Press, 1982.

Foucault, M. "Nietzsche, Genealogy, History." In *Language, Counter-memory, Practice: Selected Essays and Interviews*, edited by D. Bouchard, trans. D. Bouchard and S. Simon, Ithaca: Cornell University Press.

———. "What Is an Author?" In *Language, Counter-memory, Practice: Selected Essays and Interviews*, edited by D. Bouchard, translated by D. Bouchard and S. Simon. Ithaca: Cornell University Press, 1977.

Lacan, J. "The Agency of the Letter in the Unconscious, or Reason Since Freud." In *Écrits: A Selection*, translated by A. Sheridan. New York: Norton, 1977.

———. *The Seminar of Jacques Lacan: Book III: The Psychoses: 1955–1956*, edited by J.-A. Miller, translated by R. Grigg. New York: Norton, 1993.

Mahon, M. *Foucault's Nietzschean Genealoty: Truth, Power and the Subject.* Albany: SUNY Press, 1992.

Racevskis, K. *Michel Foucault and the Subversion of Intellect.* Ithaca: Cornell University Press, 1983.

LIST OF CONTRIBUTORS

Sharon Abbey, Ed.D., is Assistant Professor of Education at Brock University, where she teaches courses in social studies and women's studies, as well as a founding member of the Centre on Collaborative Research. Previously she spent twenty years as an elementary school teacher, curriculum consultant, and school principal. She received the Federation of Women Teachers of Ontario Ruby Kinkaid Doctoral Studies Award and the University President's Award for coordinating a speakers' series on eating disorders and body image. Currently Dr. Abbey is the president of the Canadian Association for Studies on Women in Education, the book review editor for *Teaching Education,* and a member of the Board of Directors of the National Foundation for Eating Disorders. She is the coeditor of the recently published book *Redefining Motherhood: Changing Identities and Patterns* (1998).

Douglas Sadao Aoki is an Assistant Professor in the Department of Sociology at the University of Alberta. His principal areas of teaching and research are psychoanalytic social theory and social theory of the body. He has published in such journals as *Theory, Culture & Society*; the *Harvard Educational Review*; *Cinema Journal; Body & Society*; and the *Journal of Historical Sociology*. He is currently editing a special issue of *American Imago* on Lacan, mathematics, and reading, and preparing a book manuscript, *True Love Stories.*

June Yuriko Aoki is a retired sculptor and a mother. She practices calligraphy in Vancouver, British Columbia.

Mary Kay Blakely is the author of a critically acclaimed memoir, *Wake Me When It's Over*, and a lecturer on university campuses. She has appeared frequently on national television and her articles on family life and women's and political issues have appeared in *The New York Times*, *The Washington Post*, *Vogue*, *Mirabella*, *Ms.* and other national publications. Now, in the book *American Mom* (1994), she gives an engrossing account of a modern mother's real-life experiences.

Cate Dooley, M.S., is Codirector of the Mother-Son Project and a faculty member at the Jean Baker Miller Training Institute of Wellesley College's Stone Center. She is Campus Consultant for Eating Disorders at Brandeis University Student Health Services and has been the Stone Center's relational consultant for T. Berry Brazelton's Touchpoints Project at The Child Development Unit, Boston Children's Hospital.

From 1977 to 1993 Ms. Dooley codirected the Eating Disorder Program in The Cognitive Behavior Therapy Unit at McLean Hospital, Belmont, Massachusetts. She later worked as a trainer and program developer for The Women in Prison Project at Wellesley College's Stone Center. She has twenty-five years of experience in the field of psychology, doing clinical work and research projects, designing treatment programs, and supervising clinicians. Ms. Dooley is also in private practice in Newton and Watertown, Massachusetts. Ms. Dooley has coauthored several publications including: "An Inpatient Model for the Treatment of Anorexia Nervosa" in *Theory and Treatment of Anorexia Nervosa and Bulimia*, (1985); *Mothers and Sons: Raising Relational Boys* (1998); *Relational and Social Diversity Training in a Prison Setting: A Training Manual* (1995); and *Workplace Training: Relational Intelligence and Action* (2000).

Andrea Doucet is Assistant Professor in the Department of Sociology and Anthropology at Carleton University, Ottawa, where she teaches and publishes in feminist theory and qualitative methods. Her work has appeared in numerous books as well as in several journals: *Women's Studies International Forum*; the *Journal of Family Issues*; *Community, Work and Family*; and *Canadian Woman Studies*. Her current research is on economic restructuring, fatherhood, and masculinities in a Canadian context and her daily life is filled with mothering three daughters.

Nikki Fedele, Ph.D., graduated from Cornell University College of Arts and Sciences in 1972 with a B.A. in psychology and biology. She concentrated her psychological studies on physiological psychology and her biological studies on neurobiology and behavior. Dr. Fedele received her

M.A. (1979) and Ph.D. (1983) in clinical and community psychology from Boston University. She began her studies of parenting with her dissertation on differences in parenting styles between mothers and fathers. She has spoken nationally on parenting, women's development, and application of the relational model. Currently she is Codirector of the Mother-Son Project at the Jean Baker Miller Training Institute at the Stone Center for Developmental Studies, Wellesley College. Dr. Fedele is also Assistant Clinical Professor of Psychology in Psychiatry at Boston University School of Medicine and teaches residents about a relational model of group psychotherapy at Harvard Medical School. Dr. Fedele has twenty-two years of clinical experience working with men, women, couples, groups, and children. She is also the mother of two sons.

Linda Rennie Forcey, Professor Emerita of Human Development and Women's Studies in the School of Education and Human Development at Binghamton University, is a political scientist by training. Her research focuses on the intersection of peace studies and feminist theorizing. She has authored, edited, or coedited a number of books and articles relating to women and peace, including *Mothers of Sons: Toward an Understanding of Responsibility* (1987); *Peace: Meanings, Politics, Strategies* (1989); *Yearning to Breathe Free: Liberation Theologies in the U.S.* with Mar Peter-Raoul and Robert Fredrick Hunter, Jr. (1990); *Mothering: Ideology, Experience, Agency*, with Evelyn Nakano Glenn and Grace Chang (Routledge, 1994); and *Peacebuilding for Adolescents: Strategies for Teachers, Administrators, and Community Leaders*, with Ian M. Harris (1999).

Jacqueline Haessly, mother, grandmother, and peace educator, provides training, consulting, and coaching on topics of peace and social justice through her company, Peacemaking Associates. Her publications include *Learning to Live Together* and *Mothering Teens*. She and her husband share in the fun, love, tears, and laughter of busy family life.

Claudette Lee is the Practicum Coordinator and a Professor for the School of Social Work at the University of Nebraska at Omaha (UN Omaha). She was given the UNO Chancellor's Commission on the Status of Women 2000 Outstanding Achievement Award in April 2000 for her service to women at UN Omaha and in the community. She has presented at national conferences, including the Council on Social Work Education APM and the Gender Issues in Higher Education National Conference; served on boards and committees of national organizations; taught at Iowa State University and Creighton University; presented at the Nebraska

Teaching Improvement Council Faculty College; and was the keynote speaker for the Omaha Black Family Summit, among other accomplishments.

Amia Lieblich is Professor of Psychology at the Hebrew University of Jerusalem, where she served as a chairperson from 1982 to 1985. Born and educated in Israel, she has been studying psychological aspects of Israeli society, such as the influence of war and the mandatory military service, on the lives of Israelis. She is among the pioneers of gender studies in Israel and has published two psychobiographies of Israeli female authors, one of which appeared in English: *Conversations with Dvora: An Experimental Biography of the First Modern Hebrew Woman Writer* (1997). Her most recent academic project involves studying life stories as a means to psychological understanding. Since 1993, she has coedited with Ruthellen Josselson a book series titled *The Narrative Study of Lives*, and with two of her graduate students she has published a book on qualitative methodology in psychological research: Lieblich, Tuval-Mashiach, and Zilber, *Narrative Research: Reading, Analysis and Interpretation* (1998).

Andrea O'Reilly, Ph.D., is Assistant Professor in the School of Women's Studies at York University, where she teaches courses on Toni Morrison, on motherhood, and on mothers and daughters. She has presented her research at numerous international conferences and is the author of more than a dozen articles and chapters on these topics. She is coeditor of *Redefining Motherhood: Changing Identities and Patterns* (1998), *Mothers and Daughters: Connection, Empowerment and Transformation* (2000) and the special 20th anniversary issue of *Canadian Woman Studies* (Fall 1998) on Mothers and Daughters as well as completing *Toni Morrison on Motherhood* (forthcoming). She was coordinator of the first international conferences on Mothers and Daughters, 1997 and Mothers and Sons, 1998 sponsored by the Centre for Feminist Research at York University. O'Reilly is founding president of the Association for Research on Mothering, (A.R.M.) and is founding editor/publisher of the ARM journal. In 1998 she was the recipient of the "University Wide" Teaching Award at York University. She has conducted numerous community workshops on motherhood, mothers and daughters, and mothers and sons and has been interviewed widely on these topics. O'Reilly and her common-law spouse of sixteen years are the parents of a fifteen-year-old son and two daughters ages ten and thirteen.

Janet Sayers is Professor of Psychoanalytic Psychology in the Sociology Department of the University of Kent at Canterbury, where she also works part-time as a therapist both privately and for the National Health Service. Her books include *Mothering Psychoanalysis, Freudian Tales,* and, most recently, *Kleinians: Psychoanalysis Inside Out* (2000).

Alison M. Thomas writes on the mother-son relationship from a vantage point which combines both the academic and the personal. As a feminist researcher studying the social construction of gender, she is also the mother of boy/girl twins. Her research publications encompass diverse aspects of gender relations and include work on sexual harassment (*Sexual Harassment: Contemporary Feminist Perspectives,* 1997, coedited with Celia Kitzinger), and on "Feminists Mothering Sons" (a special feature for *Feminism and Psychology,* 1996, coedited with Robyn Rowland). She is currently an Adjunct Associate Professor with the Sociology Department at the University of Victoria.

Jess Wells is the editor of *Lesbians Raising Sons,* an anthology by Alyson Publications that examines the ways in which boys are being raised in lesbian households. It was a finalist for the coveted Lambda Literary Award in 1998.

Ethel Hill Williams, Ph.D., is an Assistant Professor in the University of Nebraska at Omaha's (UNO) College of Public Affairs and Community Service, Department of Public Administration. She has a doctorate in political science, with an emphasis in public administration and public policy from the University of Nebraska-Lincoln. She holds a master's degree in Public Administration from the Graduate School of Public and International Affairs at the University of Pittsburgh. Dr. Williams offers more than twenty-five years of experience in the fields of public administration, public policy, and personnel administration, especially affirmative action and diversity issues. She has edited a volume of *Public Productivity and Management Review* devoted to affirmative action and diversity issues. Her chapter, "Managing Diversity in the New Millennium: Organizational Resistance to Change" is forthcoming in *Global Trends in Administration.* She was recently invited to serve on an intercultural research and cultural exchange team to travel to Vera Cruz, Mexico, to study and increase cultural interactions and communication between African-American, Mexican-American, and Hispanic academics and public administration professionals.

INDEX

Abbey, Sharon, 10, 265
abortion, 34
Achilles, 107–108, 185, 203, 214
activism, 241–42; political, 82
ADD (Attention Deficit Disorder), 191
ADHD (Attention Deficit Hyperactivity
    Disorder), 205
adolescence (*see also* boys, adolescent),
    36, 51, 66, 73, 76, 109, 208–211,
    221, 224; stages of, 47 (*see also*
    developmental stages)
adolescents, 198–99 (*see also* boys,
    adolescent)
adoption, 42–55, 158, 162
Adult Children of Alcoholic and
    Dysfunctional Families, 44
adult role models, 129–30; gendering
    of, 131
adulthood, 168, 200, 225, 236
African-Americans (*see also* blacks),
    59–61, 62, 68, 77, 112; culture, 56;
    women (*see* women, black)
Agammemnon, 92
aggression, 130, 145, 172, 192, 194
AIDS, 34, 36, 160
Alda, Alan, 94
alienation, 71, 198, 208, 212
Almog, Oz, 246
Althusser, Louis, 91
anger, 194, 208
anxiety, 209, 213
Aoki, Douglas Sadao, 17, 265

Aoki, June Yuriko, 17, 251, 253, 265
Apollo, 92, 145
Arab(s), 248, 249n. 1; states, 235
Arcana, Judith, 4–5, 100–101, 104–105,
    115, 147, 149–50, 152, 153; *Every
    Mother's Son*, 4, 94–98
Aries, Phillippe, 76
Association for Research on Mothering
    (ARM), 2, 19n. 2
Athena, 92
attachment: and loss, 217–234; theory,
    217 (*see also* Bowlby, John)
Attention Deficit Disorder. *See* ADD
Australia, 127, 137n. 1
authenticity, 194, 203, 210, 214

Backes, Nancy, 1–2
Balbo, Laura, 169
Baldwin, James, 113
Barker, Pat: *Regeneration,* 219–20
Barnett, Rosalind, and Caryl Rivers, 84
Barr, Roseanne, 159
behaviors: acting out, 206, 208, 210;
    aggressive, 78, 123, 128, 192; boy,
    189, 205; high-risk, 198–99, 205;
    macho, 130; nurturant, 128
    (*see also* nurturance; nurturing);
    phallocentric, 129; relational, 206;
    traditional forms of masculine, 136
Bennington, Geoffrey, 262
bereavement, 247
Bergman, Steve, 191

Bergman, Steve, and J. L. Surrey, 192
Bernard, 98
Bhavnani, Kum-Kum, 86
Bion, Wilfred, 218
bisexuals, 63
black matriarchal family structure:
     myth of the, 56–70, 93
black(s) (*see also* African-American),
     82, 86, 112; assimilation, 63; boys,
     65, 111, 115, 130; community, 57,
     64, 112, 114, 169; culture, 56,
     57–59; families, 56–70, 93;
     feminism (*see* feminism, African-
     American); girls, 65;
     identities, 112; matriarchy, 56–70;
     men, 7, 56–70, 93, 111–12, 114;
     migration to the North of, 57;
     mortality rate of, 60; narratives,
     112; religious experience, 63;
     southern, 57; women, 7, 56–70,
     75, 93, 169
blackness, 58
Blakely, Mary Kay, 5–6, 7, 266
Bly, Robert, 9, 20n. 5, 93, 110, 149;
     Iron John, 8, 93–94
Blye, Frank, 146
Bottoms, Sharon, 158
Bowlby, John, 217 (*see also* attachment)
Boy Code, 151, 174
boys, 1, 7, 12, 14, 15, 18, 40, 51, 65, 71,
     76, 95–97, 103–104, 108–110, 113,
     122–24, 126, 135–36, 147–51, 154,
     155, 159–61, 165, 174–75, 187,
     189–94, 199–200, 202–204,
     210–211, 225, 240; adolescent,
     194, 208–211, 226, 233 (*see also*
     adolescence; adolescents); and
     self-glorification, 225–32, 233;
     black, 65, 111, 115, 130;
     development of, 185–86, 189, 192,
     199; entitlement of (*see* entitle-
     ment, boys); expectations for, 190;
     growing into mothering, 163–82;
     hyperactive, 191, 203, 205–206;
     Israeli, 236; mama's, 211;
     mothers' rejection of, 109 (*see also*
     mother-son, separation);
     nonsexist, 105; pampering,
     236–39; raising relational,
     185–216; recurring nightmares in,

220–21, 233; self-division in,
     221–24, 233; stammering in,
     219–20, 233; wild, 201
Braden, Jophie, 54n. 4
Brannen, Julia, and Peter Moss, 122
Branovski, Matti, 18
bravado, 151, 187, 192–93, 200, 205,
     206, 208
Brazelton Touchpoint Project, 187
breadwinner, 122, 124, 165
Britain, 127, 161, 164, 171, 175, 224
Brown, Rosellen, 37
Buddha, 256
bullying, 193, 200, 204, 206, 207
bullyproof curriculum, 207
Burton, John, 87n. 8
Butler, Judith, 148

California Spur Posse, 37
calligraphy, 253–54, 258, 260–62
Canada, 18, 127, 175, 256
Cannon, Nona, 48
Caplan, Paula: *The New Don't Blame
     Mother*, 20n. 4
Caraway, Nancie, 61
care. *See* caregivers; caring
caregivers, 166, 168, 210; daytime, 171;
     primary, 13, 42, 172, 175, 218;
     women, 218
caring, 155, 165, 167–68
Caron, Ann, 152
CATC hold, the, 51
child care, 84, 149, 164, 166, 170, 218;
     men's involvement in, 84
child custody, 27–28, 158, 160; joint,
     131
child rearing, 100–101, 122–24, 134,
     136, 168–69, 171, 174, 198; black,
     59, 64; feminist, 6, 67, 97; shared,
     101
childhood, 29, 31–32, 36, 43, 76, 77,
     168, 202, 236; early, 202, 218;
     middle, 204–207; stages of, 47, 76
     (*see also* developmental stages)
children, 3–4, 7, 38–39, 71, 76, 96,
     97–99, 105, 121–22, 124, 136, 141,
     158, 164–65, 167, 169, 170–72,
     189, 207, 217, 240–41, 244–45,
     252; abused, 44; adopted, 42–55;
     attachment and, 217–34; black,

56–70, 113, 169; custody of (*see* custody); development of, 168, 187; gender identity in, 143–46, 162; Japanese-Canadian, 253; of color, 86, 158; of lesbians, 13, 157–62; racial identity in, 78; regulation of, 105; special needs, 6, 42–55; white, 78, 86

Chodorow, Nancy, 83, 99, 106, 116n. 1, 144, 218

Christian, Harry, 135

Civil War, the, 57

class, 13, 56, 61–62, 81, 86, 147, 166, 169, 186

Cleage, Pearl, 60–61

Clinton, President, 86

Clytemnestra, 8, 91, 93, 105, 110, 114, 115

code of silence, 190, 193–94

Cole, Johnetta, 135

Collins, Patricia Hill, 61–63, 78, 85–86

communication, 209

compassion, 204

competitiveness, 42, 46

conflict resolution: nonviolent, 43, 45, 48, 51; techniques, 78–79, 80

connection, 151, 187–88, 194–95, 198, 207, 208–212, 214; avoidance of, 192; emotional, 199; mother-daughter, 106; mother-son, 3, 14–17, 185, 192, 199; strategies of, 193

Connell, R. W., 146, 148, 163, 172

conquest mentality, 38

consumerism, 46, 52

Cooper, Baba: *Politics of the Heart*, 3–4

countermemory, 17, 251–64

criminal justice system, 77

crying, 246–48

cultural: expectations, 201, 211; models for development, 183, 200; narratives, 106; practices, 106; theory, 186

culture, 38–39, 57, 189, 191, 195, 202, 207, 211–12; black, 56, 57–59, 112; boy, 15, 187–88, 189–94, 201, 203, 204–207, 209, 213; contemporary, 51; dominant, 12, 77, 129, 132, 195; Euro-American, 58, 64, 101; female, 13; hypermasculinization

of, 18; Israeli, 245–47; male, 10, 97, 103, 150–51, 187; patriarchal, 3, 62, 100, 104, 106, 108, 114, 153; peer, 199; popular, 93, 130, 132; Western, 10, 14, 76, 108, 246; women's, 170

custody. *See* child custody

dating, 210

daughters, 4, 13, 65, 71–72, 73, 75, 81, 82, 86, 96, 103, 106, 113, 124, 127, 141, 143–44, 151, 153, 154, 166, 173, 211, 217, 236, 244, 256

de Beauvoir, Simone, 75, 98

de Saussure, F., 17, 260, 262

DeFrabrizio, Lucy, 258

Demeter and Persephone, 106–107

denial, 192, 209

Deny It, 34

depression, 209, 213

Derrida, Jacques, 261–62

detachment, 220 (*see* also mother-son, separation)

developmental: models, 192; stages, 47, 192, 213, 236 (*see also* adolescence, stages of; childhood, stages of; men's developmental stages)

Deviri, Manuella, 247–48

dichotomization: of women and men, 83, 84

Dinnerstein, Dorothy, 116n. 1

disconnection, 8, 186–87, 189, 192, 195, 205, 208–209, 211–12, 214; mother-son, 14–17, 205, 211

discrimination, 56, 57, 59, 114

diversity, 147, 158

divorce, 74, 159

Donnerstein, Edward, 38

Dooley, Cate, 266

Doucet, Andrea, 13–14, 266

drug use, 36, 60

Du Bois, W. E. B., 112

Durkheim, Emile, 225E

education, 51, 78, 155

educators, 78–79, 153–54, 199, 206

emotions (*see also* individual emotions), 147, 149, 152, 154, 155, 161, 188, 191–93, 198, 201–203, 204, 206, 207, 208, 211–13, 218–19, 221–22,

237–38, 246; and relationship, 192; denial of, 209, 213; disconnection from, 205, 206; expression of, 193, 213; incestuous, 91, 221–22; uncontained, 221–22; vulnerable, 205, 208

empathy, 194, 198, 201–203, 204, 206, 213, 241

empowerment, 86, 194, 199, 213; black, 63; female, 4, 6, 106–107; of daughters, 4, 6, 107

Enders, Louise, 128–29, 132, 133

entitlement, 96–97, 150, 161; of boys, 95; of men, 95

Etheridge, Melissa, 162

ethnicity, 65, 166, 169, 186, 195

Faludi, Susan: *Stiffed: The Betrayal of the American Man*, 10, 11, 110

Family Life Educators for Peace, 48

family(ies), 5–6, 42, 51, 54, 83, 84, 100, 122, 125, 134, 136, 145–46, 161–62, 169, 174, 186, 189–90, 196, 202–203, 207, 210, 213–14, 240, 246, 248; adoptive, 42–55; American, 28; black, 56–70, 93; breadwinner, 124; Canadian, 259; dual-earner, 124, 134; dysfunctional, 42; Japanese, 259; lesbian, 157–62; nuclear, 5, 29, 82, 160; patriarchal, 161; patterns, 122, 124; peacemaking and the, 42–55, 72; role models, 145; sexual division of labor, 134, 165; single-parent, 29; values, 28, 34, 39, 112, 195, 199, 205

father's rights movement, 94

father(s), 7, 10, 11–12, 13, 15, 17, 36, 39, 51, 74, 76, 79, 81, 82, 87, 99, 103, 110, 123–24, 127, 131, 134, 136, 142, 145, 150, 163–82, 177n. 24, 188, 210, 219, 225, 236, 243, 246, 248, 259–60; absent, 77, 116n. 1, 122–23, 137n. 3, 245; as primary caregivers, 175; at home, 13; breadwinner, 122, 124, 165; castration by the, 92; distant, 135; figure, 136; hunger, 93, 135; roles, 122, 133–36; single, 171, 175; younger, 135, 175

father-son: attachment, 9; connection, 110; identification, 123, 126, 127; relationship, 79, 85, 135–36, 143

fatherhood, 164, 175, 177n. 18

fathering, 9, 93, 136, 165, 171, 174, 177n. 18

fear, 194

Fedele, Nikki, 266–67

Fedele, Nikki, and Cate Dooley, 16, 107

feelings. *See* emotions

feminine: roles, 125; the, 9, 10, 11; traits, 151

femininity, 9, 123, 125, 143–44, 149, 151, 164, 171; ultra-, 10

feminism, 1, 7, 10, 57, 60–61, 62–65, 81, 85, 93–94, 99, 103–104, 126, 132, 133, 144, 146–47, 150–51, 161, 252; African-American, 7, 8, 56–70, 86, 92, 111–14, 115; Anglo-American, 8, 61–62, 63, 91–92, 94–110, 113–14, 115; exclusionary, 61; second wave, 76

Feminism and Psychology, 11, 135, 163, 173

feminist(s), 1, 9, 64, 76, 81, 82, 84, 86, 99, 106, 126, 146, 152, 217, 233; child rearing (*see* child rearing); ideals, 173; Israelis, 249n. 6; maternal, 11; mothering of sons, 4; movement, 61, 75; narrative on mothers and sons, 8, 110, 115; scholarship, 4, 76, 99, 169, 241; theory, 9, 14, 42, 76, 83, 104, 105, 116n. 1, 217; values, 42, 50; Western, 86

Fisher, Bernice, 167

Forcey, Linda, 7–8, 104–105, 114, 267; *Mothers of Sons*, 2, 74, 75, 94, 98–101

Foucault, Michel, 251, 257, 262

Four Mothers protest movement, 242, 249n. 8

Frazer, Elizabeth, 87n. 12

Freud, Sigmund, 74, 77, 92, 108, 219

Friday, Nancy: *My Mother/My Self*, 106

Friedan, Betty, 75–76, 98

Furies, The, 92

games (*see also* sports), 51, 54n. 2; competitive, 51

Gandhi, Mohandas K., 80

gays. *See* homosexuality
gender, 13, 40, 63–64, 71, 81, 86, 104, 121, 124, 136, 142, 148, 154, 155, 159, 161, 173, 175, 189; -differentiated family patterns, 124; -neutral language, 50; -specific roles, 50; and schools, 12, 153–54, 155, 158, 189–90, 201; categories, 13, 83; construction of, 145, 148, 154; crossing, 174; differences, 17, 50, 165, 174; equality, 50, 110, 134, 144, 165; identities, 15, 83, 122–23, 142–46, 149, 154, 155, 164; inequalities, 128; relations, 100, 104, 123, 146, 175; restructuring, 149–53; roles, 100, 121, 123–24, 137n. 1, 153; socialization, 3, 9, 122, 137n. 1; stereotyping, 50, 154
gendered: behavior patterns, 121; characteristics, 173; social relations, 164
Gilbert, Robert, and Pam Gilbert, 147, 149, 154
Gilligan, Carol, 83, 99, 191, 193–94, 225
Gilligan, James, 194
girls, 4, 65, 122, 154, 155, 161, 174–75, 189–91, 192, 219, 238
Golden, Marita, 111–13
Good Mother, the, 40, 77, 99, 102–103
grandfathers, 145
grandmothers, 145, 258
grandparents, 11, 145, 158
Greenson, Ralph, 217–18
Grinberg, Rui Zvi, 245
growth, 168–71

Haessly, Jacqueline, 6, 7, 48, 267
Harris, Judith Rich, 77
Harris, Sidney, 26
Hartley, Ruth, 125, 135
Hearn, Jeff, and David Morgan, 147
Hercules, 145
heterosexuality, 127, 159
homemakers, 122, 124, 165
homophobia, 13, 144, 158–59, 161
homosexuality, 34, 36, 63, 225
hooks, bell, 60–61
househusbands, 172
Howard, Jeff P., 60

hyperactivity, 203, 205–206
hypermasculinity, 9, 18

identity, 84, 86, 109; masculine, 93, 116n. 1, 124, 142, 144–45; self-, 100–101
Iliad, 185
Illich, Ivan, 124
in, 260
independence, 191–92, 200, 204, 209
International Conference on Mothers and Daughters, 169
Iphigenia, 92
isolation, 187, 199, 206, 209, 212, 213, 220, 228
Israel, 16, 248; mother-son relationships in, 235–50
Israeli: Defense Force, 236, 243, 244; War of Independence, 245
Israelis, 235–50
issei, 256

Japan, 256
Japanese, 253, 255
Japanese-Canadians, 251–64
Jay, Elsie, 11, 128
Jews, 235–50; orthodox, 236, 241
Jocasta, 8, 91, 92, 93, 100, 105, 110, 114, 115
Johnson, Miriam, 93
Jordan, Judy, 192
Joyce, James: *Portrait of the Artist as a Young Man,* 223
Judson, Stephanie, 48
justice, 42, 43, 48, 50, 72, 80, 165; and black men, 59–60

Kaufman, Judith, 154
Kaufman, Michael, 9, 146–48, 151–52
Kildwick, Tony, 218
Kimmel, Michael, 148
King Jr., Martin Luther, 80
King, Joyce Elaine, and Carolyn Ann Mitchell: *Black Mothers to Sons,* 111, 113
Kitaen-Morse, Beverly, 51
Komarovsky, Mirra, 122
kore ga oitoma, 255–58, 260–61

Lacan Jaques, 231, 253, 262

Lacey, Nancy, 87n. 12
Ladner, Joyce, 58
Lantieri, Linda, 87n. 2
Lasch, Christopher, 77
leave-taking, 251–64
Lebanon, 242–43, 247
Lee, Claudette, 267–68
Lee, Claudette, and Ethel Williams, 7, 114
lesbian(s), 63, 127, 157–62; mothers, 3–4, 12–13, 19n. 2, 157–62; raising sons, 157–62
Let's Pretend, 6, 34–35
Letzter, Irit, 243
Lewinsky, Monica, 86
Lieblich, Amia, 16–17, 268
Limbaugh, Rush, 28
Livna, Neri, 247
Lorde, Audrey, 6, 91, 113
Lynn, D., 135

Mac an Ghaill, Martin, 174
machismo, 128, 130, 132, 137n. 4
Mahon, Michael, 258
Malamuth, Neil, 38
male: -female bond, 150; bonding, 9, 151; dominance, 145, 150, 189; identity, 16, 217–18, 225; mothering, 11; role models, 130, 135, 142, 150; the new, 131 (see also New Man, the); violence, 26, 86, 87n. 2
maleness, 144, 152–53, 218
manhood, 9, 10–11, 14, 18, 92, 93–94, 108–109, 112–13, 123–24, 147, 152, 174, 236; black, 61; idealized, 10; maternal conception of, 11; traditional, 5
manic self-glorification, 225–32, 233
Martin, Elmer, 62
Martin, Joanne Mitchell, 62
masculine: ideal, 172; norm, 128; role models, 136; roles, 125; self-differentiation, 123; traits, 129–30, 149
masculinities, 11, 146–48, 163, 165, 172, 174; and men, 8–14
masculinity, 4, 5, 8, 9–13, 65, 95, 102, 110, 123–24, 127, 128–29, 130, 132, 135, 137nn. 1, 141–42, 144–54, 155, 163, 171–73, 175,

239; and matriarchy, 56–70; crisis in, 18, 110; definitions of, 12, 146–49, 151, 153; hegemonic, 13, 134–35, 143, 163, 172; literature, 9, 10, 14; new, 107, 128–29, 131, 133, 135; nonpatriarchal, 115; patriarchal, 95, 97, 113, 114; sabotaging, 131–33; sons, 141–56; traditional, 3–4, 9, 95, 97, 107, 110, 115, 125, 131, 137n. 7, 145, 149, 153
maternal: authority, 104–105, 110, 115, 116n. 1; connection, 107, 188; countermemory (see countermemory); displacement, 8, 92, 94, 104–105; erasure, 8, 92, 105, 116n. 1; identities, 5, 100, 106, 110; loss (see mother-son separation); manhood, 11; practices, 7, 13, 83, 96, 98, 102, 114, 115, 164, 167, 171, 173; responsibility, 98–101, 110, 115, 145; role, 5, 100, 103, 107, 143, 164; separation (see mother-son, separation); thinking, 79, 163–82, 243; work, 101, 167, 175
matriarchy and masculinity, 56–70
McCray, R., 62
McGinnis, James and Kathleen, 48
McGuire, Jacqueline, 123
McLaren, Arlene, 128, 131–32
media, 12, 56, 61, 123, 129–30, 135, 153, 186, 189–90, 202, 212, 242, 246; violence, 18
men, 4, 10, 11, 15, 18, 26, 74, 86–87, 94, 96, 105, 109, 122, 124–25, 142–50, 155, 162, 165, 169–73, 175, 187, 189–90, 218, 225, 236, 239, 246; and masculinities, 8–14; and mothering, 163–82; black, 7, 56–70, 93, 111–12, 114; entitlement of, 95; feminine, 94; new (see New Man); nonsexist, 4, 96, 125, 135; schizophrenia and, 224–27; soft, 149; traditional roles for, 125; violence in, 194
men's: adulthood, 212; developmental stages, 187, 213; estrangement from women, 110; mythopoetic movement, 93; narratives, 167
Middle East, 16, 235–50
Miedzian, Myriam, 87n. 2

militarism, 17, 18, 42, 46, 52, 87, 239
military: aggression, 52; service, 17,
    236–50; the, 52, 74–75
Miller, Jean Baker, 83; *Toward a New
    Psychology of Women*, 186–87, 188,
    193, 195
Miller, Jean Baker, and Irene Stiver:
    The Healing Connection, 187, 192
Miller, Sue, 40
Miron, Dan, 245
misogyny, 93, 94, 123
momism, 93
Morgan, Robin, 1
Morris, William, 221
Morrison, Toni, 5, 106
mother: blame, 76, 99; right, 92
mother-daughter: connection, 106;
    identification, 106; literature, 4;
    master narrative, 106–107;
    relationship, 6, 67–68, 83, 106
mother-son: attachment, 2, 14, 92,
    107–108; attachment and loss,
    217–34; connection, 3, 8, 14–17,
    91, 107–110, 142–43, 185, 192,
    199, 203, 214, 228; disconnection,
    14–17, 18, 191–92, 205, 211–12;
    equality, 97, 104–105, 115, 134;
    separation, 8, 14, 91, 92, 108, 143,
    191, 195, 199–200, 217–18,
    217–34
mother-son relationship, 2, 4–5, 8,
    14–17, 25–41, 66–67, 75, 85, 99,
    102–110, 111–14, 142–43, 186,
    188, 191, 195–96, 198–200, 210,
    211–14, 244; African-American,
    56–70; and peacebuilding, 71–90;
    in Israel, 235–250; marginaliza-
    tion of, 10–11; war and, 235–50
motherhood, 2–8, 10, 11, 18, 19n. 2,
    25, 27, 30–31, 33–34, 36, 40, 68,
    85, 95–98, 100–101, 104, 105,
    114–15, 164–65, 176n. 3, 241, 256,
    260; black, 169; insititution of, 5,
    6, 7, 27–28, 97; of soldiers,
    235–50; oppression of, 101, 110,
    143; patriarchal, 3–4, 6, 97;
    traditional, 4, 6, 28, 97, 100, 114
mothering, 2, 3–8, 9, 14, 19n. 2, 72, 74,
    78, 84, 85–87, 93, 97–99, 101, 102,
    105, 110, 113, 126, 161, 165–66,
    168–69, 171, 173–74, 194, 201,

241, 258; black, 58–59, 64, 111,
    114; feminist, 11–13, 97, 98, 114,
    121–40; feminist influence on,
    64–65; for African-American
    women, 56–70; good, 75, 99; good
    enough, 87n. 12; gynocentric, 4,
    97, 106; lesbian, 3–4; male, 11;
    radical, 3–4; role models, 158
mothering of sons, 4, 127, 175; African-
    American, 7; feminist, 14, 121–40;
    lesbian, 157–62
motherland, 244
motherline, 17, 106
mothers, 3, 7, 10, 12–15, 29, 36, 39–40,
    51, 79, 81, 82, 87, 100, 103, 105,
    123–24, 134, 149–54, 164–65, 168,
    170, 172, 185, 201–202, 204–205,
    207, 210, 239, 243, 246, 259; as
    agents of gender restructuring,
    149–53; as mourners, 17, 235,
    244–49; attachment and, 217–34;
    black, 7, 56–70, 111–14, 115; co-,
    13; divorced, 6, 145; feminist, 3, 6,
    99, 125, 126, 127, 128–29, 132–33,
    136, 137n. 7, 141–56, 163;
    feminist academic, 141–56; First
    Nations, 19n. 2; Hispanic, 66–67;
    homemaker, 122, 124, 165;
    immigrant, 19n. 2; Israeli, 235–50;
    Japanese, 251–64; Latino, 66, 67;
    lesbian, 12–13, 19n. 2; of color,
    19n. 2, 64–65, 85–86; role of, 76,
    96, 115; single, 5, 27, 142, 145–46,
    240, 245; stay-at-home, 5, 124;
    white, 57, 66–67, 68, 149, 195;
    with disabilities, 19n. 2; working,
    19n. 2, 145
mothers and daughters, 1, 107
mothers and sons: 1960s, 102–104;
    African-American perspectives on,
    91–118; Anglo-American
    perspectives on, 91–118; Japanese,
    251–64
mothers of sons, 11, 40, 73, 77, 80, 82,
    86–87, 186, 187, 189; African-
    American, 7, 65, 111; with special
    needs, 42
motherwork, 86
mourning, 246–47
Moynihan report, the, 93–94
Moynihan, D. Patrick, 56, 57

Musil, Robert: *Young Törless,* 223
mutuality, 194, 210
mythology, 56–70, 91–93, 106, 203, 214

National: Association of Criminal
    Defense Lawyers, 59–60; Center
    for Lesbian Rights, 160; Insitute
    of Mental health, 84; Institute of
    Child Health and Human
    Development, 199; Urban
    League, 60
New Man, 131, 135, 157–62
nisei, 251–52
nonviolence, 44, 72, 80, 83, 86
North America, 144
nurturance, 133, 151, 167, 185
nurturing: children, 51, 66, 73, 82, 84,
    96, 99, 101, 105, 112, 136, 161,
    168, 173; touch, 50–51
Nussbaum, Hedda, 37

O'Brien, Margaret, 171
O'Reilly, Andrea, 268
Oedipal complex, 92
Oedipus, 8, 91, 92, 93, 115, 145
Omolade, Barbara, 75
oppression, 56, 58–59, 81; gender,
    62–63, 84; of black women, 62; of
    women, 76, 85, 94, 97, 99, 101,
    143, 147; patriarchal, 106; racial,
    64, 86, 114; sexist, 61, 82
Orestes, 8, 91, 93, 115
Orlick, Terry, 54n. 2

Palestinians, 248
parenthood, 198
parenting, 14, 42–44, 67–68, 103, 105,
    121–22, 136, 157–58, 175, 198,
    210; -in-connection, 186, 198–200,
    201, 204; and peacemaking,
    48–53; black, 59, 65; co-, 166;
    feminist, 6, 42; good enough, 80;
    practices, 43, 54; queer, 161;
    shared, 136, 175; sons, 67–68
parents, 77, 79, 121, 161, 175, 189, 194,
    199, 207, 208, 210, 236–37, 240,
    244, 252; abusive, 44; black, 59;
    co-, 134, 166; same-sex, 122;
    single, 144
patriarchal: masculinity (*see* masculinity,
    patriarchal); narratives, 8, 91,

92–94; power, 92; thought, 17
patriarchy, 1, 42, 61, 65, 95, 129, 131,
    152, 160, 162; white, 86
Patti, Janet, 87n. 8
peace, 242; education, 43, 48–49, 77,
    80; movements, 241, 246; politics,
    164–65
peacebuilding, 71–90
peacekeeping, 71–72, 74, 77–78, 83
peacemakers, 42–55, 77, 79; women's
    roles as, 7, 72
peacemaking, 6, 7–8, 42–55, 71–90;
    and parenting, 48–53; family,
    42–55; mothering as, 8
pedophiles, 67
peer groups, 77, 114, 142, 148, 152,
    189, 191, 193–94, 196, 199, 208,
    210; mediation with, 79–80;
    pressure of, 7, 12, 51, 129–30, 154,
    207
people of color, 10, 78 (*see also* African
    Americans; blacks; Hispanics;
    Latinos)
Peters, M. F., 58
Peters, Marie, and G. C. Massey, 58
Pleck, Joseph, 122
Pollack, William: *Real Boys,* 10, 15,
    109–110, 146, 149, 151, 153, 174
poverty, 7, 18, 36, 57
power, 172–73, 187, 195, 206, 211; -over
    model of boyhood, 208; relations,
    142, 147–48, 151
preservation, 167–68
prison populations, 59–60
private sphere, 16–17, 71, 235
privilege, 96–97, 147, 151, 161, 173;
    male, 153, 228; racial, 78, 195
Prutzman, Priscilla, 48
public sphere, 16–17, 235, 246

race, 13, 61–62, 65, 81, 86, 158, 186,
    195, 199
Racevskis, Karlis, 262
racism, 7, 18, 56, 58–59, 61, 65, 86, 114,
    130, 195, 206; and black men,
    59–60; white institutional, 93;
    white women's support of, 86
rationality, 146, 154
reconnection, 195, 198, 212
Reconstruction, 57

recurring nightmares in boys, 220–21, 233

relational: dread, 191; learning, 188–89; models, 151; mothering, 201; needs, 152; patterns, 187; skills, 202–205; theory, 188; traits, 149

relationships, 199, 207–209; conflicts in, 196; ebb and flow of, 194–98

Remembrance Day, 18

Rich, Adrienne, 5, 6, 27, 71, 95–97, 126, 153; *Of Woman Born: Motherhood as Experience and Institution*, 3, 97

Richardson. B. B., 58–59

rights: civil, 44, 94, 158; individual, 165

Rivers, W. H. R., 219

Robinson, Lillian, 10

Rosenberg, Jack Lee, 51

Rowland, Robin, and Alison M. Thomas: *Feminism and Psychology*, 11, 163, 173, 175

Rowland, Robyn, 126, 127

Ruddick, Sara, 7, 79, 83, 96, 98, 105, 114, 169, 176n. 3, 241, 243; *Maternal Thinking*, 13, 95, 111, 163–65, 167, 171

Said, Edward, 82

sansei, 251, 253

Sayers, Janet, 108, 269; *Boy Crazy*, 15–16

schizophrenia and suicide, 224–27

Schlafly, Phyllis, 34–36

schools: gender and, 12, 153–54, 155, 158, 189–90, 201; peace education and, 78, 207; system, 129–30, 155

Segal, Lynne, 83, 85, 87

self: -divsion, 221–24, 233; -empathy, 192; -esteem, 49, 59, 65–66, 72, 96, 112, 150, 187; -sufficiency, 109, 161; -worth, 195, 204

selfhood, 83

Sentencing Project, the, 60

separation. *See* mother-son, separation

Sevenhuijsen, Selma, 167

sex, 34, 223–24; roles, 124

sexism, 4, 61, 110, 114, 130, 233, 259; anti-, 4, 98

sexual: abuse, 46; dominance, 145, 200, 208; fantasy, 223–25, 228; harassment, 123; intimacy, 211;

orientation, 186; partners, 210

sexuality, 36, 61, 169, 210–211

shame, 194, 204, 206, 209, 211, 213

Sharma, Ursula, 169

signatures, 251–64

signified, 17, 253, 260, 262

signifier, 17, 253, 260

signs, 253

Silverstein, Olga, and Beth Rashbaum: *The Courage to Raise Good Men*, 14, 15, 18–19, 107–110, 123–24, 143, 150, 188

slavery, 57, 59, 62, 64

Smith, Babette: *Mothers and Sons*, 1, 94, 102–105, 114, 115, 150–52

social: change, 80–81, 85; control, 80; practices, 83; status, 147; values, 189

socialization, 26, 58, 121, 142; gender, 3, 9, 95, 122, 124, 135; in the school system, 129–30; masculine, 3–5, 14, 72, 95, 97, 98, 122–24, 129; of black children, 58; of daughters, 106; of sons, 73, 75, 135

society: male-dominated, 129; misogynist, 94; nonpatriarchal, 99; patriarchal, 3, 11, 65; postpatriarchal, 165; sexist, 131; Western, 124, 142; white-dominated, 58

soldiers: motherhood of, 235–50

sons, 1, 3, 9, 14–17, 81, 82, 86, 97–98, 110, 112, 124, 127, 134, 142, 145, 149, 151–54, 160, 163, 165, 167, 173, 188, 195–96, 200–201, 211–12, 218, 239, 244, 247, 256; adult, 188, 200, 211–14; attachment and, 217–234; black, 56–70, 111, 113–14; deceased, 17; feminist, 133, 135; masculinity, 141–56; nonsexist, 125, 131; of lesbians, 13; post–1960s, 102–104; with special needs, 42–55; women raising, 20n. 5, 25–41, 66–67, 173, 183–216

Sophocles, 92

sports (*see also* games), 18, 154; competitive, 130; contact, 51; cooperative, 54n. 2

stammering: in boys, 218–20, 233

Starobin, Robert, 73
Stein, Nan, and Lisa Sjostrom, 207
Steinberg, Joel, 37
Steinberg, Lisa, 37
Steinem, Gloria, 146, 150
stepfathers, 127
stereotypes, 195; all-powerful-mother, 75, 82, 83–85; cultural, 211; gender, 50, 154; masculine, 127, 133, 149; racial, 59
suicide, 73, 209, 217, 233; and schizophrenia, 224–27; loss of attachment and, 224–27
superhero figures, 200, 202–203

Tavris, Carol, 9, 142, 145
Taylor, Ula, 60, 62
teasing, 204
Thetis, 107–108, 185
Thiele, Bev, 129, 131
Thomas, Alison *(see also Feminism and Psychology)*, 11–12, 269
Thorne, Barrie: *Gender Play,* 173–75
Three Fathers, 243
Ticknor, J. Ann, 82
Tomo, Yoshido, 255
Tong, Rosemary, 82
Tronick, Ed, 187
Tronto, Joan, 167

Ungerson, Clare, 167
United States, 18, 61, 72, 76, 127
University of Alberta, 262

values: community, 199, 205–206; feminist, 42, 50; masculine, 99, 104, 109, 130, 132; peacemaking, 54; social, 189; spiritual, 52; systems, 207
VanDeburg, William, 63
Vasquez, Carmen, 60
violence, 36, 37–39, 44, 77, 79, 86, 112, 128, 152, 155, 189, 194, 199, 209, 243; desensitization to, 190, 208; domestic, 37; male, 26, 86, 87n. 2; media, 18; sexual, 38
vulnerability, 152, 167, 185, 194, 203, 205, 208, 214

Walkerdine, Valerie, and Helen Lucey: *Democracy in the Kitchen,* 105
Wallace, Michelle, 93
Wallerstein, Judith, 27
war, 17, 74–75, 243, 244, 246, 256; mother-son relationship and, 235–50; toys, 52
Wayne, John, 94, 145
Wedekind, F.: *Spring Awakening,* 223
Wellesley College, 84
Wells, Jess, 12–13, 269
West Bank, the, 241
white(s), 59, 61, 68, 113; women, 61, 62–63, 65, 68
whiteness, 63
Williams, Ethel Hill, 269
Willis, Paul, 174
Wills, Gary, 86
Winnicott, D. W., 87n. 9, 220
womanhood, 106, 241; black, 62
womanism, 62–64, 67, 68
women, 4, 15–16, 63, 81, 85–86, 96, 105, 125, 145–46, 160, 162, 163–65, 169, 172, 192, 217, 224, 236, 239–40, 245, 248; Afrisporic, 111; as peacemakers, 7, 8, 72; autonomy of, 149; battered, 35; black, 7, 56–70, 75, 93, 169; development of, 186; domination of, 163; in service to boys, 115; Israeli, 241; of color, 61, 78, 85–86; oppression of, 2, 76, 85; white, 61, 62–63, 65, 68
Women in Black, 241
Woodacre, Grace, 160
work: domestic, 125, 166, 169; kin, 169; paid, 125; women's servicing, 169
World Health Organization: *Maternal Care and Mental Health,* 217
World War I, 57, 219
World War II, 93
Wylie, Phillip: *Generation of Vipers,* 93

yonsei, 259
York University: Centre for Feminist Research at, 1, 2

Zeus, 92, 145